Security Dynamics in the Former Soviet Bloc

This book focuses on four former Soviet sub-regions – the Baltic Sea region, the Slavic republics, the Black Sea region, and Central Asia – to explore the degree to which 'democratic security' has been established. It discusses the idea of democratic security, which includes depoliticisation of, and civilian oversight of, the military, resolution of conflicts by international cooperation, and involvement in international organisations. It examines how far states in these regions have developed cooperative foreign and security policies towards their immediate neighbours and key Western states and organisations, explores the interplay between internal and external aspects of democratic security building, and uses case-study examples to show how inter-state bi-lateral and multi-lateral relations are developing.

Graeme P. Herd is a Professor of Civil–Military Relations at the George C. Marshall European Center for Security Studies, Garmisch-Partenkirchen, Germany. He has published extensively on aspects of post-Soviet security politics in the *Journal of Peace Research, Security Dialogue, European Security, Journal of Slavic Military Studies, Co-operation and Conflict, Mediterranean Politics* and *The World Today*. His latest book is entitled *Russian Regions and Regionalism: Strength Through Weakness* (RoutledgeCurzon, 2003).

Jennifer D. P. Moroney is an Associate at DFI Government Services and an Adjunct Professor and Research Associate in the Elliott School of International Affairs, George Washington University, in Washington, DC. She has written and published widely on the politics and security of the former Soviet Union, particularly Ukraine and Central Asia, defence and military relations between NATO/the US and Eurasia, and the status of the NATO aspirants relative to NATO enlargement.

Security Dynamics in the Former Soviet Bloc

Edited by Graeme P. Herd and Jennifer D. P. Moroney

RoutledgeCurzon
Taylor & Francis Group
LONDON AND NEW YORK

First published 2003
by RoutledgeCurzon
11 New Fetter Lane, London EC4P 4EE

Simultaneously published in the USA and Canada
by RoutledgeCurzon
29 West 35th Street, New York, NY 10001

RoutledgeCurzon is an imprint of the Taylor & Francis Group

Editorial matter and selection © 2003 Graeme P. Herd
and Jennifer D.P. Moroney
Individual chapters © the contributors

Typeset in Times by Taylor & Francis Books Ltd
Printed and bound in Great Britain by Antony Rowe Ltd,
Chippenham, Wiltshire

British Library Cataloguing in Publication Data
A catalogue record for this book is available from the British Library

Library of Congress Cataloging-in-Publication Data
Security dynamics in the former Soviet bloc/edited by Graeme P. Herd
and Jennifer D. P. Moroney.
p. cm.
Simultaneously published in USA and Canada.
Inlcudes bibliographical references and index.
1. National security–Former Soviet republics. 2. Post-
communism–Former Soviet republics. 3. Democratization–Former
Soviet republics. 4. Former Soviet republics–Foreign relations. 5.
Former Soviet republics–Politics and government. I. Herd, Graeme P.
II. Moroney, Jennifer D. P., 1973–
DK293.S43 2003
355'.03301717–dc21   2003040931

ISBN 0–415–29732–X (hbk)

Contents

Contributors

The editors

Herd, Graeme P.: Prior to assuming his duties on 1 September 2002 as a Professor of Civil–Military Relations at the George C. Marshall European Center for Security Studies, Garmisch-Partenkirchen Germany, Dr Graeme P. Herd was Deputy Director of the Scottish Centre for International Security (SCIS) and Lecturer in International Relations at the University of Aberdeen (1997–2002). Among his previous posts he was Lecturer in Central and East European Politics, Staffordshire University (1994–97) and Projects Office, Department of War Studies, King's College London (1993–94).

Dr Herd is a Research Associate of Conflict Studies Research Centre (CSRC), Royal Military Academy Sandhurst, and was a British Council Scholar at the Institute of Russian History, Russian Academy of Sciences (1991–92), a Visiting Research Fellow at the Copenhagen Peace Research Institute (COPRI) in 1999, and a Socrates Lecturer at the University of Lapland in 2000 and 2001. He holds an MA and PhD from the University of Aberdeen and has published extensively on aspects of post-Soviet security politics in the *Journal of Peace Research*, *Security Dialogue*, *European Security*, *Journal of Slavic Military Studies*, *Co-operation and Conflict*, *Mediterranean Politics* and *The World Today*. His latest book co-edited with Anne Aldis is entitled *Russia and the Regions: Strength through Weakness* (London: RoutledgeCurzon, 2003).

Moroney, Jennifer D. P.: Dr Jennifer Moroney, an Associate at DFI International's Government Practice, is a project manager for contracts with the Office of the Secretary of Defense, US Department of Defense. Most recently, Dr Moroney conducted a strategic reassessment of US and Allied Security Cooperation programmes in Central Asia, the Caucasus, Ukraine and Moldova, and, prior to that, she led an assessment of Bulgaria, Romania, Slovakia and Slovenia's readiness to join NATO for OSD NATO Policy. Prior to joining DFI, she worked in NATO Policy at the Defense Department. Dr Moroney is also an adjunct professor and a Research Associate in the Elliott School of International Affairs, George Washington University.

Dr Moroney was a NATO Fellow from 1999–2001, and has published numerous articles on European security and Ukraine, and the impact of NATO/European Union enlargement on the post-Soviet states. She co-edited a book published in May 2002 entitled *Ukraine's Foreign and Security Policy: Theoretical and Comparative Perspectives* (with Taras Kuzio and Mikhail Molchanov), and is a contributor to a forthcoming book entitled *Almost NATO: Partners and Players in Central and Eastern European Security*, with a chapter on NATO–Ukraine relations. Dr Moroney is a frequent presenter at academic and policy conferences in the US and Europe. She received her PhD from the University of Kent at Canterbury, United Kingdom, in 2000, and her MA in European Integration from the University of Limerick, Ireland, in 1996.

The authors

Akerman, Ella: Ella Akerman is currently a PhD candidate at Mediterranean Studies, King's College London, having formerly been a Research Associate at the Scottish Centre for International Security (SCIS), University of Aberdeen. Her area of expertise includes Central Asian and Middle Eastern politics, political Islam, as well as Russian foreign and security politics. Her articles have been published in the *Review of International Affairs*, *The Journal for Conflict, Security and Development*, and *Security Dialogue*. She graduated from the University of the Sorbonne in Contemporary History (MA), and from the University of Aberdeen in Commercial Law (LLM).

Chudowsky, Victor: Dr Victor Chudowsky is a Program Officer at Meridian International Center in Washington, DC, a major contractor to the US Department of State and other federal agencies. He received his PhD in 1998 from the University of Connecticut in international relations and comparative politics. In 1996 he was a visiting scholar at the National Institute of Strategic Studies in Kiev, under a Title VIII grant from the US Department of State. His area of academic specialisation has been Ukrainian foreign policy, public opinion and relations among members of the Commonwealth of Independent States. He has taught courses in comparative politics and has hosted and produced local television programmes on international relations.

Darchiashvili, David: Dr David Darchiashvili is a lecturer in the International Relations Department at Tbilisi State University. Currently he is also Head of the Research Department of the Parliament of Georgia, Director of the Centre for Civil–Military Relations and Security Studies, and a member of the Board of the Caucasian Institute for Peace, Democracy and Development. During 1996–2001 Dr Darchiashvili participated in the Executive Program at the George C. Marshall European Centre for

Security Studies (2001), was awarded a MacArthur Fellowship (1998), and a Research Fellowship at CISAC, Stanford University (1997). He is author of number of articles published in international journals and magazines.

German, Tracey: Dr Tracey German is a graduate in Russian from the University of Edinburgh and was awarded a PhD by the University of Aberdeen on the topic of Russia's conflict with Chechnya. She has lived in Russia and Ukraine, and also speaks French and German. She is a part-time Senior Lecturer, Department of War Studies, Royal Military Academy Sandhurst, Defence Academy of the United Kingdom.

Grissom, Adam: Adam Grissom is an associate policy analyst at RAND. His primary research areas are defence planning, military strategy and low-intensity conflict. His recent research includes contributions to RAND studies on *The War on Terrorism: Preliminary Implications for the Army*, *The Contribution of Land Power Across the Spectrum of Operations*, and *The Future of Army Security Cooperation*. Before joining RAND, he was a civil servant in the Office of the US Secretary of Defense. His assignments included stints as Regional Director for Southern Africa, Operations Officer on the Kosovo Refugee Task Force, and Regional Security Specialist on the Balkans Task Force. In 1998 he was seconded by the Department of Defense to the Office of the High Representative in Brcko, Bosnia, as a Special Projects Officer. He has a Masters degree in Public Policy from the John F. Kennedy School of Government, Harvard University.

Huang, Mel: Mel Huang is a freelance analyst and a Research Associate of the Conflict Studies Research Centre (CSRC), Defence Academy of the United Kingdom. He formerly served as a Baltics analyst for Radio Free Europe/Radio Liberty, founding its Baltic States Report, as well as the Baltics Editor for the award-winning online journal *Central Europe Review*. His analytical works have been published frequently in various media in both English and Estonian, and he has frequently lectured at the United States Foreign Service Institute. His main areas of interest are Baltic party politics, the history of the interwar period in the Baltics, and Baltic civil–military relations.

Morgese, Frank: Colonel Frank Morgese is a serving United States Army Foreign Area Officer, and currently the United States Army Attaché to the Czech Republic. He recently completed a Fellowship at the Atlantic Council of the United States. From 1997 to 2001 he was responsible for managing United States security cooperation with Ukraine, Belarus, Moldova and the Caucasus for the United States European Command in Vaihingen, Germany.

Oldberg, Ingmar: Ingmar Oldberg is the Associate Director of Research at the Swedish Defence Research Institute (FOI) in Stockholm. He has published many reports, chapters and articles on Russian and East

European foreign and regional affairs; for example, *Kaliningrad: Russian Exclave, European Enclave* (Stockholm 2001); *In Dire Straits: Russia's Western Regions between Moscow and the West* (Stockholm 2000, with Jakob Hedenskog); *At a loss. Russian Foreign Policy in the 1990s* (Stockholm 1999, editor and co-author); and 'The Kaliningrad Oblast – a Troublesome Exclave in Unity or Separation' (2001).

Pataraia, Tamara: Tamara Pataraia graduated from Tbilisi State University and, in 1992, after completion of post-graduate courses, she received the degree of candidate of sciences in Physics and Mathematics. Since then she has continued to work at the university as a lecturer. In 1994 she started working as Researcher and Programmes Coordinator in the field of security studies at the Caucasian Institute for Peace, Democracy and Development (Tbilisi, Georgia). She was one of the editors of the monthly bi-lingual bulletin 'Army and Society in Georgia'. During 1996–2001 she participated in training programmes on international security and civil–military relations at the Center for Non-proliferation Studies, Monterey Institute of International Studies, the Naval Postgraduate School (Monterey) and Aberdeen University. Tamara Pataraia is author of a number of articles on the problems of national security and civil–military relations in Georgia.

Puglisi, Rosaria: Dr Rosaria Puglisi is currently a Political Affairs Officer, EU Mission, Kiev, having at the time of writing been Research Fellow at the Centre for European Political Communications, University of Leeds, where she is involved in an EU-funded project on mobilisation and unemployment in Europe. She obtained her PhD from the Institute of Russian and Eastern European Studies, University of Glasgow, with a thesis on the role of economic élites in relations between Russia and Ukraine. Her main areas of interest are the political economy of post-Soviet transitions, foreign policy and international relations in the FSU and the Russian regions.

Rontoyanni, Clelia: At the time of writing, Clelia Rontoyanni was an ESRC post-doctoral fellow at the Russia and Eurasia Programme, Royal Institute of International Affairs (London). Since January 2003, she has been working for the European Commission in Moscow. Her current research concerns the external relations of Russia, Ukraine and Belarus, particularly with the European Union and NATO.

Waters, Trevor: Dr Trevor Waters is a senior analyst at the Conflict Studies Research Centre (CSRC), Defence Academy of the United Kingdom. He is the author of a wide variety of articles in several English-language journals, military publications and books, and has written extensively on Moldova. His work has also been published in Bulgarian, Russian, Romanian, Slovak and Ukrainian. He served for more than twenty years in the UK Volunteer Reserve Forces.

Preface

In the early 1990s the expectation amongst most scholars, analysts and policy practitioners was that the newly independent states, which emerged and in some cases re-emerged from the collapse of the Soviet Union, would move from authoritarian state-building towards democratising their political systems, economies and foreign and security policies. Democratic security building would result in the reduction of tensions and cleavages within and between the states in the region, as all undertook a gradual strategic re-orientation Westwards and re-integrated into a globalised economy. The cooperative capacities of the former Soviet Union (FSU) have been used by researchers as a litmus test of the ability of these states to respect and uphold sovereignty and international law, and to integrate into the international system. With a few exceptions, this perspective represented the mainstream interpretation of how post-Soviet political developments would unfold. The only contested issue was the speed at which the process would occur, with an acknowledgement that variable-speed democratic transitions and consolidations were likely. Broadly speaking, the Baltic states were expected to undertake the transition first and move furthest fastest, whilst the five Central Asian ships of state would take up the rear of this Westwards-steaming convoy.

What, then, has been the experience of the former Soviet bloc from the Baltic region through to Central Asia? How might we best understand the condition of security, stability and interstate relations in the former Soviet space? To what extent have these states developed cooperative foreign and security policies towards their immediate neighbours? What is the nature of the relationship and interplay between internal and external aspects of democratic security building? How might we characterise the main dynamics in shaping inter-state bilateral and multilateral relations in post-Soviet space?

Clearly, with a multiplicity of contemporary perspectives, interpretations and paradigms which now abound – to say nothing of the alphabet soup of ever-changing acronyms and the sheer complexity of the issue – any one book which seeks to give a comprehensive and definitive answer to these questions is doomed to failure from the outset. Instead, this book has gathered together analysts from academia, government service, international organisations and NGOs who all have a professional interest in security developments in the newly independent states. We have sought only to identify current trends and dynamics and demonstrate the manner in which they influence the internal stability and international relations of these states. The focus is not primarily to capture the nature of relations between former Soviet republics and the West, but rather relations between these independent states.

This book is split into five parts. Part I introduces the notion of a transition or transformation from authoritarian to democratic stability, and Chapter 1 explores the nature of Soviet foreign policy and explains conceptual and theoretical issues relating to democratisation and democratic security building. Part II examines case studies in the foreign policy approaches in the most clearly delineated sub-region within the former Soviet bloc – the Baltic states. Chapter 2 assesses the extent to which the Baltic security agenda is being shaped by NATO integration, whilst Chapter 3 carries forward this analysis by focusing on intra-Baltic foreign policy cooperation within the military–security sector. Chapter 4 identifies pressures that shaped Russia's Baltic policy through the 1990s and into the new century – in particular geo-economic considerations.

Part III then directs our attention to what might be called the core of the Commonwealth of Independent States (CIS) – the three Slavic republics of Russia, Ukraine and Belarus. Chapter 5 explores more deeply the impact of geo-economics on Russian foreign policy towards the CIS, allowing a contrast with geo-economic considerations and Russia's Baltic policy in the previous chapter. Chapter 6 compares and contrasts the impact of NATO and EU enlargement on both Russia and Ukraine. Chapter 7 analyses Russia's relations with Ukraine through the prism of realism and imperialism. Chapter 8 brings Part III to a close by providing an assessment of the Belarus-Russia Union.

Having analysed the core CIS in Part III, Part IV proceeds to direct our focus towards the periphery of the CIS, beginning in Chapter 9 with an evaluation of the foreign and security policy of non-aligned Moldova. Chapter 10 takes us from the east to the west coast of the Black Sea, where an analysis of Georgian foreign policy sheds light on many of the key security dynamics at work in the south Caucasus. Chapter 11 introduces an emergent dynamic in Central Asia that increasingly will shape the security environment there – namely, US bilateral and multilateral relations with states considered hitherto to be under Russian hegemony. Part V takes us to the conclusions and Chapter 12, which tries to offer insights into the characteristics of security dynamics in the former Soviet bloc.

Although analysts of contemporary events are presented with a fast-moving stream that is difficult to bridge within any single framework, we offer our insights as landmarks for today by which to chart tomorrow's course.

As with all volumes that cover a vast region – especially one that for the most part uses a non-Roman alphabet – the issues of transliteration and spelling are always at the forefront. The editors have opted to use a translit-eration of names that are country-specific; i.e. for Ukrainian names a Ukrainian transliteration is used (Volodymyr rather than Vladimir), and for Belarusian names a Belarusian transliteration is used (Alyaksandr rather than Aleksandr). Most of all, consistency and clarity has been the primary objective and motivation for the editors.

Acknowledgements

Our thanks are due to the Scottish Centre for International Security (SCIS) at the University of Aberdeen, which brought the contributors to the current volume together for a conference in Aberdeen (November 2000), and to the International Studies Association (ISA) annual conference (March 2002) in New Orleans, allowing a panel to discuss conference 'first draft' presentations. We would like to pay particular tribute to Mel Huang, an SCIS Research Associate, for his superb and tireless effort in style-editing the chapters in conformity with RoutledgeCurzon specifications.

It is only possible to research and produce studies such as these with the help and understanding of the institutions for which the contributors work. In many cases, they supply not just salaries and research infrastructure, but also the network of contacts and the opportunities to meet and collaborate with others in what must necessarily be a dispersed discipline.

Contributors also acknowledge support from the following:

- United Kingdom Ministry of Defence;
- US Department of Defense;
- DFI Government Services, Washington, DC;
- Caucasus Institute for Peace, Democracy and Development, Tbilisi, Georgia;
- Conflict Studies Research Centre, Royal Military Academy, Sandhurst, UK;
- The Elliott School of International Affairs, George Washington University;
- RAND Corporation;
- Swedish Defence Research Establishment;
- Department of Politics, University of Glasgow;
- Meridian International Center;
- George C. Marshall European Center for Security Studies, Garmisch Partenkirchen, Germany.

The views contained in each chapter are those of the chapter's author, and do not represent the views of all contributors, of the organisations in which they work, or of any government or governmental department.

Part I
Introduction

1 From Soviet bloc to democratic security building?

Ella Akerman and Tracey German

Introduction

The disintegration of the Soviet Union in December 1991 precipitated fundamental changes in the geopolitical space, transforming the fifteen Soviet republics into independent actors on the international stage and necessitating the modification of their relations with each other from 'domestic' to 'foreign'. Subsequently, the former Soviet sub-regions of Central Asia, the Slavic republics, the Caucasus and Baltic Sea regions have all developed cooperative foreign and security policies towards their immediate neighbours and key Western organisations. These policies reflect the ongoing process of transition within the former Soviet Union (FSU), although attitudes and objectives vary dramatically from country to country, reflecting different stages of the process.

As governments across the former Soviet bloc by and large turned their backs on communism at the beginning of the 1990s, there was misplaced optimism amongst the international community that these newly liberalised states would simultaneously re-align themselves with the West. However, the reality has been very different. In order to understand contemporary politics in the region it is important not only to apply the democratisation paradigm and transition theories to the study of the post-Soviet space, but also to take into account their common past and political culture shaped by the Soviet experience. This introductory chapter will examine the historical legacy bequeathed by communism and the impact of the Soviet experience on foreign policy objectives. It will also provide a theoretical appraisal of the transition process, as a state strives to adopt the rhetoric and practices required to move towards its aspirations of democracy.

The Soviet Union: peaceful co-existence?

Following the success of the Soviet Revolution in 1917, the Bolsheviks were convinced that it was neither possible nor necessary for revolutionary Russia to formulate a foreign policy towards the existing capitalist order. This attitude was summarised by Leo Trotsky, the first peoples' commissar for foreign affairs, when he predicted that he would issue a few revolutionary proclamations and then close up shop (Carr 1966: 28). The Bolsheviks believed that revolutions would break out across the West, and saw little need to establish diplomatic relationships with governments whose days were numbered. However, as the anticipated revolution in the West failed to materialise, the Bolsheviks began to formulate and pursue a policy of 'co-existence', establishing trade ties and securing political recognition from neighbouring countries and the major international powers. Nevertheless, the Bolsheviks still expected an international proletarian revolution and perceived foreign policy as a very temporary expedient. The peaceful co-existence of 'socialism in one country' in 1924 had served several purposes. First, it afforded the new leadership flexibility in domestic and foreign policies and narrowed the gap between doctrine and reality. At the same time it represented a move away from the belief in imminent revolution, the *raison d'être* of the international communist movement.

Changing conditions within the Soviet Union, together with the failure of revolutionary attempts abroad and Lenin's death in January 1924, brought the first phase of Soviet foreign policy to a close and set the stage for a major doctrinal shift. Stalin unveiled the new doctrine in an article entitled 'The October Revolution and the Tactics of the Russian Communists', published in December 1924. The new tenet of 'socialism in one country' argued that the world revolution had merely been postponed because capitalism had managed to stabilise itself temporarily. Thus the best course of action was to abandon efforts to promote revolution abroad and to concentrate on building the USSR's economic and military capabilities. While proclaiming this new approach to foreign policy, Stalin retained Lenin's doctrine of the inevitability of war, based upon the argument espoused by Marx and subsequent 20th-century Marxist theorists that private property and the existence of social classes were the causes of war. Even though victory in the Great Patriotic War (1941–45) and the establishment of communist regimes in Central and Eastern Europe (1945–48) necessitated certain modifications to this doctrine, Stalin continued to promulgate the inevitability of war until his death in 1953.

The Cold War paradigm projected a bi-polar international system based on military, politico-ideological and economic competition between the capitalist (the US and its allies) and communist (the USSR and its allies) 'first' and 'second' worlds. Proxy wars and an ongoing battle for influence were waged by the superpowers in the non-aligned 'third' world. Within the Soviet bloc, which included the USSR and Central and Eastern Europe, Moscow ensured a high level of integration and conformity of the foreign and security policies of the those states and regions under its rule. For example, although the USSR was allocated three UN seats (RSFSR, Ukraine and Belarus), there was but one acceptable vote as a larger bloc.

Stalin's successors initiated important changes in Soviet foreign policy doctrine and practice. Malenkov and later Khrushchev argued that a protracted period of co-existence between the communist and capitalist systems was feasible. During this period, the Soviet Union and its allies actively sought to undermine the capitalist system, adopting policies that included the exploitation of 'contradictions' within the Western world, supporting wars of national liberation in the third world and efforts to outstrip the West in economics and technology. In his report to the 20th Party Congress in February 1956, Khrushchev pointed out that 'as long as capitalism survives in the world, the reactionary forces may try to unleash war. But war is not fatalistically inevitable. Today there are mighty social and political forces possessing means to prevent the imperialists from waging war' (Khrushchev 1959).

In the late 1950s Khrushchev advocated the idea that communism's final victory would be achieved through, or at least facilitated by, economic and technological competition with the West. Although the concept of peaceful coexistence remained the principal basis for Soviet foreign policy, Khrushchev's successors Kosygin and Brezhnev undertook significant modifications to this doctrine, not least because Khrushchev's optimistic assumptions about the USSR's economic and technological progress proved to be wrong.

In early 1968, the Czechoslovakian Communist Party, under the leadership of Alexander Dubček, attempted to introduce a number of reforms, including the abolition of censorship. The Soviet Union adopted a policy of combating 'anti-socialist forces'. The policy became known as the 'Brezhnev Doctrine'. Soviet leader Leonid Brezhnev gave the following justification. 'When forces that are hostile to socialism and try to turn the development of some socialist country towards capitalism, it becomes not only a problem of the country concerned, but a common problem and concern of all socialist countries'. This effectively meant that no country was allowed to leave the Warsaw Pact. The Brezhnev Doctrine of limited sovereignty was used to justify the invasions of Hungary in 1956 and Czechoslovakia in 1968, and strongly reinforced the 'bloc' identity of the Soviet Union and Central and Eastern Europe. The doctrine was officially abandoned by Mikhail Gorbachev in 1988.

Following American involvement in Vietnam, the Dominican Republic and Israel, the Soviet leadership deferred further cutbacks in non-strategic forces and launched major new strategic programmes. Kosygin and Brezhnev also downplayed Khrushchev's claims about overtaking the US economically and talked more openly about the danger of war and the West's aggressive policies. By the early 1970s Brezhnev, who had assumed a dominant position in the Soviet leadership, began to develop a militarised foreign policy doctrine that tied global political and social change to the growth of Soviet might. At the 25th Party Congress in 1976 Brezhnev declared that 'the passage from Cold War and from the explosive confrontation of the two worlds to detente was largely connected with the changes in the world correlation of forces' (Pravda 25 February 1976). Furthermore, he developed the concept of a 'restructuring of international relations', which would occur as a result of the shift of the correlation of forces (Mitchell 1978). However, after 1979 it became clear that Brezhnev's policy would not allow the Soviet Union to shift the military aspects of the correlation of forces in its favour. In addition, the slowdown of the economy, the war in Afghanistan and the weakness of the Soviet leadership under Brezhnev and his two short-lived successors demonstrated the widening gap between Soviet rhetoric and reality, Western modernisation and Soviet stagnation.

One of the major characteristics of Soviet foreign policy was the extent to which policy-making was insulated from domestic political pressure. Soviet leaders had considerable autonomy in devising and pursuing their foreign objectives. However, the political arena was dramatically altered by the extensive domestic reforms implemented by Mikhail Gorbachev. His desire to open up political debate presented an increasing challenge to the leadership on virtually all of its policies, both domestic and foreign. When Gorbachev assumed power in spring 1985, there were growing symptoms of economic decline as the USSR fell further behind the West and a growing number of industrialising Asian states. Other serious problems included spiralling levels of environmental degradation, alcoholism and infant mortality, as well as declining life expectancy.

In terms of foreign policy, the massive expenditure on new weapons systems had failed to enhance Soviet security. Furthermore, the weakness of the Soviet economy raised questions about a possible overextension of international commitments and the USSR's limited role in helping to resolve pressing global problems. Gorbachev's policies of *perestroika* and *glasnost* were based on a recognition that the USSR's international status depended upon an improvement in its political and economic systems. This new approach to world affairs led to a reorientation of Soviet foreign policy between 1986 and 1989 that included major initiatives in relations with the West and crucial agreements on arms reductions, the withdrawal of Soviet troops from Eastern Europe and an acceptance of the anti-communist revolutions throughout the region in 1989. These initiatives significantly contributed to the liberation of the communist states of Eastern Europe from Soviet dominance and an end to the global confrontation between the USSR and the United States. They also had a positive impact on the opening up of political and economic contacts between the USSR and the West.

Great expectations

The collapse of the outer Soviet empire in 1989, followed by the disintegration of the Soviet Union in 1991, elicited a surge of confidence amongst the liberal democracies of the industrialised West, who claimed victory over the communist ideology ('the West is best'). This was exemplified by Francis Fukuyama's manifesto that the fall of the communist empire amounted to the 'end of history', on the basis that non-democratic regimes had recognised liberal democracy and the capitalist economic order as 'the final form of human government' (Fukuyama 1992). The spread of democratic forms of governance has been acclaimed as a significant tool in the promotion of global peace and security. Noting in his 1994 State of the Union address that no two democracies have ever fought a war against each other, US President Bill Clinton argued that support for democratisation – or, to be more precise, the proliferation of 'market-democracy' – would be an anti-dote to both international war and civil conflict.[1]

However, would democracy become the banner under which manifold groups would be united by a leader primarily interested in personal gain, not only unsympathetic to democratic objectives, but fully conversant with the mobilising power of popular democratic slogans? Would the collapse of communism reduce conflict? Would former Soviet republics adopt democratic security-building projects and embrace cooperative foreign policy objectives?

Democratisation has been defined as 'the advance of liberal-democratic reform, implying, in particular, the granting of basic freedoms and the widening of popular participation and electoral choice' (Heywood 1997: 28). Over the past century there has been a tendency for an increasing number of countries to pursue supposedly democratic forms of government, Huntington's so-called 'Third Wave', and by 1992 the number of 'democracies' was in a majority for the first time, totalling 91 of 183 states (Chang 1995: 56). Giuseppe Di Palma challenges the assumption that there has been a dramatic rise in democratic administrations, with his assertion that 'the proportion of democracies among independent nations is no greater today than it was after World War I' (Di Palma 1990: 3). The process through which states democra-tise, their success in consolidating their democratisation projects and the relationship between democratisation, security, stability and warfare are thus highly contested issues.

Before a country can embark on a democratisation project it must first move away from its previous non-democratic regime, whether authoritarian, totali-tarian or communist, in what is defined as the transition process. Democratisation is not a solitary consequential event; it is comprised of several different stages that occur over an indefinite period of time: the breakdown of undemocratic rule, transition, consolidation and, if successful, the perpetuation of a stable democratic political order. Thus, transition or 'transformation' is merely an intrinsic stage in the complex development of a democratic state. Rose *et al.* believe it is misleading to describe new democracies as being in 'transition', as this implies a known start- and end-point. In their opinion the term 'transformation' is more consistent with the 'catalytic process of funda-mental and pervasive change' (Rose *et al.* 1998: 7). A state is deemed to be undergoing transition, from the moment critical flaws initially become discernible in the regime, until it successfully attains democratic stability, an accomplishment often taking many years.

It is essential to clarify the distinction between liberalisation and democratisation in order to ascertain how the FSU republics measure up. Liberalisation constitutes an expansion of civil rights and a loosening of restrictions, such as abandoning censorship of the media, whilst democratisa-tion takes this process further towards the establishment of a popular political regime, with regular free and competitive elections. Aleksandr Gelman has elucidated the difference between the two interlinked processes: 'Liberalisation is an unclenched fist, but the hand is the same and at any moment it could be clenched again into a fist. Only outwardly is liberalisation sometimes reminiscent of democratisation, but in actual fact it is a fundamental and intolerable usurpation' (Brzezinski 1989: 45–6).

Thus liberalisation does not necessarily lead to a process of democratisation – it may merely restore the authority of a weakened regime and allow it to pursue its restrictive policies anew. Huntington believes that liberal reformers in the late twentieth century tended to view liberalisation merely as a means of defusing opposition to the regime without launching complete democratisation: 'They wanted to create a kinder, gentler, more secure and stable authoritarianism without altering fundamentally the nature of their system' (Huntington 1991: 129). He views a liberalised authority as unstable, inasmuch as it risks stimulating a desire for a further loosening of restrictions amongst certain groups, simultaneously increasing a desire for repression amongst others, notably the ruling elites.

The transition process in post-communist states

The legacy of various undemocratic regime types that exist prior to the initiation of transformation will have a specific impact upon efforts to introduce democratic changes. The starting point of individual transition attempts will have profound consequences on the eventual outcome. Democracy is transplanted into very different circumstances – whether it flourishes or not depends partly upon the ground in which it is sown, together with the prevailing climate and the level of care bestowed upon it during the initial stages of its development. In order to understand the nature of post-Soviet transition, and the different degrees of democratic development across the region, it is pertinent to examine the impact of communist rule.

Totalitarianism, which was central to the communist concept of governance, reached a peak with the large-scale purges and deportations that characterised Stalin's Soviet Union, before his successors recognised the impossibility of attaining totalitarian ideals of communism and gradually relaxed the harshly repressive system. This led to the development of what have been labelled 'post-totalitarian regimes', which were slightly less repressive but still accountable to a political elite as opposed to an electorate that was accustomed to the undemocratic use of mass terror to force compliance with state dictates (Rose *et al.* 1998: 41). Thus the post-communist countries are commonly considered to have embarked upon the democratic transformation of post-totalitarian regimes and share common attributes.

Lilia Shevtsova has ascertained characteristics that, in her opinion, are shared by all post-communist societies, including a poorly developed system of party formation, fragile coalitions among the ruling elite, continuous confrontation between the executive and legislature and an ideological vacuum resulting from the repudiation of socialism (Shevtsova 1995: 33).

Each of these attributes constitutes an obstacle to the successful realisation of democratic reform. Leslie Holmes interprets post-communism as a 'rejection of the communist power system' rather than a 'clear-cut adoption of an alternative system', arguing that it is impossible to comprehend it without an understanding of communism as a political system. In his opinion, post-communist countries broadly share three common factors: 'a similar starting point and legacy; the comprehensiveness of their attempts at transition; and the global context in which such attempts have been made' (Holmes 1997: 15). Moreover, Taras Kuzio has referred to the transition process in the FSU, with Ukraine in particular in mind, as the 'quadruple transition', specifically that state- and nation-building, marketisation, and of course, democratisation, are all major challenges currently confronting the FSU (Kuzio *et al.* 1999: 1). Despite the introduction of democratic reforms, civil society remains very weak and underdeveloped in most post-communist countries, a legacy of totalitarian rule.

A particular complication with post-communist transitions has been the necessity of conducting wide-reaching economic reforms whilst simultaneously attempting to institute the norms of democratic government and society. Dahrendorf argues that, because transitional periods are highly politicised, economic issues tend to be neglected: 'Political transition leads to economic frustration, resulting in instability and unrest' (Dahrendorf 1990: 139). Economic change frequently results in great personal hardships for the majority of the population (the 'veil of tears'), and as a consequence it increases popular disillusionment in the transition process. At least a 'triple' transformation is imperative (if not Kuzio's notion of quadruple transition), incorporating both political and economic reform, as well as the introduction of institutions to implement these changes. The newly established countries of the FSU had the additional complication of being obliged to forge relationships with the international community, developing foreign and security policies with little experience to draw upon. Popular dissatisfaction with the transition process has often been translated into antagonism or isolationism in terms of foreign and security politics.

There are many obstacles to the successful emergence of a democratic system in both post-authoritarian and post-communist countries. They can be difficulties of a systemic, functional or contextual nature, encompassing problems with the establishment of democratic institutions or an acceptable constitutional framework, as well as public opinion. The stability of immature democracies may also be threatened by problems inherited from the previous regime, such as a failing economy, poor infrastructure or a weak civil society.

Systemic crises arise as a direct result of the change in political orientation away from (or towards) non-democratic methods of governance. [2] They stem from a failure to institutionalise the new political order and include problems with the establishment of new constitutional and electoral systems, as well as the parallel existence of old and new state institutions. Without vital institutional support, attempts to reform a political system are likely to fail, as they are unable to function in a vacuum. Democratic transformation will be undermined if corresponding alterations to the institutional framework of a state, such as the constitution, are not made and the institutions of the previous regime persist.

The transition of post-communist countries is further hampered by the fact that many members of the former socialist regime have retained positions of authority within political structures. Therefore, political development is strongly influenced by the often-undemocratic political cultures, attitudes and strategies of elites, instilled under communist rule, and the character of the parties and other institutions through which they vie for power (Parrott 1997: 21). Whilst elite continuity is not a problem exclusively associated with post-communist transitions, it does pose a greater threat to a fledgling democracy attempting to root itself in the soil of a former communist state. Authoritarian regimes are not formulated around any specific ideology, in contrast to pervasive totalitarian dogma. Communism, as an ideology, encompassed all areas of daily life, particularly for those working within the Party hierarchy. The current leaders of so-called 'democratic' groups in post-communist states were cultivated to be archetypal representatives of the previous regime's repressive state system. They may have changed the explicit political slogans under which they operate, but transforming ingrained attitudes and behaviour is a far more onerous task.

Dankwart Rustow, who argued that 'the vast majority of citizens in a democracy-to-be must have no doubt as to which political community they belong to', identified the idea of national unity as an essential condition for the initiation of transition. He established a link between homogeneity and democracy that implies that democratic transition is virtually impossible within a multinational state, such as the Soviet Union, because liberalisation encourages nationalist separatism (Rustow 1970). Thus, successful transition requires a certain degree of national unity, a concord of conflicting interests for the sake of peace. However, whilst a certain degree of nationalism or national pride is necessary for the cohesion of a modern state, extreme forms accompanied by violence are destabilising and dangerous. Unfortunately the fundamental liberalism inherent in democratic ideology promotes the free expression of a wide spectrum of grievances, thereby fostering nationalistic tendencies. Existing underlying ethnic tensions are particularly prone to exacerbation during a transitional period. Previously repressed national groups push for increased autonomy, whilst political leaders exploit these rifts and utilise populist, ethnic rhetoric in order to win support for their faction. Instead of the moderation and cooperation essential to avoid conflict, extremist rhetoric is employed.

It has been suggested that democratisation provides a pertinent occasion to resolve ethnic conflict, as it encourages open discussion and the possibility of negotiation. However, this is qualified by the assertion that '[d]emocratisation is most likely to succeed in mitigating ethnic tensions if ethnic issues are addressed early in the transition process' (De Nevers 1993: 39). John Stuart

Mill concluded that democracy is 'next to impossible in a country made up of different nationalities' (Mill 1959: 486), whilst Huntington contends that the introduction of democracy creates a 'democracy paradox' – it allows groups that appeal to indigenous ethnic and religious loyalties to come to power, and yet these groups are then likely to be anti-democratic (Huntington 1996: 6). He points to the examples of the former Soviet Union and Yugoslavia as manifestations of this 'paradox'. Zakaria is also highly critical of the common assumption that the forces of democracy are forces of ethnic harmony and peace, observing that 'without a background in constitutional liberalism, the introduction of democracy in divided societies has actually fomented nationalism, ethnic conflict or even war' (Zakaria 1997: 35).

Belligerence or insecurity?

Despite the hopes of the international community that the spread of democratic forms of governance would enhance global security, some analysts regard the increased possibility of armed conflict or war, stemming from the instability and uncertainty of a transition period, as a serious threat to the progress of successful democratic reform. The most notable advocates of this proposition are Mansfield and Snyder, who argue that the characteristic instability of a transitional period greatly increases the likelihood of war:

> [C]ountries do not become mature democracies overnight. More typically, they go through a rocky transitional period, where democratic control over foreign policy is partial, where mass politics mixes in a volatile way with authoritarian elite politics, and where democratisation suffers reversals. In this transitional phase of democratisation, countries become more aggressive and war-prone...

They have identified four conditions that, they argue, increases the propensity of a democratising state to engage in war: elite disunity and conflict; mobilised mass politics; a constricted marketplace of ideas; and an unfavourable international environment (Mansfield and Snyder 1996: 5).

Huntington also suggested that democratisation can increase the probability of war, supporting the work of Mansfield and Snyder in this field. In his opinion, war can be triggered by the same motives to make communal appeals that also stimulate ethnic conflict within democratising states (Huntington 1996: 7). As mentioned above, the transitional period can witness a dramatic rise in nationalism, particularly amongst ethnic minorities within a multinational state. This exacerbates the volatile nature of a partially democratised state, often culminating in war. A recent study of conflicts involving global minorities concluded that states undergoing democratisation are more prone to ethno-political conflict, as they lack the proper mechanisms through which national groups and minorities can channel their grievances (Gurr 1993).

Mansfield and Snyder believe that one reason for the aggressive tendencies of democratising states 'lies in the nature of domestic political competition following the break-up of the autocratic regime'. Elites from both the old regime and those representing the new democratic forces compete for power and survival. They need to muster as many allies as possible, an objective often achieved by utilising nationalist slogans. Exploiting nationalistic sentiments and insecurities – in a process that could be termed 'nationalist-outbidding' – is a simple means of uniting people as it requires little from them other than membership of a particular ethnic group. However, once mobilised, these groups frequently prove very difficult to control and armed conflict may ensue, particularly if other grievances with democratic reforms exist, such as economic inequalities. Nevertheless, it is the unscrupulous misuse of power by elites that stimulates the tendency for war, not public opinion. This exploitation is facilitated by the weak institutionalisation of the democratising state. The lack of any formal regulatory mechanisms encourages abuse of power within state structures, as officials and other members of the ruling circle cannot be held fully accountable to the public.

The research by Mansfield and Snyder triggered a debate amongst scholars in the field of democratisation, and in particular, the relationship between democratisation and war. [3] This focused on the notion of the 'exportation' of democracy; Mansfield and Snyder contend that Western governments should concentrate on devising strategies for managing democratic transitions in ways that minimise the risk of war. Snyder expanded his study to explore the link between democratic transformation and internal conflict, investigating in more detail how the democratisation process can actually exacerbate nationalist fervour and ethnic conflict if the conditions permitting a successful transition are not in place (Snyder 2000).[4] He argues that it is imperative to distinguish between the early phase of democratisation and the subsequent consolidation of democracy. In his assessment, it is in this initial phase that factors rendering a state more prone to war can be located. He particularly stresses the negative impact of fragile, weak or even non-existent institutions necessary for the functioning of an effective democracy, as noted above. This is a period when the masses have begun to play a role in the political life of the state, but democracy has yet to be consolidated. It is during this period that mass nationalist movements are most active and effective, as political elites frequently employ nationalistic appeals in order to mobilise popular support for their programmes. According to Snyder, it is this instrumental usage of nationalism by self-interested elites, so-called 'elite persuasion', which links the early stages of transition with an increased potential for ethnic conflict. The motivation to utilise nationalism depends on how threatened the elites are by the introduction of democracy. Furthermore, when powerful groups feel threatened by democracy they seek to keep their states' institutions weak and easy to manipulate, which results in a 'partial democracy' (Snyder 2000: 55). The consequent impotency of supposedly democratic institutions allows ruling elites to avoid being fully accountable to the electorate.

Snyder believes that nationalism reflects a need to establish an effective state that is capable of achieving a group's economic and security goals. According to his analysis, the most aggressive nationalist movements arise when states fail to fulfil these tasks, inciting people to create more effective states for themselves. He argues that nationalism is usually weak or absent, typically arising during the earliest stages of democratisation when elites are competing for popular support. Snyder rejects the 'ancient hatreds' view, asserting that 'nations are not simply freed or awakened by democratisation; they are formed by the experiences they undergo during that process' (Snyder 2000: 36).

Conclusions

The events across Eastern Europe and the former Soviet Union in the early 1990s emphasise the immense complexity of democratic transition and the fundamental weaknesses of existing democratisation theories when applied to post-communist regime transformations. The demise of communism and subsequent redrawing of international boundaries has necessitated the rapid conception of foreign and security policies by the countries of the former Soviet Union. This has elicited many changes in forms of governance and policy-making, as the new dynamic of democratic security building has begun to shape their foreign policies. Nevertheless the impact of this dynamic varies across the region, reflecting different stages of progress in democratic development.

The outcomes of transition are inherently unpredictable, and it appears unrealistic to expect post-communist regimes to evolve in a similar manner to authoritarian ones, particularly as the former are undergoing a double transition to both a political democracy and a market economy. Theoretical models of post-communist transitions are still in an embryonic form, so it is conceivable that the turbulence experienced in all spheres of public and private life since 1991 can be regarded as an integral part of the transition process. To paraphrase Mansfield and Snyder, countries typically undergo a rocky transitional period during which democracy may appear to be in jeopardy, and it could be argued that most of the former Soviet states have not deviated from this paradigm.

In the proceeding chapters the authors will draw on some of the theoretical perspectives raised in the introduction from a regional standpoint. This book addresses the debates surrounding external and internal aspects of democratic security building and addresses three core themes:

- the extent to which states within these regions have developed cooperative foreign and security policies towards their immediate neighbours and key Western states and organisations;
- the nature of the relationship and interplay between internal and external aspects of democratic security building;

- the main dynamics in shaping inter-state bilateral and multi-lateral relations in post-Soviet space through the use of case-study examples.

Although each author brings his/her own unique perspective to bear, it is generally accepted that democratic security building process in the FSU is an uphill road, and while the challenges are somewhat unique to each post-Soviet sub-region, there are challenges that are prevalent in all. Key among those is the need for these states to focus on state/institution and nation building, and for the West to continue to encourage these partners to continue along the road to true democracy, and integration into the market economy.

Notes

1 For further information on the 'democratic peace' debate with regard to international war see: Doyle 1986, Russett *et al.* 1993, Gleditsch 1992, Schweller 1992, Macmillan 1996, Oneal and Russett 1997, Reiter and Stam 1998.
2 The term *systemic change* pertains to necessary modifications in the actual mechanisms of government and institutions of state, such as governmental ministries, during a transformation of the regime. It should be noted that the term *systemic change* can refer to a change in political orientation, either democratisation or away from democracy to more authoritarian forms of rule.
3 See Wolf 1996, Enterline 1996, Mansfield and Snyder 1996, Neil and Pravda 1996.
4 See also Byman and van Evera 1998.

Part II

Baltic security politics

2 The post-Prague strategic orientation of the Baltic states

Adam Grissom

Introduction[1]

Outsiders have dictated the security orientation of the Baltic peoples for most of the past two centuries.[2] The modern form of this trend was established by the incorporation of the Baltics into the Tsarist Russian Empire in the early 19th century. It continued with the Molotov–Ribbentrop Pact of 1939 and the post-war settlement at Potsdam, which embedded the Baltics in the Soviet inner empire.[3]

In one sense, history repeated itself in November 2002 when the member states of NATO gathered in Prague to consider the alliance's enlargement. If – as is now expected – NATO issued invitations to Estonia, Latvia and Lithuania, the Prague summit will be a watershed on a par with the episodes in Brest-Litovsk and Potsdam during the last century (Dempsey 2002). And, once again, neither Tallinn, nor Riga nor Vilnius had a vote.

On the other hand, it is a stark contrast between the 2002 summit and the events of 1939 and 1945. Over the past decade, external involvement in the Baltic region has been accompanied by serious efforts to help the Baltic states develop their own capacities to build and sustain democratic polities at home, influence their security environment, and play a role on the European stage.[4] Where previous eras in Baltic security were dominated by the principles of imperial politics and bipolar Cold War, the post-Prague era will be built on the principles and practices of democratic security building.

This chapter explores the interplay between democratic security building and the external security orientation of the Baltic states. The first section briefly reviews the evolution of the Baltic governments' security orientation since the restoration of independence. The second considers the Baltic countries' strategic orientation in the post-Prague era, focusing on the Euro-Atlantic agenda and potential security challenges arising in the Nordic–Baltic region. The third explores the interaction between democratic security building in the Baltic states and their post-Prague security orientation, noting that while the past decade of democratic security building has been very successful, the task is not yet complete. The Baltic governments do not yet have the capacity to simultaneously sustain security cooperation at both the Euro-Atlantic and Nordic–Baltic levels. As a result, the massive requirements of Baltic integration with Euro-Atlantic institutions may preclude the development of security cooperation in the Nordic–Baltic region – with deleterious consequences for the Baltic states and the region as a whole.

Baltic security orientation in the post-Cold War era

Phase 1: Independence (1988–91)

The Soviet Union treated the Baltics as a buffer zone. In so doing, the Soviet political and security *nomenklatura* followed the lead set by Russian imperial officials since at least the time of Peter the Great (Puheloinen 1999:14–22). As the Cold War security system matured, Soviet planners also increasingly viewed the Baltics as a coherent region intimately linked to the Kola Peninsula to the north. Under Soviet rule the Baltic region was a highly militarised defensive screen for Moscow, Leningrad and the military facilities in the Murmansk region. The air defence network in the region, consisting of a number of important radar installations, communications nodes and airfields, was particularly important to the Soviet Union's military posture (Puheloinen 1999: 55).

The Soviets' approach to the Baltics helped create a sub-regional identity where previously there had been a pastiche of Nordic and Central European religious, linguistic and cultural identities (Norkus 1998b: 265). As the Latvian ambassador to Washington has remarked, '…Baltic identity is not a phenomenon with deep historic roots. The identities of the Baltic nations were formed in the first half of our century as the basis of the respective nation-states. However, the similar conditions in the three countries that prevailed under Soviet rule formed a strong component of joint Baltic identity that co-exists with the Estonian, Lithuanian and Latvian national identities' (Ronis 1996). As a result, the Baltic states worked closely in the post-independence era and adopted a similar strategic orientation.

In the initial months of independence, the Baltic leaders' primary objective was to compel the Soviet Union to continue to decentralise power while establishing their own institutions in its place. Citizenship quickly became a fundamental political issue. By the time the Soviet Union collapsed, more than thirty per cent of Estonian and Latvian residents were members of the Russian-speaking minority (Semjonov 1996). Many ethnic Estonians and Latvians wished to confer citizenship upon only pre-1940 inhabitants, effectively excluding Russian speakers (the non-titular minority) from political life (De Nevers 1998: 121–4). The citizenship status of the 'Russian' minorities would become a serious and longstanding point of contention with Moscow (De Nevers 1998: 121–4).

Phase 2: Internationalisation (1991–94)

The collapse of the Soviet Union threw the strategic orientation of the Baltic states into profound uncertainty. The inchoate nature of the Baltic states' relations with the new authorities in Moscow was their most immediate concern. Initially, there were prospects for cordial, if not warm, relations between the Baltic governments and Russia. However, the relationship quickly began to sour amid controversies involving the plight of Russian-speaking minorities in Baltic states, the final status of borders between the new countries, the disposition of Russian forces on Baltic territory, and economic relations across the new boundaries (Archer 2000). As Baltic–Russian relations deteriorated, the primary goal of the Baltic governments became the withdrawal of Russian military forces from their Cold War garrisons. Russia prevaricated on this issue to place pressure on the Baltic governments to settle citizenship and financial disagreements on terms amenable to the Russian government (Bleiere 1998: 120). Russo–Baltic relations settled into a long-term pattern of antagonism.

At this stage, the involvement of outside powers and institutions in Baltic issues became a vital element in the resolution of disputes in the region and the development of the Baltic states' strategic orientation. In particular, the contribution of long-term missions established under the Organisation for Security and Cooperation in Europe's High Commissioner on National Minorities (HCNM) in Latvia and Estonia in 1993 were a classic case of democratic stability building.[5] These missions provided expert advice to the Baltic governments (at times directly shaping legislation and administrative instructions) and played a key role in mediating negotiations between Russia and the Baltic states on citizenship for Russian minorities.[6] But the HCNM did not act alone. The OSCE Forum on Security Cooperation, the EU, the Western European Union and the Council of Europe provided similar assistance to the Baltic states. NATO and Western governments were instrumental in creating viable compromises between the Baltic countries and Moscow on citizenship issues (Norkus 1998a: 152). A similar pattern of internationalisation was applied to other outstanding issues in the region, most prominently the withdrawal of Russian forces from Baltic territory.[7]

In addition to internationalising their disputes with Russia, the Baltic states also began to seek membership in international forums. They joined the UN shortly after re-gaining independence in late 1991. In March 1992, an initiative led by the German and Danish governments resulted in the establishment of the Council of the Baltic Sea States, consisting of Latvia, Lithuania, Estonia, Germany, Denmark, Finland, Norway, Poland, Russia, Iceland, Sweden and the European Commission. The CBSS agenda was specifically and purposefully limited to 'soft security' issues, such as trade, economic development and cultural exchanges.[8] In May 1993, Lithuania and Estonia were admitted to the Council of Europe; Latvia followed in February 1995.

This phase in the Baltic states' security orientation concluded with the final withdrawal of Russian forces in 1994. Internationalising the issue had significantly strengthened the Baltic case. It was a lesson they would take forward into the future.

Phase 3: Seeking European sponsorship (1994–97)

The withdrawal of Russian troops from the Baltics in 1994 did not end contentious interactions between the Baltic states and Russia. Provocations and alleged provocations continued on both sides. The strategic orientation of the Baltic countries was fundamentally shaped by these disagreements (Blank 1998a: 13–14). Russian threats, coupled with prior Baltic experience with internationalising Russian troop withdrawal, increased the interest of the Baltic governments in EU and NATO membership (Herd 2000). The three Baltic states began active involvement in NATO's Partnership for Peace programme in 1994, and each signed a Europe Agreement in 1995. Before long, EU and NATO membership had become an important element in Baltic identity (Feldman 2000).

The Baltic countries turned to their European partners, and particularly Germany, for assistance in their pursuit of membership of NATO and the EU. The German government, with a long history of involvement in the region and a key role in both organisations, was naturally one of the Baltic states' top priorities for engagement. Many in the Baltic governments perceived Germany to be a viable counterbalance to Russian pressure (Blank 1998a: 27). Early in this period, the German government reacted positively to requests for assistance from the Baltic states. Indeed, in 1992 the German Foreign Ministry played a central role in the establishment of the CBSS (Heimsoeth 2000). However, German support for Baltic aspirations had its limits, which became increasingly evident as Russia intensified its objections to greater Baltic integration with the West. Russia's policies significant influenced Germany's stance. By the middle of the decade, German decision-makers were advising the Baltic countries to abandon thoughts of NATO membership in the near term. Instead, they should accept a role as a bridge between the West and Russia, as distinct from members of the West in their own right (Blank 1998a: 28). Eventually the German government would settle on a policy opposing both Baltic membership of NATO (at least in the near term) and the involvement of the EU in 'hard security' issues in the Baltic region (Archer 2000).

The Baltic states were obliged to turn elsewhere in their search for security sponsorship. Although a spectrum of foreign observers advocated that the Nordic states (particularly Sweden and Finland) undertake this role, the Nordics declined (Blank 1998a). While Sweden and Finland provided critical support to regional cooperation on 'soft security' issues, they had no interest in becoming the providers of 'hard security' to the Baltic countries – nor did they have the capability to do so (Archer 2000).

Nevertheless, the Nordic and Baltic governments pursued a significant number of regional 'soft security' initiatives in the mid-1990s. Many of these initiatives established regional institutions, through which 'soft security' cooperation could be enhanced over the long term. The earliest example was the CBSS (Heimsoeth 2000). It explicitly eschews 'hard security' issues, instead focusing on such areas as democracy building, humanitarian assistance, environmental management, etc. While the CBSS does have a limited central secretariat – its main administrative workload being borne by the country holding the annual presidency – it supports a number of important initiatives through working groups, special task forces and other methods.

The Baltic Round Table was established in 1994 to support negotiations on the OSCE Pact on Stability in Europe. The Round Table members included the three Baltic governments, Poland and Russia. The OSCE, EU, CBSS and interested outside governments were also invited to participate. While the Round Table produced several promising proposals, discussions effectively ceased with the subsequent signature of the Pact.

The Baltic Council was established in 1994 to provide a forum for functional cooperation between the three Baltic governments. The Council works primarily through ministerial meetings convened under its Council of Ministers, and discussions between parliamentarians under the auspices of the Baltic Assembly (Norkus 1998b: 279). Unlike many other regional forums, defence and security issues are firmly embedded in the Council's agenda. Indeed, a proposal for a Baltic Defence Union was floated in 1995, but ultimately rejected (Vareikis & Žygelytė 1998).

The primary Nordic–Baltic cooperative mechanism for security issues has been the '5+3' ministerial process. The '5' are the members of the Nordic Council: Denmark, Finland, Iceland, Norway and Sweden. The '3' are the Baltic Council members: Estonia, Latvia and Lithuania. The '5+3' arrangement allows the full scope of economic, political and security issues to be discussed without the political difficulties that might attend the establishment of a formalised forum focusing on hard security issues. Despite its lack of institutionalisation, the '5+3' ministerial process has become extraordinarily important to the security dynamics of the region. The Foreign and Defence ministries of participating governments regularly address developments in Baltic–Russian relations, Baltic integration into European and North Atlantic institutions, and the enhancement of Nordic–Baltic regional cooperation (Norkus 1998b). However, the effectiveness of the '5+3' construct is significantly limited by the informal nature of discussions and the lack of Russian participation. These factors put portions of the region's security agenda out of reach.

The Nordic and Baltic governments have also invested in specific regional military capabilities. The first of these initiatives was the Baltic Peacekeeping Battalion (BALTBAT), created and supported by the Nordics, Germany, the UK, the US, France and the Netherlands. In addition, the Baltic Air

Surveillance Network (BALTNET) was established in 1997 to link the air traffic control radar and communications networks in Estonia and Latvia with a regional air traffic control centre in Lithuania. A year later, the Baltic Naval Squadron (BALTRON) was established to prepare Baltic naval personnel to operate to NATO standards, and the Baltic defence ministries and their major counterparts (primarily the Nordics, UK, France and US) began to meet thrice yearly under the Baltic Security Assistance (BALTSEA) initiative. Last, and perhaps most important from a long-term perspective, the Baltic Defence College (BALDEFCOL) opened its doors in 1999 to train staff officers from Baltic militaries in the procedures used in the West. Each of these important initiatives served to enhance security relationships within the region while bolstering a specific military capability.

However, despite this flurry of regional activity, in mid-1997 the Baltic countries still lacked a strong European sponsor to advocate their membership in Euro-Atlantic institutions. Moreover, the German 'prime mover' driving the first round of NATO enlargement was explicitly opposing their membership in that organisation. (Szayna 2001: 18–19). The ultimate result was that the Baltic states did not achieve their primary objective of integration into the Euro-Atlantic community. At the NATO Summit in Madrid in July 1997, the first round of NATO enlargement was limited to Poland, Hungary and the Czech Republic. The European Commission's recommendations on enlargement released less than two weeks later included only Estonia from the Baltic region. A combination of Russian antagonism and European reluctance had denied the Baltic states their primary foreign policy objectives – membership of NATO and the EU. The Madrid Summit and EC declarations marked the beginning of a new phase in Baltic strategic orientation.

Phase 4: Expanding emphasis on Washington and Brussels (1997–2002)

In 1997, the failure of the Baltic states to secure NATO membership at Madrid and the exclusion of Lithuania and Latvia from the European Commission's list of first-echelon states to be integrated led to a reassessment of Baltic security orientation. In the absence of European sponsorship, the United States began to assume an increasingly prominent position in the calculations of the Baltic countries.[9]

Up to that time, the US had played an ambiguous role in post-Cold War Baltic security issues. Washington's approach was defined by a desire for greater cooperation between the Baltic states, stronger Nordic–Baltic links on security, Baltic accession to the EU, and a 'credible' open-door policy for NATO (Asmus 1996). Washington took little direct interest in the Baltics. In the lead-up to Madrid, Washington had been no more willing than the Germans or other European members to take up the cause of Baltic membership in the first round. However, the Madrid communiqué language confirming the alliance's 'open-door' policy essentially invited the aspirants to press their case – which the Baltic countries exploited to the fullest in Washington. In time, there was a discernible redirection of the Baltic states' strategic orientation toward the US, and greater interest on Washington's part.

In September 1997, the US government unveiled its Northern European Initiative (NEI), aimed at promoting cooperation within the region (including Russia and its north-western provinces) and increasing the involvement of major external powers (particularly the US, EU, Germany and Poland) (Browning 2001). The NEI was unusual for an American initiative because it addressed 'soft security' issues and embraced the involvement of sub-state actors (Karp 2000). NEI highlighted six functional areas for increased co-operation – trade, crime, civil society building, energy, the environment, and public health (Sergounin 2002). NEI was also explicitly intended to improve the Baltic countries' preparedness for NATO membership. The initiative was hamstrung by its second agenda, which guaranteed Russian opposition (Browning 2001). The NEI was followed in 1998 by the US–Baltic Charter, a formal agreement signed by the leaders of Estonia, Latvia, Lithuania and the United States. The Charter made explicit US interest in seeing stability in the region, and committed the signatories to '...consult together, as well as with other countries, in the event that a Partner perceives that its territorial integrity, independence, or security is threatened or at risk.' While the Charter did not formally commit the US government to support Baltic membership in the next round of NATO enlargement, the document was a striking and important statement of political support.

The Baltic governments' relationship with the EU also moved in a positive direction in this period. Finnish Prime Minister Paavo Lipponen utilised Finland's presidency of the EU to launch the Northern Dimension (ND) in 1997. The purpose of the ND was to focus attention and resources on the 'soft security' challenges facing the Baltic Sea region and the Nordics (Archer 2000). The ND serves to encourage cooperation on functional issues such as transportation, telecommunications, energy, natural resource management, the preservation of the environment, education, vocational training, public health, social welfare and the prevention of crime.[10] The NEI and ND overlapped in many areas, but ND enjoyed more success because it was not linked to NATO enlargement, allowing a more robust programme of cooperation with Moscow (Sergounin 2002).

By all accounts, reorientation of the Baltic countries' security alignment towards Washington and Brussels has paid off handsomely. Their internal capacity for participating in Euro-Atlantic institutions is steadily increasing with considerable outside assistance, they are on track for eventual membership in the EU, and (most important to Baltic decision-makers) they will likely be invited to join NATO at the Prague Summit in November 2002.

Post-Prague strategic orientation of the Baltic countries

The Prague Summit inaugurated the fifth phase of the Baltic states' post-Cold War strategic orientation – the consolidation of their relationships with NATO and the EU. The vital national security interests of the Baltic countries will be much more secure in this phase than at any time in the recent past. By achieving their primary goals, the leadership of the Baltic governments has averted the worst-case scenario for their countries – subordinate status in the Russian near abroad. They will also have averted the second-worst result of purgatory in a grey zone between East and West. This is a striking accomplishment for Baltic diplomacy. But it does not represent the totality of Baltic security needs. A variety of secondary security challenges will persist that are difficult to resolve through Euro-Atlantic channels, or are a poor fit for existing regional soft security institutions.

Russian military vulnerability

Though it may seem ironic, the Baltic membership of NATO will inadvertently create significant challenges to Russia's military security. Over the past decade, as Russian military planners have observed Western precision air campaigns against Iraq, Yugoslavia and Afghanistan, they have become increasingly concerned by this capability (Kaufman 2001). The air defence radars and communications sites in the Baltics were, during the Cold War, the Soviets' primary (if not wholly impressive) defence against such attacks. The withdrawal of Russian forces from the region forced Moscow to reconstitute the north-west air defence network on an *ad hoc* basis, amid crushing budget austerity. The ability of this network to protect the many high-value facilities found in Moscow, St Petersburg and the Pskov Military District is at best questionable. Baltic membership of NATO will exacerbate this vulnerability. While Moscow clearly does not fear the Baltic governments' national military capabilities, the 'Zapad-99' exercise demonstrated a deep concern regarding the West's ability to launch air and missile strikes from the direction of the Baltics.

This may be particularly true regarding the survivability of Russia's nuclear retaliatory capability. At least sixty per cent of Russia's nuclear capability is based at facilities on the Kola Peninsula near Murmansk, a figure that is likely to increase over time (Blank 1998a: 16). Moreover, a very high proportion of Russia's second-strike capabilities reside in the Submarine-Launched Ballistic Missiles (SLBMs) deployed aboard submarines based at Kola. While these facilities are a considerable distance from current Western airfields, tactical aircraft operating from Baltic airfields would be within easy un-refuelled striking distance. Aircraft based in the Baltic countries would also be within an hour's flying time to political and military command centres in the Moscow and St Petersburg metro areas (Blank 1998a). Given Moscow's increasing reliance on its nuclear deterrent, the vulnerability of its Murmansk facilities is an issue of regional and global significance. The potential for misunderstandings, particularly given the quality of Russia's air defence network in the region, is quite real. Baltic membership of NATO may increase the potential for such a misunderstanding or mistake to escalate unnecessarily.

A carefully constructed programme of confidence- and security-building measures might help manage these dynamics. Potential measures might include collaborative airspace control, agreed limits on military deployments and exercises of particular types in particular areas, and increased transparency through data and planning exchanges. There are clear NATO–Russian aspects to such an agreement. However, there is also room for a regional contribution. The national capabilities, infrastructure and airspace of Sweden and Finland are relevant to this problem (as are the Baltics', prior to full membership), but cannot be integrated into a NATO–Russian arrangement. A Nordic–Baltic–Russian regional understanding, or even CSBMs, might prove a useful contribution to military stability in the region.

Kaliningrad

The Russian enclave of Kaliningrad will also continue to be a significant security concern for the Baltic region. The oblast's population is heavily dependent on commercial contacts with the surrounding countries to sustain its flagging economy. For example, eighty per cent of Kaliningrad's electricity comes from a nuclear power plant in Lithuania (Kramer 1997). The current epidemic of organised crime and smuggling is destabilising to the oblast and surrounding areas. If economic conditions continue to deteriorate, the political consequences could be dire. Yuri Fedorov has outlined this scenario in some detail:

> Since the financial crash in August 1998, the economic and social situation in Kaliningrad has deteriorated dramatically, with unemployment in the region affecting 25% of the economically active population and about half of the total population living below the poverty line. Some Russian experts believe that Moscow's economic policy towards Kaliningrad is aggravating the already tragic social and economic conditions there as well as encouraging secessionist ambitions. According the Russian estimates, approximately 30% of the region's population support the idea of the Kaliningrad oblast becoming a so-called Baltic Republic that would have its own President and Parliament and be a kind of 'associate member of the Russian Federation.' It is, of course, only natural that such attitudes are perceived in Moscow as a clear sign of secessionism which is absolutely unacceptable to Russia's elite. Thus, the roots of potential conflict are already there and the further degradation of the economy and falling living standards may promote regional separatism which, in turn, could provoke large-scale repression and instability.
>
> (Fedorov 2000)

Fedorov leaves implicit the effect that such a crisis would have on relations between Russia and the West. Baltic membership of NATO would completely encircle Kaliningrad with alliance territory. Russia's sole landward route of access into Kaliningrad runs through Lithuanian territory, and its seaward link passes through Estonian territorial waters, ensuring that the Baltic governments would be thrust in the midst of this crisis from its opening moments. A miscalculation in these conditions could be potentially disastrous for regional stability.

A carefully arranged programme of confidence- and security-building measures could significantly contribute to stability in times of crisis. The establishment of clear Russo–Baltic procedures for land, air and maritime transit would be a valuable start. The institutionalisation of crisis consultation mechanisms would also benefit the region. Above all, a comprehensive dialogue – encompassing 'hard security' issues, as well as 'soft security' issues – is a pre-requisite for long-term stability in Kaliningrad. Such a dialogue would likely be more successful in the Nordic–Regional context than in the NATO–Russian context, to minimise perceptions of NATO aggrandisement in the region.

Military environmental hazards

The environmental threats to the Nordic–Baltic region are well publicised. They are being addressed through a number of existing regional 'soft security' forums and programmes. However, there is a 'hard security' component to many of these issues that can prove quite problematic. Examples include nuclear test residue and nuclear waste on Novaya Zemlya, radioactive pollution at ex-Soviet naval bases in the Baltics, abandoned hazards such as the hulks of the Komsomolets and Kursk submarines, chemical weapons dumps from the Soviet era, and residual pollution from a variety of fuels (jet, liquid rocket and solid rocket) (Yablokov 2000). These problems pose a day-to-day threat to the health of all the inhabitants of the Nordic–Baltic region and northwest Russia.

If these issues are to be managed effectively, mechanisms will need to be established for managing their 'hard security' aspects – to include the exchange of sensitive data, inspections of sensitive sites, access to cleanup operations, monitoring of military activities with environmental relevance, and demilitarisation/destruction of weapons and other dangerous materials. Any approach to these 'hard security' issues must include the defence ministries of area states and a variety of non-state actors, such as intergovernmental organisations, non-governmental organisations, provincial and local governments, and corporations. The established NATO–Russian 'hard security' channels are unsuited to these issues, as are the existing regional 'soft security' mechanisms. A Nordic–Baltic regional 'hard security' mechanism might fill this important gap.

Current state of Nordic–Baltic regional security cooperation

In the post-Prague security environment, the Nordic–Baltic region is less prepared than it might be to respond to these issues. This is particularly true in the 'hard security' arena and where Russia's involvement is required. Though several confidence- and security-building schemes have been proposed by Poland, Russia, Finland, Sweden and other states, the Baltic governments have been unwilling or unable to participate; and existing regional institutions are unsuited to the task in their current form (Trenin 1998: 121–4). The Council of the Baltic Sea States limits itself to 'soft security' issues. The Baltic Round Table has lapsed into disuse. The Baltic Council involves only Estonia, Latvia and Lithuania, and the '5+3' mechanisms (now changed to '8') bring only the Nordics to the table. There is an evident need for a Nordic–Baltic institution capable of working with Moscow to manage the 'hard security' issues posed by, *inter alia*, the vulnerability of the Russian military in the region, instability in Kaliningrad, and military–environmental issues. Unfortunately, the particular dynamics of democratic security building in the Baltic states may prevent them from undertaking this type of regional cooperation.

Prospects for future Nordic–Baltic regional cooperation

The principles and practices of democratic security building have served the Baltic states extraordinarily well. Over the past decade, these governments have, with outside assistance, been able to institutionalise democracy and the rule of law within their societies and build sufficient capacity to participate meaningfully in Euro-Atlantic institutions. However, there is reason to believe that the process of democratic security building is not yet complete. The institutions responsible for foreign and defence policy in the Baltic countries may not yet possess sufficient capacity to participate in security building at the Nordic–Baltic level, as well as the Euro-Atlantic level.

The requirements of EU and NATO accession

The security orientation adopted by the Baltic governments places top priority on Euro-Atlantic membership. These priorities will impose enormous demands on Baltic foreign and defence policy institutions in coming years. In the case of EU accession, the Baltic governments began negotiations with the EU in 1993 and 1995, and membership is a reasonable prospect starting in 2004 (Bradley 2002). Evidence is already mounting that the Baltic governments lack the personnel and expertise to implement EU policies at home while participating fully in the union's many organs. The demise of the Baltic Round Table and the anaemic implementation of the Baltic Free Trade Agreement are also suggestive in this regard (Ozolina 1999).

The capacity of the Baltic governments will be strained even more severely by the NATO accession process, which will occur concurrently with the EU process (Szayna 2001). The most evident burden of NATO accession will be financial. The Baltic governments will be expected to provide their share of the common fund for allied headquarters, support for international personnel, and specialised capabilities such as the NATO Airborne Warning and Control force. Additionally, the Baltic defence ministries will be expected to provide national funds for upgrading the interoperability and capabilities of their armed forces, participation in the rather heavy schedule of NATO exercises, and in NATO operations. This may come on top of resources already devoted to international military activities – a burden one Estonian observer estimated to be 25 per cent of that country's defence budget, leading to 'PfP coma'. Robertas Sapronas has published the most comprehensive (publicly available) analysis of the financial implications of NATO member-ship (Sapronas 2000). He estimates that the additional costs for Estonia will total USD 31.5 million, for Latvia USD 52.5 million, and for Lithuania USD 78 million. If undertaken in a single year, these expenditures would comprise 34, 69 and 42 per cent of their annual defence budgets respectively.[11] Clearly, this represents a significant burden, even if spread over several years. Moreover, these estimates were made under the assumption that the Baltic militaries will be as interoperable with NATO in 2004 as the Visegrad members were in 1999. This is an optimistic assumption – the defence expen-ditures of Visegrad members are twenty-two times as large as the collective Baltic defence budgets.[12] NATO membership represents a massive burden on the Baltic national budgets, which are already under pressure from popula-tions growing restless for greater social spending (Sapronas 2000).

In addition to its financial commitments, NATO accession will also severely stretch the defence expertise of Baltic governments. NATO membership requires large numbers of highly trained officers and civilians (Hoff 2001). This burden is difficult even for well developed militaries to meet. The three Visegrad militaries have failed to fill their assigned slots in NATO headquarters by an alarming margin, despite a collective uniformed end-strength fourteen times that of the Baltics' armed services.[13] Indeed, the Baltic militaries may have as few as 4000 officers between them. The Baltic governments are also woefully short of civilian defence experts – the entire Latvian Ministry of Defence has less than 150 personnel. This small group of Baltic officers and defence civilians will be spread over a large number of headquarters with actual or potential command responsibilities in the Nordic–Baltic region, including:

- NATO Headquarters, International Military Staff, Brussels, Belgium
- Supreme Headquarters, Allied Force Europe, Mons, Belgium
- Regional Headquarters Allied Forces North Europe, Brunssum, Netherlands
- Joint Headquarters NORTHEAST, Karup, Denmark

- Allied Naval Forces North, Northwood, UK
- Allied Air Forces North, Ramstein, Germany
- Joint Command North, Stavanger, Norway
- Multinational Corps Northeast, Szczecin, Poland
- Polish 12th Division (constituent of MNC-NE)
- German 14th Division (constituent of MNC-NE)
- Danish Division (constituent of MNC-NE)
- Allied Command Europe Mobile Force (Land)
- Allied Command Europe Rapid Reaction Corps
- Reaction Corps Centre, Heidelberg, Germany
- SFOR Headquarters, Sarajevo, Bosnia
- KFOR Headquarters, Pristina, Kosovo

(Hoff 2001)

Additionally, the Baltic defence establishments will need to staff national missions in Brussels and participate in the truly astounding number of alliance working groups, commissions, agencies and schools. If the personnel burdens borne by other small NATO militaries are any guide, NATO-related assignments could account for as many as 200 officers from each Baltic military – nearly twenty per cent of Estonia's officer corps and about ten per cent of Latvia's and Lithuania's. Recent efforts to rectify this situation through the creation of the Baltic Defence College are, while admirable, totally inadequate at present. The College produces only ten staff-qualified officers per year for each Baltic military.

Clearly, the requirement for Euro-Atlantic integration will severely tax the financial and human capacity of Baltic defence institutions. This is not to suggest that the Baltic countries will be unable to execute their duties as members of NATO and the EU. Over the past decade, they have proven capable of extraordinary accomplishments in the cause of Euro-Atlantic integration. Rather, the strategic orientation of the Baltic states toward Euro- Atlantic institutions will have the unintended effect of eliminating the institutional capacity for participation in Nordic–Baltic regional security mechanisms.

Conclusion

The Baltic countries have achieved remarkable success in their process of democratic security building. Ten years of diligent work have brought the Baltic states close to accomplishing their primary foreign and security objectives – membership in NATO and EU, and a close strategic relationship with the US. However, the Euro-Atlantic strategic orientation adopted by the Baltic governments will place extraordinary demands on the financial and human capacities of their defence establishments. The most probable, though unintended, consequence is that the Baltic governments are unlikely to pursue Nordic–Baltic regional security cooperation. This will leave the region more exposed than it need be to such challenges as Russian military vulnerability and instability in Kaliningrad.

The Euro-Atlantic and Nordic partners of the Baltic states ignore this situation at their peril. They would be well advised to take steps to expand the capacity of the Baltic defence establishments as quickly as possible. These steps might include increased security assistance resources to fund additional Baltic civilian defence staff, contract staff or military officers (perhaps bringing retired officers back onto the rolls). They might also consider seconding their own civilians and officers to the Baltic defence ministries, or accepting additional burden for existing activities to lighten the load on the Baltics. In the long term, a significantly expanded Baltic Defence College is likely to be the most sensible alternative.

When the Baltic defence establishments attain sufficient capacity, the Nordic–Baltic partners should collaborate with Russia to build the long-delayed and much needed mechanisms for managing 'hard security' challenges in the Nordic–Baltic region. Potential measures for decreasing the vulnerability of Russia's north-west regions might include collaborative airspace control, agreed limits on military deployments and exercises of particular types in particular areas, military data and planning exchanges, and inspection visits in excess of the Vienna Document. Potential measures for decreasing the likelihood of a crisis over Kaliningrad include the establishment of clear Russo–Baltic transit procedures, the institutionalisation of crisis consultation mechanisms, and a comprehensive dialogue – encompassing 'hard security' as well as 'soft security' issues – on the future of Kaliningrad. Potential measures for improving environmental security in the region might include institutionalising procedures for exchanging sensitive environmental data, conducting inspections of sensitive sites, monitoring cleanup operations and demilitarisation of weapons and other dangerous materials.

Democratic security building in the Baltics will have accomplished its full objective only when the Baltic states are fully capable of participating in such regional security cooperation. As eminent Swedish strategist Bo Huldt has stated,

> Debate tends to center on the main elements of the architecture – that is NATO and the European Union…It is all very well to refer in general terms to a European 'security community' as our goal but such a community will have to be made up of a number of building blocks including sub-regional and regional arrangements and unless 'security communities' are established in the various regions and sub-regions of Europe…then the grand design will also fail.
>
> (Huldt 1996)

Notes

1 The author would like to thank Jeffrey Lewis, Olya Oliker and Thomas Szayna for their insightful comments on this piece. Of course, responsibility for any errors remains solely with the author. The views expressed in this chapter are the author's own; they do not reflect the views of RAND Corporation or its research sponsors.

2 See, for example, Holoboff 1995. For the purposes of this chapter, 'security orientation' is defined as a government's dominant external balancing strategy.
3 For an overview, see McGwire 1997.
4 This paper uses the terms 'Baltic states' and 'Baltic countries' interchangeably to refer to the nation-states of Estonia, Latvia and Lithuania.
5 Texts of HCNM recommendations are available at: www.osce.org/hcnm/documents/recommendations/index
6 For example, see Gracheva 2000.
7 See, for example, Archer 2000 and Kauppila 1999.
8 'Soft security' is defined for the purposes of this chapter to be the non-military aspects of security; 'hard security' aspects are considered to be largely military in nature.
9 The effectiveness of this strategy is described in Larrabee 2001.
10 Summary at: http://europa.eu.int/comm/external_relations/north_dim
11 According to the Baltic defence white papers, the 2001 Baltic defence budgets are roughly: Estonia: 92.4 million, Latvia: 76 million, Lithuania: 184 million in US dollars.
12 Szayna 2001 estimates the Visegrad defence budgets to be: Czech Republic 1.175 billion, Poland 3.144 billion, Hungary 715 million in US dollars.
13 Visegrad information from Simon 2001, total end-strength data from Szayna 2001.

3 Security

Lynchpin of Baltic cooperation

Mel Huang

In the post-Cold War security architecture of Europe, the cooperation among the Baltic countries of Estonia, Latvia and Lithuania occupies a unique place among the myriad of different manifestations of cooperative security.[1] The latter term, the modern buzzword of choice to describe any form of international cooperation to increase security, has been applied to just about every security relationship ranging from the Partnership for Peace (PfP) scheme to the NATO–Russia partnership. It has even been characterised as an 'idealistic' approach in bringing security strategies into the post-Cold War era (R Cohen 2001: 3).

To define and characterise Baltic cooperation beyond this catch-all term becomes more difficult for various reasons. First, the cooperation among the three is difficult to evaluate due to its rather unique nature, one that can be described as an overlapping development of internal defence capabilities and external interoperability (Linkevičius 1999: 91). Second, many of the more detailed concepts suffer from seriously varying definitions. A recent definition of 'collective security', for example, focused on the maintenance of security within an internal space, separating it from the 'collective defence' against external threats (R Cohen 2001: 6–7). However, even the weakened definition of collective security sans mutual defence only partly describes the Baltic case.

Ironically some of the best criteria offered about associations and alliances – such as collaboration over a mutual concern, probability of mutual assistance, aggregation of capabilities to pursue foreign affairs, perception of a common foe and mutual interest of preserving the status quo (Friedman 1970: 4–5) – would better characterise the Baltic case, although the relationship among the three is far from one of alliance. The aforementioned and other security-strategy-related literature have largely analysed the nature of security in the Baltic region from a NATO perspective and in terms of these under-theorised security concepts, and thus the Baltic security environment has been poorly served by existing categories of definition.

This chapter will argue that Baltic security cooperation is best depicted as based on the 'twin pillars' of internal development and external integration (Linkevičius 1999; Dalbiņš 1996: 7), with the two efforts interconnected and mutually supportive. The realisation that a threat to one would equate to a threat against all (Dalbiņš 1996) is thus the driving force in this example of cooperative security, giving Baltic cooperation a *raison d'être*. In order to demonstrate this contention, let us briefly identify the characteristics of the region, threat perception, and the nature of current defence cooperation between the three Baltic states.

Is there a 'Baltic' region?

To most observers, Estonia, Latvia and Lithuania for a variety of reasons, ranging from shared geography to common historical development, naturally fall within a region called the Baltic states. The three countries are situated on the eastern shore of the Baltic Sea and have endured a similarly traumatic experience of occupation and loss of independence in 1940, and emerged together from the collapsing Soviet Union a half-century later. The world remembers their common plight and struggle, indeed perceiving the 'Baltic revolutions' as an inter-related phenomenon, and that memory continues to translate into and shape current security perceptions of the three countries.

In line with historical memory, foreign states and international organisations often perpetuate this categorisation with policy-making that treats the trio as a collective unit in the post-Cold War era. However, increasingly throughout the 1990s the three states – especially the periphery countries Estonia and Lithuania – diverged in their foreign policy approach, seeking external state recognition that the three countries are individual states rather than some externally-constructed concept (Clemens 2001: 4). The three countries' foreign policy goals are very similar – re-integration with Europe via NATO and EU membership – though divergences in the level of development and policy emphasis within each country have encouraged different paths towards the same goals.

Geography has also played a major role in the divergence of the three countries' paths towards Western integration: Lithuania gravitated towards its former commonwealth partner Poland, most notably following Poland's 1999 invitation to join NATO, whilst Estonia has oriented further towards its northern neighbours, especially after the accession of Finland and Sweden to the EU in 1995 (Väyrynen 1999: 211–15). Former Estonian Foreign Minister Toomas Hendrik Ilves (1996–98 and 1999–2002), for example, was a key factor in Estonia's re-orientation away from the common Baltic mould, continually advocating that evaluation of the countries must be based on merit ('single-state capability') rather than being fixed on some arbitrarily-designated sub-regional division with all three states being perceived as a single echelon. Ilves went as far as to place Estonia into a mythical 'Yuleland' with the Nordic countries, away from their Baltic and Slavic neighbours (Ilves 1999). Former Estonian Defence Minister Hain Rebas, however, warned that if Latvia is isolated by the continual diversion of the two periphery countries at the expense of pan-Baltic initiatives, it could fall back into Moscow's orbit, in fulfilment of the so-called 'Karaganov- or Kozyrev Doctrine' (Rebas 1999: 31).

The decision by the European Commission in 1997 to begin accession negotiations with Estonia, without Latvia or Lithuania, marked the first significant sign of international recognition of the three countries as individual states with different levels of achievement, rather than a homogenised geographical bloc. Even as the Helsinki European Council opened up the EU enlargement process into a 'regatta' process in 1999 by beginning accession talks with all candidates, there was no reason whatsoever to treat the three as a collective unit again; the 'healthy competition' among the three gave little incentive for deep cooperation in this pursuit.

However, when viewing the Baltic states through the prism of security and defence, their remained a continual perception amongst external states that the three were to be understood as a single regional unit. Moreover, the Baltic states themselves adopted this perspective, understanding that one country's security would depend on the security of the region as a whole (Dalbiņš: 8). This acceptance of the regional grouping in turn allows for active cooperation to develop.

Perceiving the threat – what sort of security?

Clearly the driving force for a range of security cooperations in the Baltics is the shared sense of insecurity in all three countries. Michael Mihalka has argued, for example, that, after the Cold War, Western Europe changed its focus from the survival of the state ('hard' security) to economic well-being ('soft' security) due to the perceived decline in threat posed by Moscow (Mihalka 2001: 34). Clive Archer and Christopher Jones correctly noted that the issue of pure survival in a Hobbesian sense is no longer the prevailing issue for the three Baltic countries (Archer and Jones 1999: 167), and this notion was affirmed on the record with defence concepts confirming no imminent threat from the East. For example, the draft Estonian Defence Concept referred to issues like regional instability, terrorism and ecological disasters as more of a threat, and noted that there was no immediate threat from neighbouring states (Huang 2002: 31, 37). However, the realist perception that Russian revanchism would pose a major threat influences them towards striving for 'hard' security guarantees (Hubel 1999: 249).

Cohen suggested that 'damage to the security of individuals' in countries results in a diminished sense of security by others and the government (R Cohen 2001: 8). Though Cohen focused this assertion on the issue of human rights and the internal source of instability, it can easily be adapted for use in the external sense. At the basic individual level the sense of insecurity that is derived from both individual and collective psychological baggage remains high, due to historic memory of the loss of independence and atrocities committed by the Soviet Union over decades of occupation. As an example of psychological baggage, in Estonia an estimated 5 per cent of the population were deported by Soviet authorities during the twelve months of occupation in 1940–41, including most of the country's civilian and military leaders. President Konstantin Päts was sent to a mental hospital in Kalinin, Defence Forces Commander-in-Chief General Johan Laidoner died in a Vladimir prison, and about twenty-five generals and admirals – a large majority of the officer corps – lost their lives from this era of terror (Õun 2001).

The issue of NATO membership, viewed as the ultimate safeguard of the Baltic states' independence, is supported by the entire mainstream political spectrum in Estonia, Latvia and Lithuania. Peeter Vihalemm, for example, depicts the need to integrate with Western security structures as resistance to 'contemporary Russian attempts to keep Estonia in its sphere of influence', adding that Estonia cannot survive outside of it (Vihalemm 1996: 135). The same psychological fear was exacerbated by reports in the Estonian media of various Russian opinion polls, including an overwhelming positive response on the justification of Russian military aggression against Estonia if it joins NATO. To give one example, the Russian survey polled people from six cities, in which 93 per cent of respondents supported the military justification against Estonia's NATO entry (Mihkelson 1996). This psychological lack of security is projected to the state, and the security deficit experienced by all three countries has bonded them together. Therefore the issues of defence and security have become the lynchpin of the entire cooperation scheme, as this primary mutual concern is privileged above and overrides petty differences on other issues.

How deep is the cooperation?

For ardent champions of Baltic cooperation – particularly those who remember the human chain which, on 23 August 1989, linked Tallinn, Riga and Vilnius in protesting against the Molotov–Ribbentrop Pact of fifty years earlier – the level of cooperation has diminished drastically. To individualists such as Ilves, there was little reason to accelerate cooperation unless practical benefits could be identified; cooperation for cooperation's sake lacked an underlying utility. In defence and security matters, however, joint cooperation remained paramount, and even for cooperation detractors there is an easily demonstrable rationale to continue to pursue cooperation in this sector.

Cohen describes cooperative security as 'practical' and 'transparent', and emphasises dialogue amongst the cooperative unit on a wide basis (R Cohen 2001: 12). His criteria for a broader view of security to encompass more than defence include political consultations, free and open trade relations, and closely-aligned foreign and security policies including integrated or multilateral military formations. To what extent does Baltic cooperation in security and defence conform to this conception?

At the most basic level, mechanisms have been in place for trilateral consultations on various levels between the three Baltic states. The three governments, under the framework of the Baltic Council of Ministers, coordinate policies ranging from improving the rail network to combating the smuggling of contraband. The meetings of specific ministers are supplemented by frequent gatherings of working groups at civil service and government departmental levels. Presidential summits also occur regularly, usually to discuss foreign policy matters. The cooperation extends to the military, the national guards and other institutions, including the joint parliamentary body, the Baltic Assembly. Though the latter has been criticised as a 'talk-shop', the frequent sharing of ideas and consultations helps to forge ties at the important inter-state working or expert group levels.

However, the level of inter-state cooperation has not deepened in either qualitative or quantitative terms through the last decade, despite the frequent consultations and meetings. Though a common visa zone was adopted in 1992, the much discussed and debated customs union never came to be – a telling lack of cooperation, particularly when viewed in the context of continuing EU integration. When Estonia was elevated into a front-runner for EU membership in 1997, for example, the possibility of having to erect a Schengen border with Latvia for the short period until Latvia too became an EU member demonstrated the problems and tensions in harmonising Baltic cooperation with the drive to EU integration. The three countries did eventually institute a common transit procedure to ease customs and border procedures in 1999. However, the free trade agreement among the three, which came into effect in 1994 and was extended to agricultural goods in 1997, plays a less important role in stimulating pan-Baltic (north–south) trade flows, and the level of inter-state trade remains weak. For example, Estonia's export to Latvia was a modest 8.3 per cent in 1999 and 7.1 per cent in 2000, while for the same years exports to Lithuania was a paltry 3.4 per cent and 2.8 per cent of total trade (Eesti Statistikaamet 2001).

So, if not in the economic sector, upon which issues does substantive cooperation occur? Unsurprisingly, the deepest level of cooperation among the three countries is directly related to issues arising from the security sector, and is particularly notable in matters relating to national defence. The ministerial links among the defence ministries, the militaries and the national guards are especially high, with the primary strategic objective of NATO membership as the driving force. This 'second pillar' of Baltic cooperation serves as a demonstration of their capacity for military interoperability (infrastructure, materiel and personnel) that is vital for any collective defensive structure.

A significant amount of interest in security cooperation is reflexive and is shaped by historical lessons learned. The lack of a joint Baltic military effort in the late 1930s helped contribute to the three countries' capitulation to Soviet occupation, and the interwar dispute between Poland and Lithuania over the status of Vilnius destroyed any opportunity of true regional security cooperation. Though Estonia and Latvia signed a defence pact on 1 November 1923 (Tarulis 1959: 70), the extension of this pact to Lithuania and/or Poland failed because of these ongoing security-related disputes; at the same time, Finland increasingly sought to distance its foreign and security policies from those of its southern neighbours. The 'Baltic Entente', signed in September 1934, failed to advance cooperation to an effective level, even to the extent that it gave Estonia and Latvia op-outs in common positions on Lithuania's difficult territorial issues with Germany over Klaipèda and Poland over Vilnius.

Simply put, the level of inter-state cooperation in the Baltic region depends very much on a shared perception by each state that such cooperation is necessary and will provide security benefits for all three states. The race towards EU membership is depicted as 'healthy competition' among the three countries in the post-Helsinki regatta enlargement strategy, and the emergence of 'zero-sum' state behaviour naturally limits inter-state cooperation. However, unlike EU membership, issues within the security and defence sector and the objective of joining NATO are perceived in terms of a collaborative process, providing the impetus for cooperation in this field and giving it a strong and dynamic *raison d'être*.

Active defence cooperation

Throughout the 1990s and into the new century, the three countries have continually deepened their level of cooperation in the defence sphere, fortified by the 'twin pillars' of strengthening trilateral defence capabilities and jointly working towards NATO integration. The trend in Baltic defence cooperation is underpinned and characterised by the construction of both joint forces and joint institutions, in what Andrius Krivas called 'an indispensable element' of 'interoperability-related homework' for their mutual aim to join NATO (Krivas 1999: 113). Thus, many of the cooperative projects are designed to demonstrate both Baltic interoperability and the ability for that interoperability to be integrated into a larger – NATO-centred – framework. The so-called 'BALT-' projects, covering both the integration of forces and the creation of joint infrastructure and institutions, serve as effective models of regional collaborative security that have been praised by countries from both West and East.[2]

BALTBAT

The first major project of Baltic defence cooperation is the joint Baltic battalion, BALTBAT. This flagship project was born out of trilateral discussions held in 1993–94 at which it was decided that international interest and collaboration in the Baltic military sector was an effective strategy to engage the still-occupied Baltic countries in the wider post-Cold War security framework without directly addressing the issue of NATO integration.[3] The three Baltic prime ministers signed the agreement creating BALTBAT on 13 September 1994, complementing the signing of a multinational support agreement in Copenhagen two days earlier.[4] The creation of this first cooperative project was designed to help promote cooperation both among Baltic states and with Western countries (Møller 2000: 38), while others argued it served as 'shock therapy', exposing the Baltics to the issue of multilateral defence cooperation (Sapronas 1999: 58).

Though BALTBAT actually featured three distinctive national companies, the command structure is united. The BALTBAT established its headquarters at the Latvian army base in Ādaži, just outside Riga. The joint command posts are rotated among the three companies (commander, deputy commander, chief-of-staff) and the *lingua franca* of the command staff and the battalion itself is English. Their activities are regulated by consensus of the three defence ministers. Funding for BALTBAT comes both from the participant countries and foreign partners; equipment donation and language training all feature in the support provided by foreign partners.

However, the small size of BALTBAT – numbering around 700 – made their deployment as a battalion problematic (Møller 2000: 38). Rotation would be impossible if the full battalion were deployed, for example. Therefore in the Balkan operations individual national companies within BALTBAT served within other peacekeeping contingents for the companies to gain peacekeeping experience and contribute to the continent's security. In order to re-invigorate Baltic cooperation, the three governments chose to restructure BALTBAT from a peacekeeping unit to a fully-active 'peace-enforcing' force, into what former Estonian Defence Forces Chief-of-Staff Major General Ants Laaneots called a 'normal, standard infantry battalion' with a notable increase in firepower (Tali 1999). The increase in size and applicability of BALTBAT would allow for effective deployment as a unit, capable of being self-sustaining beyond one rotation.

Though BALTBAT is widely perceived as the flagship of Baltic military cooperation and was hailed as a successful model from its inception, the unit itself has achieved rather little in substantive terms over the years. The lack of deployment opportunities allowed the budget-makers to overlook BALTBAT's primary purpose; instead of functioning as a deployable peacekeeping force BALTBAT has basically turned into a giant PR tool. Indeed, Daniel Austin has characterised BALTBAT as 'worthless' save for its symbolic and political value (Austin 1999: 1). However, Sapronas argued that BALTBAT served its importance in developing Baltic cooperation, engaging foreign assistance, and in 'Westernising' the Baltic militaries (Sapronas 1999: 59–60). Whether the revamping of BALTBAT into a full infantry unit would allow it to be fully deployable is dependent on the continual commitment – especially budgetary – of the three countries.

BALTRON

Although it has received less attention from analysts and the media, the more successful of the joint forces projects has proved to be the joint naval squadron, BALTRON. Though all three navies are minute and boast no real offensive maritime capability, the non-fighting nature of BALTRON activities at the present time have greatly contributed to enhancing security and stability in the Baltic Sea.

Despite the fact that the Baltic navies first cooperated in joint maritime exercises in 1995, the 16 April 1998 agreement among the three defence ministers created the joint naval squadron. Launched in August of the same year, essentially as a naval version of BALTBAT, its activities are focused on mine-clearing, patrolling and search-and-rescue activities. Each country contributes one or two ships and crew for a six-month period in the joint activities, with a joint command structure based in Tallinn, modelled on the same lines as BALTBAT. Various foreign countries support BALTRON with equipment and training, much in the same spirit as BALTBAT.

The joint squadron continues to train together in trilateral and larger international exercises, such as the annual PfP Open Spirit exercises, often involving major mine-clearing endeavours. The clearance of the large amount of unexploded ordinance that still litters the Baltic Sea, estimated to number tens of thousands, is the best example of the applicability of this cooperation project; it has opened up many new shipping lanes to merchant and passenger ships in the busy shipping area. MCOPEST (Mine-Clearing Operation Estonia) took place in November 2001 off the Estonian coast and brought ships from eleven countries into the mine-clearing exercise, ridding the waterways of thirty-five mines and eighteen unexploded shells (Oolo 2001).

BALTNET

The cooperation of Baltic militaries, especially for international deployments and exercises, serves effectively as a PR tool to demonstrate the active cooperation; however, the development of integrated infrastructure provides the key foundations for longer-term sustainable cooperation. The primary project in this vein is the joint Baltic airspace surveillance network, BALTNET. This was developed through the US-led Regional Airspace Initiative in 1994, and was designed to be fully compatible with NATO systems.

BALTNET shares very detailed three-dimensional airspace data among the three countries, providing each of the national radar centres the most accurate picture of the airspace of the other countries and the region itself. The coordination centre was established in Karmelava, Lithuania. It was opened in 2000 and the infrastructure developed to support and service BALTNET allows for its further development through the gradual increase of its role and its integration into a larger system. With a well-coordinated airspace surveillance system in place, BALTNET has the capability to become integrated into NATO's joint airspace defence system.

BALTDEFCOL

Another excellent example of structural cooperation is the Baltic Defence College, BALTDEFCOL. The creation of a joint Baltic senior military education institution in Estonia's university city Tartu not only builds institutional cooperation through the administration of the college, but it also develops long-term cooperation among the officers from the three countries and other allies. Though each of the three countries boasts its own military academy system, BALTDEFCOL provides the internationalism needed in the future interoperable security structure in what Swedish Defence Minister Björn von Sydow called 'openness and free meetings of minds' (Von Sydow 1999: 9).

The cost of building and running BALTDEFCOL is shared among the three Baltic countries, while thirteen allies[5] offers direct (instructors, equipment) and indirect (foreign student sponsorship) assistance. The bulk of instructors come from NATO member states, keeping the education experience commensurate with NATO levels. The involvement of foreign students, especially those from NATO countries, adds to the educational value. BALTDEFCOL is also designed to play a larger role in helping to develop both BALTBAT and BALTRON to create a better tactical doctrine for the cooperative forces.[6]

The education scheme is crafted closely towards achieving maximum result on the three countries' mutual goal of NATO membership, thus the language of instruction is English and the instruction staff are largely experts and officers from NATO member states. The inclusion of students from other countries, including NATO members, also helps to build practical working relationships among officers. As Graeme Herd puts it, 'political and economic capital has been spent creating this military interoperable capacity in order to underscore a Baltic commitment to "producing security within NATO, rather than simply consuming" it' (Herd and Huang 2002: 5). Danish Brigadier General Michael Clemmesen, commandant of BALTDEFCOL, expressed another important rationale, observing that BALTDEFCOL must break the Soviet attitudes predominant among Baltic officers (Oolo 1999).

The year-long senior staff officer education course began in August 1999, with thirty-two officers from eight countries completing the course. The following year included thirty-seven officers from ten countries, and the course due for completion on 21 June 2002 featured forty-one officers from fourteen countries. A colonel-level course was also introduced in 2001, featuring six senior officers from five countries, to focus on those officers too senior for the staff course. Clemmesen stressed that the colonel's course in the coming five to seven years should fill a gap, and then be transformed to take into account those finishing the staff officer course and reaching the level of the colonel's course (Clemmesen 2001: 7). In the same year a short-term civil service course was also introduced focusing on the development of security policy and the complexities of civil–military relations.[7]

Others

These four cooperative projects are the most visible and successful demonstrators of defence cooperation. Other projects remain in discussion, including the joint air transport squadron, BALTWING, and the personnel database system, BALTPERS. The BALTSEA project to coordinate foreign and security policy for Baltic Sea states would expand the scope of Baltic cooperation to a new dimension. Another important aspect in the long-term planning of all the 'BALT-' projects is the long-term 'Baltification' – the eventual commitment of full financial and resource support to the Baltic states themselves (Sapronas 1999: 63). This aspect of planning demonstrates a longer-term commitment to cooperation that would extend beyond NATO membership.

Joint training exercises within the scope of the aforementioned projects and of the forces at large are common, often as part of PfP exercises. The annual Amber Hope exercise brings together thousands of troops – the largest such exercise was held in September 2001 and included 2800 soldiers from fourteen countries.[8] Estonian Defence Forces Commander Rear-Admiral Tarmo Kõuts emphasised that the successful organisation of such a large-scale exercise shows NATO the abilities of the Baltics to rise to the challenge (Eelrand 2001). Smaller exercises involving communications, search-and-rescue and planning are held frequently throughout the calendar year, sometimes trilateral, other times multilateral.

A product of the ministerial meetings was the agreement to examine joint procurement of expensive military equipment. For the most part the Baltic countries receive their equipment as donations from allies, ranging from outdated and heavy M-14 rifles from the United States to refitted *Lindau*-class minehunters from Germany. The agreement of the three governments in 2001 opened up a new opportunity, though it has not been fully tested yet. Estonia and Latvia took the initiative to make a joint order for their high-tech 3-D airspace surveillance systems (as a part of BALTNET) from US defence contractor Lockheed-Martin. However, also from Lockheed-Martin, Lithuania chose to go it alone in acquiring a small order of the Javelin airspace defence system. The Baltics still depend on donations, even of larger items such as tanks and anti-aircraft weaponry. However, the future acquisition of modern equipment fit for a NATO border state would require a better pooling of resources, the foundation of which was laid out in the radar purchase.

Clearly these projects have proved to be a successful, albeit qualified, demonstration of interoperability among the three Baltic militaries, and each of them can be projected onto a larger interoperability with NATO. Danish General Clemmesen suggested that the Baltics would soon have a higher average level of interoperability than other CEE countries (Clemens 2001: 211). BATLBAT trains in PfP exercises with other allied countries, as does BALTNET. BALTRON is modelled upon a NATO-compatible system, while BALTDEFCOL is clearly designed as a NATO-internal institution. Though sometimes the cooperation intensity is lacking, especially in finance, this level of trilateral cooperation is already remarkable in comparison with other regional geographical groupings of states in Europe and beyond.

Losing the raison d'être?

In examining Baltic security strategies it has been argued that strategic security objectives rest on 'twin pillars', namely internal development and external integration. A clear and consistently held driving dynamics within Baltic defence cooperation has been the mutual goal of joining NATO. The inevitable question arises: what will happen to the quality and volume of Baltic military cooperation when the three are eventually integrated into NATO? With the security guarantee offered by Article V of the Washington Treaty, one of the two pillars is essentially toppled. Does this also undermine the *raison d'être* for Baltic cooperation?

As the three Baltic countries all reach the goal of spending two per cent of GDP on national defence, further expansion of military spending would be solely dependent on the growth of the national economies; the entire process of reaching two per cent of GDP was perceived as a target for NATO despite the pressure it placed on other under-funded areas, and moving beyond that number would threaten the tense budgetary equilibria. Would these 'PR projects' become the sacrificial lambs on the altar of budgetary prioritisation – for example, increased funding towards other uses, such as equipment acquisition? Or would Baltic trilateral military cooperation actually be perceived to be both necessary and cost-effective?

Despite these critical questions, there is little reason to believe that the moment the three countries join NATO would entail an immediate and drastic change in their policy towards trilateral military cooperation. In the run-up to NATO integration the three countries have asserted that the Baltics are already contributing to regional stability and security, and that this would be magnified upon their joining of NATO. Moreover, the extent of progress achieved within the four main cooperative projects provides, alongside the prospect of having to cut foreign involvement in their funding and activity programmes, a strong political, economic and military disincentive to disregard or downgrade such cooperation. Indeed, the cooperation projects could easily be structurally integrated into NATO, rendering current interest in their continued development doubly advantageous.

BALTNET is designed to integrate into the NATO airspace surveillance network, while the BALTDEFCOL could become a regional centre for military academia. Indeed the medium- and long-term internal planning of both structures involves post-NATO membership activities, including their gradual 'Balticisation' and – especially – the continual development of BALTDEFCOL into a regional beacon for military studies. Although BALTBAT has been characterised as a 'white elephant' – more a PR exercise, without serious deployment options – the 1999 decision to restructure BALTBAT into a functional, deployable unit especially crafted for NATO-style 'peace-enforcing' efforts indicates a serious attempt to guarantee the continuation of the flagship project into the future. In essence, BALTBAT and BALTRON are joint units already able to work within larger interoperable units, as demonstrated by the many PfP exercises already held.

Future joint acquisition of military equipment will certainly remain, especially as equipment donations dry up over time. Even with NATO membership, there is little change in the means of one Baltic country to afford expensive NATO-compatible arms compared against the current cost benefits of joint purchase. These joint acquisitions could also pave the way to increasing the scope of BALTNET, as discussed above, from being simply a surveillance network into a defensive system. The possibilities of increased cooperation, especially under a NATO framework, are far from exhausted.

Though the second 'pillar' of Baltic cooperation would have been consolidated through NATO membership, the foundations built during the accession period would nevertheless remain strong. Just as Dalbiùš suggested that a threat to one Baltic country entails a threat to all, NATO membership would not change that underlying dynamic nor the need continually to strengthen the defensive capabilities of the countries – the 'first pillar' of Baltic cooperation. NATO membership has not hindered other newly integrated members from cooperating in NATO operations, such as Poland and Denmark in the Balkans. As long as there remains any remnant of a threat to the three Baltic countries' independence, there will be the *raison d'être* for further pursuit of cooperative security. The necessity of upholding the concepts of interoperability and collaborative security are not fundamentally changed with NATO membership, and security will remain the lynchpin of Baltic cooperation far into the future.

Notes

1   I would especially like to thank Dr Graeme Herd for all his help in putting this chapter together, as well as Peter K Laustsen of the Baltic Defence College. This work was originally presented at the International Studies Association conference in New Orleans on 24 March 2001.

2   Georgia, for one, has often praised Baltic cooperation and has discussed introducing a similar trilateral scheme in the Caucasus to foster regional cooperation in the troubled region.

3   The Red Army withdrew from Lithuania in 1993, and from Latvia and Estonia in 1994. Ironically, in earlier periods some used Baltics' cooperation as a way to dissuade their interest in NATO.

4   The 11 September 1994 Copenhagen signatories include the three Baltic countries, Denmark, Finland, Norway, Sweden and the United Kingdom. The Netherlands joined the agreement in 1996, while France, Germany and the United States support BALTBAT from outside the agreement.

5   Belgium, Denmark, Finland, France, Germany, Iceland, the Netherlands, Norway, Poland, Sweden, Switzerland, the UK and the USA.

6   Danish Army Major T D Møller, who played a large role in training BALTBAT, criticised various aspects of BALTBAT (Møller 2000: 40–41).

7   Unfortunately no Lithuanians participated in the first class, which diminished its value.

8   Canada, the Czech Republic, Denmark, Estonia, Finland, Germany, Italy, Latvia, Lithuania, the Netherlands, Poland, Sweden, the UK and the USA.

4   Russia's Baltic policy in an era of EU integration

Ingmar Oldberg

Introduction

Russia's transition from a communist dictatorship and planned economy to multiparty democracy and market economy – albeit incomplete, chaotic and violent – has rendered economic development and peaceful cooperation with other states an increasingly important feature of Russian policy. Deep and recurrent economic crises also seriously undermined Russia's military power and forced it to seek cooperation with former adversaries. The Baltic states have performed these transitions much more successfully than Russia, evidenced by their advanced preparations for entering the European Union. Membership negotiations are expected to be completed in 2002. EU membership entails the integration of all sectors of the Baltic societies into the strongest economic–political community in Europe, a community that includes many NATO states, thus irrevocably de-coupling from Russia. For several years ahead this EU integration process is bound to affect Russian relations with these states, at least as profoundly as their quest for NATO membership.

   The aim of this chapter is to analyse Russia's economic relations with the Baltic states within an international context. More specifically, the factors working towards conflict or cooperation will be evaluated, and trends that have emerged over time identified and characterised. This chapter focuses on the policy formation – that is, on the actions and views of official Russian representatives such as the president and his administration, members of the government, particularly the prime and foreign ministers, ambassadors, and others, who according to the constitution are appointed by the president. But the Russian State Duma and its members, representing legislative power, regional leaders, economic actors, think tanks, newspapers and public opinion, also receive some attention, since they represent the domestic context of interest and may influence the foreign policy decision-makers, for instance, before elections. By contrast, the governments in the Baltic countries depend more on the parliaments than on the presidents.

Russian pressure tactics and its background

Russia's economic relations with the small Baltic states have traditionally been dominated by transit trade through the ports on the Baltic Sea. In Soviet times, a broad infrastructure of roads, railways and pipelines was developed, connecting Russia's central regions and major cities with the ports of Tallinn in Estonia, Ventspils, Liepāja nd Riga in Latvia, and Klaipėda in Lithuania, with transit goods flowing mainly in the East–West direction. A considerable part of Soviet/Russian exports of crude oil, oil products, minerals, chemicals, metals and industrial products passed through these ports.

These transit flows continued after the Soviet Union fell apart and the Baltic states regained independence (Spruds 2002: 360–7). However, Russia soon also decided to upgrade its own ports in the Baltic Sea, notably St Petersburg and the Kaliningrad region, where the Baltiysk naval base was partly opened for foreign trade. Most importantly, Russia decided to build a new oil terminal at Primorsk on the northern shore of the Gulf of Finland, which was to be connected with a new pipeline, later known as the Baltic Pipeline System (in Russian BTS), as well as a coal and bulk export terminal at Ust-Luga on the southern side. This construction work was accelerated after Vladimir Putin became Russian president in 2000, and in December 2001 he inaugurated the terminals (*RFE/RL Security Watch* 3 January 2002). Recently, *Lukoil* decided to build another oil terminal at Vysotsk near Primorsk (*Dagens Nyheter* 29 August 2002).

Further, Russia attempted to play off one Baltic state against another with regard to transit trade. Thus, Lithuania's new oil terminal at Butingė became in 2001 the fastest growing route for Russian oil export (Stranga 1997: 223; *Izvestiya* 17 October 1997; *Rossiiskaya Gazeta* 17 August 2001). Russian trade with the Baltic states, especially imports, markedly decreased in the 1990s, and Russian tourists, who had earlier flooded the Baltic sea resorts, went elsewhere.

There were several economic motives behind this Russian policy. The Baltic states were perceived by Russia to be unduly profiting from their geographical position by charging monopoly prices for transit. The official press thus pointed out that the BTS could not only save Russia transit fees, but it would also benefit the Leningrad oblast and other regions in north-west Russia (*RG* 29 August 1997, 26 January 2001). After the Primorsk terminal was opened in late 2001, Russian oil exports through Ventspils started to diminish, and export companies were reported to ask for price cuts of two-thirds. Indeed, the official Russian press quickly noted with satisfaction that the Baltic transit fees for Russian oil were reduced (*RG* 13 February 2002). The press also rejected the environmental concerns raised in the West against the port development at Primorsk, underlining that, unlike Ventspils and the new Lithuanian oil terminal, Butingė, it utilised the most modern technology available (*Nezavisimaya Gazeta* 25 December 2001, 28 February 2002, 2 April 2002).

The BTS should be understood against the background of Russia's energy strategy in general. The pipeline is intended to bring oil from the northern Komi Republic, and also deliver products to the Russian home market. It will also be connected to other pipelines, and may – if supplies allow – be linked to the Finnish port of Porvoo, which earlier was suggested as an alternative to Baltic ports. When Putin opened the Primorsk terminal, he stressed that it would allow Russia to control the distribution of Siberian and Caspian oil, as well as open a Russian window to the European energy market in circumvention of the Baltic states. Similarly, Russia has started to construct a new gas pipeline from Yamal to Belarus and Poland in order to serve West European markets, and made plans to lay one beneath the Baltic Sea from the Gulf of Finland, which should be connected with reserves in the Arctic Sea (*RG* 11 December 2001). In addition, Russian port projects furthered the ambition of making Russia a transit country for trade between Europe and Asia. When East Asian goods began to arrive in Russia through the Baltic states, the Russian customs stopped them at the borders (*Baltic Times* 22–28 March 2001).

However, throughout the 1990s Russia also took economic measures against the Baltic states that served more overtly politico–security purposes. Particularly in relation to Estonia and Latvia, the expressed intention was to induce them to stop the 'discrimination' against their Russian-speaking minorities. For example, when Estonia passed its Law on Aliens in 1993, Russian gas deliveries were interrupted. Russia refused to grant Estonia a most-favoured-nation (MFN) status, with the result that traditional Estonian food exports to Russia, mainly to St Petersburg, incurred double customs tariffs and shrank considerably (Oldberg 1997: 168). A senior Russian diplomat later explained that, before an MFN was granted, an 'appropriate cooperative environment, including social and humanitarian aspects', had to be created (Elagin 2001: 155; *Kommersant* 18 August 2000). For similar reasons a Russo–Latvian trade agreement was not implemented. During a political campaign against Latvia in the spring of 1998, Yeltsin threatened Latvia with economic measures, such as reducing oil exports through the pipeline to Ventspils, if the situation of the Russian minority was not improved, and railway tariffs in the Latvian direction were raised, leading to a decrease in the volume of trans-border traffic (Oldberg 1999b: 37; *NG-Stsenarii* 13 November 1999). After the Primorsk terminal was opened, ex-Governor and ex-Deputy Prime Minister Vadim Gustov stated that Estonia and Latvia now have to revise their policy towards Russia and their Russian-speaking minorities, if they are to keep at least part of their transit incomes (*RG* 11 February 2002). On occasion, this 'trade weapon' was also used against Lithuania. For example, when Lithuania tried to replace the military transit agreement of 1993 with a stricter law, Russia refused to ratify the MFN agreement and threatened to reduce transit traffic to Klaipėda (Oldberg 1998: 7).

Naturally, nationalists and communists in the Russian State Duma were particularly inclined to exaggerate the value of pressure tactics. In 2000 the

Duma passed a law in two readings forbidding trade with Latvia altogether, with reference to the minority question (*Izvestiya* 28 November 2000). Liberal Democratic Party leader Vladimir Zhirinovsky once thought that, without Russia's sources of energy and infrastructure, Estonia would be annihilated as a state, so the Estonians would soon come begging to join Russia; alternatively, if they could not pay their debts, Russia would annex Estonia as compensation for losses (Morrison 1994: 109; *Baltic Independent* 14 April 1995). President Putin sought to reassure Russia's neighbours that the BTS did not signify Russia's determination to sever ties with the Baltic states, only the desire to protect Russia's security and independence (*RFE/RL Security Watch* 3 January 2002; *NG* 28 December 2001). Indeed, Russian officials also expressed the concern that Russian exports might be disrupted if the Baltic states were NATO members and NATO states imposed an oil embargo, as had already occurred against Yugoslavia in 1999 (Demurin 2001: 79; Elagin 2001: 154).

The underlying assumption that drove these pressure tactics and sanctions against the Baltic states was that they – as small states – were vulnerable and dependent on Russian transit traffic. Thus, Minister of Foreign Trade Oleg Davydov in 1996 claimed that Russia remained the main trading partner of the Baltic states, accounting for about 30 per cent of their total turnover, whereas their share of Russian foreign trade was 2.7 per cent. Russia was still the main trading partner of Latvia and Lithuania. Regarding Latvia, Russia in 1995 supplied 93 per cent of its fuel requirement, 50 per cent of its electric energy, and 90 per cent of its ferrous metals according to Davydov (*NG* 14 May 1996).[1] A Foreign Ministry spokesman claimed that Russian transit cargo constituted 85 per cent of Estonia's gross freight volume, equalling almost half its GDP (Loshchinin 1996: 51).[2] As a result, if and when Russian trade restrictions were imposed, the entire Estonian economy would be affected (Loshchinin 1996: 51). A common Russian complaint in the early 1990s was that Estonia, as a consequence of Russian transit, had become the world's fifth biggest exporter of non-ferrous metals (Jonson 1997: 313). The 'Long-Term Policy Guidelines' towards the Baltic states, issued by President Yeltsin's press service in February 1997, remarked that the opportunities of the transit and re-export of Russian goods were often deployed to the detriment of Russia. It drew the conclusion that Russian state regulation and customs control had to be strengthened and transit channels to be diversified (BBC 13 February 1997). By 2001, between a fourth and a third of the Estonian and Latvian budget incomes is calculated to derive from Russian transit export (Elagin 2001: 154; *NG* 13 January 2001), although Baltic and other sources give lower figures.[3]

This Russian economic policy *vis-à-vis* the Baltic states must be understood in the context of its military and political ambitions and the fact that Russia still defends the incorporation of the Baltic states into the Soviet Union as legally correct, refusing to accept the term 'occupation' (Elagin 2001: 159; Demurin 2001: 77; *NG* 2 March 2001; *Krasnaya Zvezda* 1 July 2000). Russian economic policy towards its Baltic neighbours can therefore be characterised as rather heavy-handed, often serving political ends, and on occasion, instrumental – at least it was bound to be perceived as such in the Baltic states.

Towards economic cooperation with the Baltic states

However, this account of Russian economic pressure towards the Baltic states must be weighed against other evidence, which points to the emergence of businesslike economic cooperation. In fact, Russian attempts to pressure the Baltic states by economic 'measures' were to an increasing extent abandoned or remained empty threats, because they backfired against Russia's own interests. Several reasons can be cited for this countervailing trend.

First, Russian economic sanctions and repeated crises, notably the August 1998 breakdown, hurt the Russian minorities in the Baltic states most, the protection of whom was a major Russian political objective. Second, the prevalence of points of conflict with Russia strengthened the desire of the Baltic states to reduce their dependence by reorienting their trade toward the West, in line with their primary strategic objective. Amazingly, much progress was attained. From greater than 90 per cent of imports coming from Russia in 1991, Estonia reduced this dependence to 21 per cent in 1994, Latvia and Lithuania making reductions to 29 and 46 per cent respectively. Estonian and Latvian leaders already then declared that Russian sanctions did not unduly concern them (IMF 2001; *DN* 8 March 1994). Since then, Latvia and Lithuania in particular have further reduced imports from Russia, and exports to Russia have shrunk to seven per cent or below.[4] Thus, economic sanctions were remarkably ineffective. Not even in 1990 – when Lithuanian economic dependence on Soviet trade was all but total – did President Gorbachev's total embargo compel the Lithuanians to abrogate their declaration of independence. Russian economic pressure was also counteracted by the assistance of Western countries to the Baltic states. The West boosted trade and invested more money by far than Russia, promoting market reforms and Baltic cooperation. A political explanation for this, at least at the outset, was that many Western states preferred to integrate the Baltic states into the EU, which Russia officially did not object to, rather than into NATO.

Estonia oriented itself primarily towards her Nordic neighbours and key partners Finland and Sweden, whilst Latvia and Lithuania shifted orientation more towards major EU states, such as Germany and Great Britain. Intra-Baltic trade grew from close to nil – a typical pattern in Soviet times – to about ten per cent in some cases (Hansson 1991: 2, *Baltic Times* no. 74 1997). Estonia and Latvia were first to implement market economic reforms, which soon led to growth and increasing internal stability, despite frequent changes of governments.

In order to reduce their dependence on Russian energy and fuels, the Baltic states began to import them from Arab states and Western Europe, and key Western companies were invited to enter the Baltic energy sector and negotiations with individual republics in the Russian federation, such as oil-rich Tatarstan (*BT* no. 74 1997), promoted diversification. Departing from their environmental concerns in the late Soviet era, the Baltic states also turned to their own, albeit limited, resources. Estonia decided to continue to exploit its oil shale, Lithuania retained its nuclear power station at Ignalina, which is of the unsafe Chernobyl type. Latvia and Lithuania renewed their interest in oil prospecting in the Baltic Sea (which, however, led to economic border disputes). Lithuania built an oil terminal at Butingė, which could handle oil from both the West and Russia. When the Mažeikiai refinery was privatised, the Lithuanian state preferred to sell a third of the shares to the American company Williams rather than to *Lukoil*. Another initiative was to reduce the consumption of energy in the Baltic states by pricing and savings measures, and by closing down old and inefficient industries (*Finansovye Izvestiya* 22 October 1996; Kramer 1993: 41).

Third, and most important, reducing transit and trade with the Baltic states ran counter to Russia's own economic interests. Throughout the 1990s, when Russia suffered a deep economic crisis and the state was unable to collect taxes, the exports of oil and gas became the most important budget revenues. As Russian exports shifted away from CIS to Western states that could pay world market prices, Russian transit through the Baltic states increased, especially through Latvia, where the modern Ventspils terminal with its pipeline to Russia came to account for up to 15 per cent of total Russian oil export, and about 30 per cent of oil exports to the West, second only to ports on the Black Sea (Spruds 2002: 361).[5]

Although Russian oil exports through Ventspils have recently diminished, Russia still needs this outlet, since oil production and exports in general are expected to grow – in defiance of agreements with OPEC and to the pleasure of Western importers – and the world market price is high. Russia has now become the world's leading oil exporter, planning increased production also in future (Jane's Foreign Report 28 March 2002). At the same time, domestic demand is not able to swallow the growing production volumes.

Besides oil, Russian officials have expressed an interest in using the Baltic ports, for example Tallinn, for other types of bulk export to the West, such as grain and fish (*RG* 21 March 2001, 11 January 2002). On top of this comes the fact that Russia is very dependent on Lithuania for transit to and from its Kaliningrad exclave.

Little by little, Russian foreign policy doctrine has been adapted to reflect these changing economic needs and interests. President Putin's foreign policy concept of 2000 emphasised that political power depends more on economics, technology and information than on military strength, concluding that Russia has to adapt its ambitions to the available resources. Russia therefore had to rely on economic cooperation with the West. Membership in international trade groups like the World Trade Organisation (WTO) became a priority in Russian foreign policy (*RG* 11 July 2000; *NG* 30 December 1999). Economic sanctions for political ends were incompatible with the principles of free trade embodied in this organisation. With regard to the Baltic states, already the presidential guidelines of February 1997 stressed the importance of developing economic ties on the basis of mutual profitability.

A further problem with the construction of new ports and pipelines in order to circumvent the Baltic countries is the high investment costs and long lead times of such projects. The completion of the BTS and the Ust-Luga terminals had to await the upswing of the Russian economy, and the projected construction of a gas terminal near St Petersburg is at a standstill. Consequently, Russia has even shown an interest in attracting foreign investments into the BTS (*NG-Dipkurier* 26 October 2000; *RG* 26 January, 15 June 2001).

Moreover, the projects are not yet completed. The rail connection to Ust-Luga has yet to be built (*Izvestiya* 24 December 2001). The oil pipeline from Primorsk so far only reaches the Kirishi refinery (270 km), and the stretch to the Pechora fields is only expected to be ready in 2006. It can also be noted that the port fees are higher at Primorsk than Ventspils, and that the Ventspils port is very efficient. Unlike Ventspils, Primorsk is ice-bound in the winter – 40 cm on the day of inauguration (*RG*, 26 January, 15 June, 17 August 2001, 11 January 2002; *NG* 25 December 2001). The government paper *Rossiyskaya Gazeta* concluded that, even when the BTS approaches the same volumes as Ventspils in 2001, it could not meet Russian export needs. The advantages of the Butingė terminal, for which Russia had not paid anything, were also noted by the Russian oil companies. Only this offshore terminal can receive tankers of up to 150,000 tons. (*RG* 17 August 2001)

Concerning the argument that some Russian regions will profit from the BTS and the use of ports in the Gulf of Finland, other regions such as the economically weak Pskov region will lose if Baltic transit shrinks (*NG* 27 September 2001). And regarding the political risks of exporting through future NATO countries, Russian officials are of course aware that Russia is already doing so in Poland and indeed is going to build more gas pipelines there (*NG* 1 March 2001).

An additional reason for Russia to increase trade with the Baltic states was the fact that they had successfully completed market economic reforms, thereby offering favourable business conditions for both transit and mutual trade (*Neue Zürcher Zeitung* 4 April 2002; SITE 2002). Estonia was first to abolish customs barriers for Russian transit export, enlarging the port of Tallinn. Russian exports through Estonia grew even though the state had (and still has) no MFN agreement with Russia (Stranga 1997: 210; *BT* no. 69, 1997; *FI* 24 May 1996). Prime Minister Viktor Chernomyrdin had already in 1996 proposed trilateral investment activities by companies and banks from Russia, the Baltic Sea states and the European Union for the development of the energy sector, ports, projects in modern technology and the banking sector (*NG* 30 August 1996).

Russian banks and companies thus established themselves in the Baltic states, often linking up with local Russian business elites, both legal and illegal. In the 1990s (before Putin re-centralised power) some regions and republics in the

Russian Federation signed their own agreements with the Baltic states and companies (*Baltic Observer* 13 July 1995; Stranga 1997: 212; Loshchinin 1996: 51). Russian energy giants like *Gazprom, Lukoil, Transneft* and *Yukos* attempted to maintain and enlarge their market positions, opening filling stations in all three countries and investing in the ports. Russian export firms switched the export of raw materials from Kaliningrad to Klaipeda, because this port offered cheap and efficient service (*FI* 22 October 1996; *BT* 21 November 1996; *NG* 6 August 1996; *NG-Stsenarii* 13 October 1999; Spruds 2002: 362).

In these circumstances, politically-motivated economic sanctions and threats from Russian state authorities tended to undermine the status and integrity of Russian private companies in the Baltic states. Thus Arkady Volsky, the head of the Russian Union of Industrialists, spoke out against mixing politics and economics. Although he complained about the Lithuanian government's reluctance to allow Russia to take part in the privatisation process, he advised both governments not to interfere (*BT* 15–21 February 2001). Indeed, Russian officials frequently praised the businessmen (both Balts and Russians) in the Baltic states in particular for wanting more trade and political dialogue with Russia, resisting NATO-mania and favouring ethnic reconciliation (*NG* 11 August 2000; Elagin 2001: 152).

Furthermore, Russian private companies conducted different and sometimes competing policies regarding the Baltic states. For example, when Lithuania in 2001 decided to sell more shares in the Mažeikiai refinery and *Lukoil* refused to accept the price and to guarantee safe oil deliveries, *Yukos* stepped in instead, acquiring as many shares as the American company Williams (28 per cent), while the Lithuanian state remained the largest shareholder (40 per cent) (*Moscow News* no. 26, 2001; *RG* 17 August 2001; *RFE/RL Newsline* 13, 17 December 2001; BBC 12 June 2002).

On balance, Russia and the Baltic states have increasingly realised that they are economically interdependent, so there is scope for developing mutually profitable relations as befits close neighbours. Even though the Baltic states' dependence on Russia has been drastically reduced and Russia tends to overestimate it, they too still depend on Russian transit traffic and energy delivery and find a certain amount of it politically and economically useful. Therefore they also compete among themselves for Russian transit. To some extent, Russia's diversification of its export routes can be seen as normal business practice. Also, Western capital has been invested in developing the Baltic infrastructure and Russian transit traffic, particularly in the ports. In both Russia and the Baltic states, private interests compete and may be at odds with those of the state. Thus normal market considerations and conditions are the key factors that influence economic relations between these states.

EU enlargement and Russian fears

Russia's economic relations with the Baltic states in recent years have been increasingly affected by the latter's ambition to become members of the

European Union. Already in 1994 the Baltic states concluded a free trade agreement with the EU. They intensified their efforts for EU membership when they were not included in the first wave of NATO enlargement in 1997, but the two processes were seen as complementary. Most West European states are members of both organisations. In 1998–99, first Estonia, then Latvia and Lithuania, opened membership negotiations with the EU, and the countries began a veritable race in fulfilling the conditions laid down in the *acquis communautaire*. Negotiations were to be completed in 2002, and accession is expected to take place two years later. They also backed the EU's evolving Common Foreign and Security Policy (CFSP), the creation of an EU rapid reaction force, and other key political decisions (Herd and Huang 2001: 15; 33; Arnswald and Jopp 2001: 45). Step by step they adapted their legal systems to European standards, for instance with regard to human rights and minority issues, taxation and crime prevention.

In preparation for joining the Schengen agreement, the three countries signed readmission agreements with Western neighbours concerning refugees, so that visa regimes were abolished in the mid-1990s. Assisted by the EU, especially its Nordic members, they constructed EU-compatible border regimes and control systems on the Russian and Belarusian borders, which had only been administrative lines on the maps in Soviet times (Herd and Huang 2001: 8). Hard pressed by the EU, Lithuania finally agreed to shut down the two nuclear reactors at Ignalina by 2005 and 2009, respectively, in return for EU compensation (Herd and Huang 2001: 8; *RG* 30 August 2001; BBC 18, 23 April, 3 May 2002; *Kommersant* 15 March 2002). Other difficult problems pertained to the EU's common agricultural policy. The Baltic states, especially Lithuania and Latvia, insisted on more EU support and quick access to the common market (Herd and Huang 2001: 8; BBC 15 March, 16 April 2002). In general, this adaptation process was by no means easy, and generated resistance to the EU in the three countries. Interestingly, the rural populations dominated by the titular nations were more negative to change, whereas the urban Russians were more positive. This caused political headaches for the governments, because EU accessions were to be decided by referendum (Herd and Huang 2001: 9, 22; *NG* 20 April 2000).[6]

As the process of Baltic affiliation with the EU proceeded, Russia gradually realised the potentially negative impact it had or could have on its own interests (see Hubel 2002; Timmermann 2000, Vahl 2001). Russia had no chance of becoming a member of the EU itself in the foreseeable future, so EU enlargement to the Baltic states might irrevocably separate them from Russia (*NG* 6 October 2000). Irritation was expressed over Estonian statements that EU membership would enable it to conduct inter-state dialogue with Russia from a firmer position and force Russia to change its policy (Elagin 2001: 155). Researcher Arkady Moshes at the Institute of Europe in Moscow has indicated the risk that countries having tense relations with Russia may influence the EU's Russian policy in a negative way (Moshes 2002: 311).

Russian officials also expressed concern about Baltic reorientation of trade from Russia to the unified EU market, or, more justifiably, a reinforcement of this trend. Russia might lose potential investments due to the higher attractiveness of the new members. Most importantly, Russia was concerned that the introduction of EU standards and regulations with regard, among others, to quality, environment, means of transport in the new member states, would amount to a *de facto* ban on some Russian exports and contribute to turning their trade Westwards. It might also impact Russian transit traffic. Russia was calculated to have lost USD 350 million a year after Sweden, Finland and Austria joined the EU in 1995 (Moshes 2002: 310–13; Elagin 2001:155; Smorodinskaya 2001: 64). According to one Russian source, the Baltic states would on accession raise import tariffs by at least half, and be obliged to coordinate export quotas on their Eastern neighbours (*RG* 7 February 2002).

Moreover, the Baltic states adapted their visa rules to complement Schengen regulations and this threatened to restrict Russian travel to, and trade with, the Baltic states. Thus Estonia and Latvia in 2000–1 extended visa requirements to the border populations in Russia, which had been exempted before (Elagin 2001:157; Demurin 2001:78; *RG* 20 December 2001, 18 April 2002). These problems were especially serious for the Kaliningrad exclave, which is about to become a Russian enclave inside the EU when Lithuania and Poland join. The region (unlike the rest of Russia) enjoyed visa-free regimes with Lithuania and Poland since 1992, which led to a very intensive border trade, engaging about a fourth of the working population. Lithuania and Latvia also allowed visa-free train transit to and from Russia. However, after an incident, Latvia introduced visas for Russian trains in transit in 2001 (after which, Russia redirected them to Belarus). Poland introduced some limitations in 1998, but the full visa regime has been postponed, and Lithuania has set the deadline for transit by January 2003 and for visits by July 2003 (*SPB Vedomosti* 29 October 2001; Oldberg 2001: 41; Timmermann 2001:16).

Russia strongly opposed the introduction of visas for Kaliningrad. First, Russia proposed a 'Baltic Schengen', which implied preserving visa freedom for Kaliningraders and even extending it to all Baltic states. In negotiation with the EU, the Russian Foreign Ministry thereafter demanded free transit through Poland and Lithuania without visas on trains, buses and cars. Reference was made to the human right of being able to visit one's own country, and claims for compensations were hinted at (Oldberg 2001: 44; Körber Foundation 2002: 43). When visiting Poland, President Putin suggested solving the problem before EU enlargement and creating a common working group to that end.[7] At a summit with the EU in late May 2002, Putin complained that Russian proposals on visa-free transit of people and goods were met by EU proposals, which made the rights of Russians freely to visit relatives in other parts of the country dependent on another country. Such practices he found incomprehensible, since the Cold War was long over. The solution to this vital question was decisive and an absolute criterion for the relations with the EU, said Putin. At the following summit of the Council of Baltic Sea States in St Petersburg, Putin repeated that Russia would never accept a division of its sovereign territory, and suggested adoption of the procedure used for transit through the GDR to West Berlin in the 1970s (BBC 29 May, 10 June 2002).

Russian negotiators also demanded free cargo transportation through Lithuania, Latvia and Poland by rail and road without customs inspection, an air corridor across Lithuania, undisturbed use of transit infrastructure, and the right to build oil and gas pipelines and electricity lines through these countries. Officials have proposed rail and bus transit 'corridors' across Lithuania in closed wagons without stops along agreed routes, which would pass through its main cities. The Russian Duma in June again made a ratification of the border treaty with Lithuania, which was signed in 1997, contingent on the solution of the transit problem (Oldberg 2001: 43; *RG* 23, 24 May 2002; BBC 16, 17 May, 11 June 2002; *NZZ* 30 May 2002; *Tagesspiegel* 30 May 2002). These demands went beyond the present rules and were resisted by Poland and Lithuania. The talk of corridors evoked special fears in Poland echoing Hitler's 'Danzig corridor' ultimatum of 1939.

EU enlargement also threatened Kaliningrad's energy links with Russia. This region depended on receiving some 80 per cent of its energy in transit from Russia. As Lithuania decided to detach its electricity grid from the ex-Soviet to the Polish and European electricity system, Kaliningrad had to choose between following suit, thereby assuming higher costs, or being isolated (Oldberg 2001: 41, Timmermann 2001: 24). On some occasions, the Russian demands for solving these problems ahead of EU enlargement appeared to resonate pressure tactics, which were echoed in press reports that Russia could delay EU enlargement to the Baltic states.

Not least, Kaliningrad's visa and customs problems were aggravated by the fact that the region had become more dependent than other Russian regions on foreign trade, especially on food imports from neighbouring states. In order to compensate for its exclave location, the region had in 1991 been declared a Free – and in 1996 a Special – Economic Zone, which meant customs-free imports to and exports from the region. However, the region was often used as a tax-free springboard to the rest of Russia and as a loop-hole to avoid Russian customs. Furthermore, Western investors preferred investing in neighbouring states rather than in Kaliningrad, as the region itself was small, lacked natural resources, and suffered more from structural problems and unstable legal conditions than most other Russian regions. These factors combined to depress the economic situation in the region below the Russian average, which constituted a key obstacle to the development of the region (Smorodinskaya 2001: 61).

Accepting Baltic EU membership

This explanation of Russian apprehensions towards Baltic EU membership can be qualified by several counter-arguments. First, the enlargement decision was decided by the parties concerned, and Russia could do little to halt it. Attempts to do so would only prove counter-productive, whereas acceptance could provide some possibilities to influence the parties to heed Russian interests. Second, Russia had for years recommended EU membership as an alternative to NATO membership for the Baltic states, since the EU was viewed as a European organisation mainly concerned with economic matters, as opposed to NATO which was seen as a military organisation dominated by the United States. Russian leaders therefore did not oppose the EU, CSDP or the creation of an EU military force, and even talked about a strategic partnership with the EU (Danilov 2001; *KZ* 6, 9 December 2000; *NG* 24 May 2001; *RG* 16 April 2002; Blank 2000:16). Third, Russia noted that the move towards EU (and NATO) membership induced Estonia and Latvia to amend citizenship and language legislation for the Russian-speaking inhabitants to conform with international standards in a way that Russian criticism and pressure failed to do (Oldberg 1997: 158). Thus a key issue which had upset Russian nationalists and democrats alike and contaminated political relations for many years lost most of its significance. Fourth, as Russia gave priority to economic development, the EU states became its most important trading partners, accounting for up to 40 per cent of Russian foreign trade. Two-thirds of Russian exports, which rose quickly in 2001, consisted of oil and gas. By contrast, the EU states were not dependent on Russia, receiving only 16 per cent of oil imports and 19 per cent of gas imports from there (*NZZ* 22 May 2002; *Handelsblatt* 29 May 2002; *Wall Street Journal* 29 May 2002).

Thus, even if Russia itself did not aspire to EU membership, it strove to develop as close relations as possible. Russia signed a Partnership and Cooperation Agreement (PCA) with the EU in 1994, formulated a medium-term strategy for developing relations in 1999 in response to the EU Common Strategy on Russia, and contacts and cooperation on all levels intensified (Timmermann 2000; Hubel 2002; Vahl 2001). A Joint Declaration of 2000 spoke in favour of boosting exchanges between the parties, as well as between Russia and the candidate countries. A year later the EU and Russia created a common working group that aimed to develop a concept for a common European economic space within five years. In May 2002 the EU recognised Russia as a market economy, which paved the way for an early entry into the WTO. In return, Russia promised to fulfil the remaining conditions such as liberalising its domestic energy market (*RG* 30 May 2002; *NZZ* 30 May 2002). The Italian Prime Minister Silvio Berlusconi even called on the EU to accept Russia as a member state (*Tagesspiegel* 27 May 2002).

With regard to the Baltic states' entry into the EU, Russian officials also identified some economic advantages. On the strength of the PCA, import tariffs would be lowered, facilitating Russian export, and the transit of goods through EU states would be free from customs and other fees, except for administration and transport (Moshes 2002: 309; Oldberg 2001: 37). It was pointed out that Russian joint ventures and business already present in the

Baltic states would gain access to the vast European market. Russian trade with Lithuania has lately grown rapidly (*RG* 5 March 2002).

Concerning the difficult visa problem, Russia could not expect the EU to change the Schengen agreements, which had taken them much effort to attain, or that the Baltic states (and Poland) should refrain from Schengen and keep their borders to the EU closed for the sake of Russia or its Kaliningrad region. As noted, Russia was not prepared to sign re-admission agreements with its neighbours. The question of illegal immigration is one of the EU's main problems and plays a major role in the domestic debates of most member states. Moreover, Russia itself imposed visa regimes on several CIS states in 2000, even though exceptions were then negotiated, and Russian visas remained much more expensive than those of EU states and candidates.

Further, it should be observed that the EU convention on implementing the Schengen agreement does in fact allow for multiple transit visas. It permits contracting parties to issue visas restricted to their national territories (articles 10 and 11) and to make exceptions for aliens on humanitarian grounds, or due to national interest or international obligations.[8] EU officials pointed out that visa regimes could actually be made quite flexible and at least as efficient as the present border controls. Thus the number of Russian travellers to Finland actually grew after that country joined the EU and the Schengen zone, so that Finland now is second only to Germany in issuing visas to Russian citizens. Presumably this growth is also due to Russia's economic recovery.

With respect to Kaliningrad, the EU gradually came to realise its specific problems, leading to a greater preparedness for compromise. An official 'communication' of January 2001 noted that all EU rules must not apply at once to the new members, and their special practices could be used. For example, visa exemptions could apply to border populations, or visas could be multiple and long-term, cheap and available at consulates in Kaliningrad. Sweden resolved to open a consulate there in 2002. Furthermore, the EU has long contributed to the improvement of the border infrastructure. The present situation at Kaliningrad's borders is very problematic, with long queues, much corruption and crime, according to frequent reports in the Russian media. Also Lithuania and Poland proved anxious to solve the visa problem as smoothly as possible and enlarged their consular services, partly in order to enable cross-border trade for their own citizens (*MN* 12 March 2002; *RG* 30 April, 16 May 2002).

Further, even if Russia complained about the economic effects of EU enlargement on Kaliningrad and the fact that it received less EU assistance than the Baltic states, this can be justified by the fact that the latter were after all official EU candidates, and as such had made great progress in meeting membership conditions. The EU could not really be blamed for the structural and legislative problems in Kaliningrad. As alluded to already, Russia could not or had not been willing to subsidise and develop the region, and therefore

Russia needed support from the EU. It called for EU investments and economic aid to Kaliningrad with reference to the impending enlargement, and most federal projects there counted on EU assistance. Indeed, the EU paid growing attention to the social, economic and ecological problems of the region that threatened the neighbouring countries. Russia also had to acknowledge that Lithuania, in spite of its small size and restructuring problems, was demonstrably cooperative concerning Kaliningrad. Like Poland, it had provided the region with humanitarian aid after the August 1998 crisis, and was interested in maintaining border trade. The two countries developed a list of common projects – for example concerning transport, border crossings, environment and education – to be implemented under the auspices of the EU Northern Dimension (the Nida initiative) (*RG* 17 February 2000). Lithuania agreed to let Russia build a new gas pipeline across its territory to Kaliningrad, and in 2001 lowered its railway tariffs for transit to Kaliningrad, to which Russia, however, was slow to reciprocate. Lithuania pledged to keep Russia informed about its negotiations with the EU, and its parliament created a special forum with the Kaliningrad Duma. Of course, this Lithuanian policy not only served to make its EU accession more palatable to Russia but also to win favours with the EU (Oldberg 2001: 41).

A final reason for Russia to accept the Baltic states joining the EU was that this did not greatly affect and might indeed promote Russia's main recent ambition *vis-à-vis* the EU, namely to establish an energy partnership with Europe and become its main provider of oil and gas (*NG* 24 January 2001; Oldberg 2001: 48). When visiting Germany, Russia's main customer, President Putin noted critically that EU states would not permit more than 30 per cent of power supply from a non-member, adding that gas at Russia's borders was four times cheaper than in Western Europe (BBC 10 April 2002). Hopes were expressed that Russia would meet 70 per cent of the EU's energy needs in 2020 (*Vremya Novostei* 3 October 2001; *ITAR-TASS* 21 November 2001). As mentioned above, Russia is already building pipelines from its fields in Siberia and northern Russia in the Western direction, and an agreement has been reached concerning a new gas pipeline across Poland. European oil companies have shown an increased interest in making investments in Russia, due to its recent legal and fiscal reforms and improving economic performance since 1999 (*Financial Times* 25 April 2002).

To realise such an energy partnership, Russia could also rely upon existing pipelines and other means of transport in the Baltic states, though preferably at lower prices. Even if the Baltic states became EU members, they remained dependent on Russian energy, and a lot of investment had been spent on improving the infrastructure for Russian transit. The future closure of the Ignalina nuclear power station offers Russia the opportunity of expanding its energy exports to Lithuania (*NG-Dipkurier* 26 Oct. 2000; *Handelsblatt* 12 June 2002). In order to solve the energy problems in Kaliningrad, Russia decided to build a huge gas-firing power plant fed from pipelines through Lithuania, and offers were even made to export electricity from this source to neighbouring countries, including Sweden. Poland was said to have shown some interest in investing in the project. Russian energy companies were more interested in export at world market prices than helping the Russian state to subsidise Kaliningrad (*MN* 26 March 2002).

Thus, even if EU enlargement to the Baltic states might create some economic losses for Russia and more problems for Kaliningrad, political considerations and the hope of becoming a major energy partner for the EU appear on balance to have induced Russia to accept the development. Attempting to halt or postpone the enlargement process would not succeed and probably cripple Russia's possibilities in influencing and profiting from it. Both Russia and the EU considered Kaliningrad a test case for their future cooperation, and both needed a solution to the problem which had to be a compromise. Hence, Russia's overall interests with regard to Europe seemed to overshadow the losses it could incur from the inclusion of the Baltic countries into the EU.

Concluding remarks

This analysis argues that Russian economic policy towards the Baltic states since 1991 has been quite contradictory. Russian officials have contradicted each other, or even themselves, depending on the situation, the time and the audience, and the policy line has changed. One is left with an impression of a short-term and reactive Russian policy, subject to various concerns, domestic or international.

Nevertheless, certain patterns emerge. Even if the differences among the actors in Russia have not been the focus of this study, one can conclude that – unsurprisingly – private companies and businessmen appear to give priority to their own economic needs, which tend to make them more interested in cooperation with the Baltic authorities than with Russian officials. The population and politicians in Kaliningrad were particularly interested in maintaining and improving economic contacts with neighbouring states (Oldberg 2001: 59 ff). Perhaps more unexpectedly, several Foreign Ministry officials appeared as hard-liners, keen on exercising economic pressure on the Baltic states. More importantly, President Yeltsin appears to have been ambivalent, both advocating economic cooperation with the Baltic states and authorising pressure on them for political aims. By comparison, President Putin has given more priority to Russia's economic interests and cooperation with the EU, including the Baltic states. It remains to be seen whether his politically motivated opposition to transit visas for travel to and from Kaliningrad will allow a compromise solution, facilitating economic cooperation with the EU.

Paradoxically, Russia became more interested in mutually beneficial economic ties with the Baltic states when these ties were weakened in the 1990s. Russian economic blackmail reinforced the desire of the Baltic states to reduce their dependence on Russia and seek integration with the West. The economic crises of the 1990s induced Russia to increase its exports, particularly of energy, to EU states. These states proved the most willing to grant credits, make investments and provide economic assistance to Russia. Russia became quite dependent on the EU and interested in as close relations as possible. If Russia thus 'lost' the Baltic states to the West, it could resume relations with them in the European framework. By accepting the Baltic states as fully independent and integrated with Europe, just as with Sweden or Poland, Russia itself becomes more European. The record since the early 1990s shows that Russia's relations with the Baltic states have been more and more influenced by its general interests and third parties, rather than by these small states themselves.

Looking to the future, Baltic EU (and NATO) membership may therefore serve to help Russia overcome residual imperial proclivities towards these small neighbours and stake on cultivating peaceful ties with them. There are innumerable personal, cultural and commercial contacts that can be developed to mutual benefit. With regard to the Baltic states, EU (and NATO) membership will not only promote their economic development and European identity. It will also make them feel more secure from Russian pressure and allow them to develop those ties with Russia that are profitable to them. Many know Russia well and speak Russian. The Russian-speaking populations are even more EU-centric (*Eurorussians*) than the titular nations, and many of them retain old contacts with their homeland. The Baltic states can thus become some kind of bridge between Europe and Russia, contributing to the integration of Russia with Europe.

The Baltic states also have strong interests in promoting European unity and progress. They have unique experiences of state building, and they will automatically draw the attention of the other EU states to the problems of the Baltic Sea region. Even if they will require structural support from the EU for several years, this need will not be as big a burden as, for example, that of Poland. The fact that the Baltic states will have external EU borders with Russia and Belarus is likely to make them more exposed to the influx of refugees and job-seekers from these and other countries. This will be a heavy responsibility for the Baltic states but also a reason to reach agreements with Russia on this issue (Arnswald and Jopp: 60).

Whilst the Kaliningrad exclave is a special problem here, and Russia and the EU must find agreement, such agreement and compromise appears possible. By contrast, neighbouring Belarus will probably become more isolated than ever as the EU enlarges into the Baltic region, even if it has a union with Russia. The regime of President Alyaksandr Lukashenka is decidedly dictatorial, and the economy of Belarus remains state-planned in the old Soviet way. The country is thus both an economic burden and a political embarrassment to Russia. EU enlargement and increased cooperation with Russia may therefore compel Russia to apply more pressure on Belarus to follow suit or lose Russian support. In short, the Baltic states' accession to the EU will broadly have beneficial effects both on the states involved and on their neighbours.

Notes

1   According to Hansson 1997: 5, 10, 17, Russia in 1996 had 22.8 and 20.2 per cent of Latvia's export and import, respectively; 23.6 and 28.8 per cent of those of Lithuania, but only 16.5 and 13.5 per cent of Estonia's.
2   Foreign Minister Primakov in January 1997 claimed that 60 per cent of Estonia's national income came from Russian transit (*NG* 11 January 1997).
3   According to Spruds 2002: 360, 20–25 per cent of Latvia's GDP is linked to transit, and 80 per cent of rail shipments were transit in 2000. According to Sutela 2002, transit transport in 1995–99 accounted for 56 per cent of the total in Estonia, 87 per cent in Latvia and 66 per cent in Lithuania, while the GDP shares for transit transport in 1999 were 7.9, 8.0 and 4.6 per cent respectively.
4   Imports from Russia in 2000 were: Estonia 21 per cent, Latvia 29 per cent, Lithuania 46 per cent. Exports to Russia: 7, 4 and 7 per cent, respectively (calculated from IMF 2001).
5   According to *RG* 26 January 2001, one third of oil exports still went through Ventspils, and almost half through Tuapse and Novorossiisk on the Black Sea. According to RG 17 August 2001, Ventspils took 13 million tons in 2000.
6   In 2000 polls on EU membership, 45 per cent of Estonians (32 per cent in 2001), 44 per cent of Latvians and 40 per cent of Lithuanians voiced support (Lepik 2002: 21).
7   From the official website of the Russian president, 16 January 2002.
8   From the convention implementing the Schengen Agreement of 14 June 1985 (22 September 2000). Official Journal L 239, Brussels: European Union.

Part III

Interstate relations in the core CIS

5   The 'normalisation' of Russian foreign policy
The role of pragmatic nationalism and big business

Rosaria Puglisi

Over the last decade, Russian foreign policy has been characterised by a gradual but distinctive shift from a geopolitical to a geo-economic dimension. Since the early 1990s, the idea that Russia's position in world politics could be determined more by its economic than by its military power has progressively gained influence within Russian foreign policy circles. The emphasis on economic cooperation as an instrument to enhance Russia's international status was the common theme threaded through the tapestry of Russian foreign policy, from the Atlanticism of the first Russian Foreign Minister Andrei Kozyrev, to the multi-polarity of Kozyrev's successor, Yevgeny Primakov (Robinson 2002). This shift from geopolitics to geo-economics, accelerated by the 1998 economic breakdown and ultimately reflected in the 2000 Russian Foreign Policy Concept and Security Concept, has enabled and fostered a growing interaction between some sectors of Russian business and Russia's foreign policy agencies.

Throughout the 1990s, a tension was manifest at the heart of Russian foreign policy decision-making between two visions – one attempted to maintain the illusion that Russia was still a great power and the other acknowledged that, after the end of the Cold War, Russia was barely able to maintain its status as a regional power. Following the 1995 Duma elections, a consensus emerged around 'Pragmatic Nationalism' as the central tenet of Russian foreign policy. This doctrine broadly reconciled nationalistic aspirations to Russia's great power status and the pragmatic prescription that all possible means had to be employed to prevent Russia from losing authority over its neighbouring countries. The parallel transformation of the Russian economy and the consolidation of powerful financial and industrial conglomerates, which were interested in expanding into foreign markets, led many observers to argue that a convergence of interests existed between Russian business and Russian foreign policy.

Pragmatic nationalism was, none the less, the first stage in a relationship between business interests and foreign policy activities that, by mid-2002, Foreign Minister Igor Ivanov defined as a 'normal process' (*Vremya Novostei* 13 May 2002). In President Vladimir Putin's Russia, energy diplomacy and assistance in promoting Russian economic interests are strongly linked to a strategy aimed at preserving Russian influence over external markets which, as Putin noted, Russia has lost to foreign competitors 'during the period of weakness'.[1] In the words of Foreign Minister Ivanov: 'the bulk of the Russian president's negotiations deal with concrete economic issues', while support to Russian business has become a priority. Indeed, major business companies, recognising the efforts of Russian economic diplomacy, have begun to 'come to us to seek advice' (*VN* 13 May 2002).

An explanation for the strategic shift from geopolitics to geo-economics is located in the interaction of three elements. First, with the collapse of the USSR, Russia faced a post-imperial identity crisis that convinced the country's foreign policy elite of the need to consolidate Russia's influence over its CIS partners via economic rather than exclusively political means. Second, the dramatic economic disintegration that characterised the post-independence years started to be framed by some Russian economists in terms of economic security; a belief was widely held that increased cooperation with the CIS could provide a means for Russia to reverse its economic decline. Third, the economic interdependence with the countries of the former Soviet Union was still intense and the perception that geo-economic and geopolitical space that had traditionally fallen beneath Russian hegemonic control could be supplanted by foreign powers fostered a sense that the survival of Russia itself was at stake. The acceptance of the need to re-think relations with the independent states of the former Soviet Union on the basis of mutual economic advantage provided Russian financial–industrial conglomerates with an ideological justification to acquire asset ownership and consolidate their presence in foreign markets.

A 'normal' foreign policy

The rise of a global economy and the consolidation of large corporations engaged in foreign markets have challenged this conventional interpretation of the relationship between foreign policy and economic activity. Lenin identified a causal link between foreign investment and the acquisition of colonies, seeing imperialism as endemic to the monopoly capitalist mode of production, and the foreign policies of the capitalist countries as naturally expansionist and interventionist (Lenin 1993). Modern scholars of international political economy, by contrast, have highlighted a 'fundamental change' that took place in the nature of diplomacy with the emergence of firms as agents of international relations. Indeed:

> States are now competing more for the means to create wealth within their territory than for power over more territory. Power, especially military capability, used to be a means to wealth. Now it is more the other way around. Wealth is the means to power – not just military power, but the popular or elected support that will keep present ruling groups in their jobs.
>
> (Strange 1992: 9)

In accordance with a different tradition, Soviet policymakers made business dependent on foreign policy priorities by employing economic factors and foreign trade as instruments to achieve foreign policy objectives. Throughout the Soviet era, the supply of raw materials, notably oil, gas and military hardware, was used to exert influence over Eastern European political partners or Third World countries, regardless of the economic disadvantages this exchange implied for the USSR (A Smith 1993).

With the advent of an independent Russia, however, a number of factors induced the national leadership to switch from 'a mission-oriented foreign policy to an interest-driven one' (Goble 1994: 42). For perhaps the first time in its millennial history Russia was left with no special mission to play in the world, no 'Third Rome' to build, no Marxist gospel to spread. Russia's leadership was instead confronted with an environment within which issues relating to domestic socio-economic and political development had become so compelling that they determined the state's foreign policy agenda. The perception that in a post-Cold War arena state power was measured in economic rather than military terms was key to convincing the Russian foreign policy elite that, if the state was to regain its lost role as a great power, its economic strength had to be increased. In a country torn apart by a domestic economic crisis and incapable of expanding into external markets, the list of foreign policy priorities had to be reconsidered (Kozyrev 1995).

In the second half of the 1990s, still struggling to define a post-Soviet identity, afflicted by a catastrophic economic decay, preoccupied by the maintenance of its influence on the former Soviet territories, the Russian leadership saw in the consolidation of economic relations a way to enhance the country's international status. In the process of 'normalising' Russia's foreign policy, the strategic importance of business and economic activity was recognised. Russia's economic power continued to be employed to influence the decisions of commercially dependent states in Russia's favour, whilst diplomatic efforts were pursued to gain access to new foreign markets for domestic companies.

Post-imperial identity crisis

The years between 1991 and 1993 were characterised by a sense of uncertainty amongst a section of the Russian foreign policy elite over the nature of Russian state interests and the meaning of national identity in the aftermath of the dissolution of the Soviet Union. Foreign Minister Andrei Kozyrev had worked to change the image of Russia as a closed and predominantly aggressive country, having realised that the politics of military confrontation was moving off the foreign policy agenda. Foreign policy was increasingly determined by the domestic reform agenda rather than the perception of Western threat, thus reducing the power of ideology and military patriotism as legitimising factors. Russia, he believed, had to be established as a 'normal state', a democratic market economy. An 'imperial syndrome' had to be abandoned, while other sorts of considerations, such as the country's position in the world economy, in science, in culture, and the living standards of its population, had to become priority issues in the process of foreign policymaking.

This switch from a strategy of military domination to one of economic influence, Kozyrev maintained, would serve a twin purpose. It would challenge the traditional mistrust and seclusion that the capitalist world had imposed upon Russia during the Soviet era, while, at the same time, it would liberate Russia from the economic burden of supporting a 'confrontational climate'. The preservation of the country's military arsenal and the establishment of a new *cordon sanitaire* with the West constituted too high a price for Russia to pay (Kozyrev 1995).

The foreign policy strategy that was adopted as a result of these considerations was perceived amongst nationalistic circles in Moscow as the embodiment of a defeatist spirit. Nationalists suggested that Russia, having lost the Cold War, was now forced into an isolationist, inward-looking policy. Many democratically oriented analysts and politicians maintained that, just as with Japan and Germany after World War Two, Russia should concentrate on its internal political and economic restoration in order to recover its international prestige (Kolchin 1995).

With the collapse of the Soviet Union, and the consequent freedom of foreign and security policymaking afforded to the newly independent states, as well as the loss of control over the former republics, it had become particularly difficult for Russians to agree on the most effective foreign policy line to pursue (Lukin 1994). Russia had undergone systemic collapse, an event even more severe than for the other former republics where, by and large, a distinct national identity had endured persecution and repression under the Russian and the Soviet empires, or, in some cases, it had been fostered by this experience. As the centre of the empire and the focus for political and economic decision-making, Russia had failed to develop its identity as a distinct nation-state.

Thus, for many Russians, the establishment of the new polity in December 1991 represented only the shrinking of Russia's historic borders, not the rebirth and enhancement of the Russian state. They found it difficult to accept that Ukraine, Belarus or the Baltics were now independent states separated from Russia by an international border (Tolz and Teague 1992). Diminished frontiers also prompted Russians to address questions relating to their core identity as confidence in the certainties of the past crumbled (Kondrakov 1996). The loss of the Empire occurred so abruptly that Russians did not have the time to develop an extra-imperial identity.

As a result, Russian nationalists, such as Aleksandr Tsipko for example, argued that decisions over the future of the Soviet state had been made by a small number of ambitious politicians over the head of the population. This represented a *de facto* usurping of 'the power to speak in the name of Russian history and the Russian Empire' (Kondrakov 1996: 18). The inability to come to terms with this new, more humble identity accounts for the difficulties in defining a foreign policy concept for independent Russia. The foreign policy elite reached consensus only in so far as outlining a set of 'fundamental interests' as survival, prosperity, and security. Russia's geography, history, culture, ethnic composition and political tradition defined the implications of these 'immutable' interests and the way they would be implemented. Yet a further layer of national interests, reflecting the 'national idea', the 'nation's self-identity', the country's 'visualisations of the national past and the national future', also presented more serious challenges to identification (Stankevich 1994). Political opinions on the essence of national interests diverged widely, ranging from 'Liberal-Westernisers' to 'National Patriots'.[2]

The prevalence of a strategy of liberal foreign policy, in the immediate post-Soviet years, was the result of the polarisation of ideology that had occurred in the late Soviet era. In order to present themselves as the only viable ideological alternative to the communists, the democrats were forced to adopt even more radical positions than those held by Gorbachev. The rejection of liberal policy and the renewed pre-eminence of nationalism once power was safely in the hands of Yeltsin's democrats, represented, in this context, the return to a natural state of being. Russia was a great power, had traditionally harboured a vision of itself as a great power, and it was only natural for it to return to the logic of great power policy (McFaul 1995).

However, after the inauguration of *glasnost*, Russians had endured almost a decade of 'self-flagellation'. Russia was faced with revelations that pricked its national pride: the scale of the horrors perpetrated in the Stalinist period, the devastation of the environment, the rise of crime, the decay of traditional social values, the condemnation of Russian colonial exploitation of the other Soviet Republics. This was combined with a 'feeling of victimisation', loss of pride and national self-assuredness that had been present in the Russian conscience since the Soviet era. The 'practice of damning Russian imperialism', along with the perception that large resources were being transferred out of Russia to promote social and economic development in the non-Russian republics, contributed to the sentiment that Russia was indeed feeding the empire while being blamed for keeping it together (Prizel 1998).[3]

Economic deterioration

Another factor that affected the change in direction of foreign policy was the deepening economic crisis. The continued deterioration of the economic situation from 1993 onwards increased the identity crisis of the Russian Federation. The failure of a pro-Western foreign policy to stabilise the economy, and the general perception that economic welfare and living standards, as low as they might have been, were at least guaranteed in the Soviet Union, served to strengthen a sentiment of nostalgia for the USSR. This mood translated into the conviction that economic interests and relations with the former Soviet republics had to be restored to a central position in the Russian foreign policy strategy.

In 1993 real GDP fell by a further 12 per cent in comparison to the previous year, after a drop of 13 per cent in 1991 and 19 per cent in 1992. Inflation reached an annual rate of 915.3 per cent after having peaked at 1353 per cent in 1992 (IMF 1994). The economic crisis was steadily deepening. Years of unsatisfactory economic reforms, of a steep decline in living standards, industrial production and patterns of trade, emphasised that the threats this never-ending crisis posed were real. Internal stability was directly influenced by Russia's 'economic security'. The chaotic and under-regulated environment resulting from the rapid pace of economic liberalisation, added to the economic degradation and structural deformities of the years of stagnation, created a dangerous combination that threatened to explode into social and political unrest at any time.

In his 1995 speech on the state of the nation, President Yeltsin also recognised that 'Russia will not have reliable guarantees of sovereignty, independence and territorial integrity until it overcomes the economic crisis' (*Rossiiskiye Vesti* 17 February 1995). A number of Russian academics writing in two special issues of *Voprosy Ekonomiki* raised the alarm.[4] Comparing Russian economic indicators to those in the West signalled a situation of risk, and one of them pointed out that Russia was already beyond the critical threshold (see Table 5.1). Leonid Abalkin warned that, in halting the structural deterioration of the country, timing was essential. National authorities were urged to act while resources and reserves were still available, the human capital was still highly qualified, and a reorganisation of the industrial base was still possible (Abalkin 1994).

Vladimir Medvedev argued that the striking contrasts of the model of development pursued in the post-independence years condemned Russia to a

Table 5.1   Indicators of economic security in 1994

Indicators	Critical level in Western economies	1994 levels in the Russian Federation	Possible consequences at socio-political and economic levels
Fall in GNP	30–40	50	De-industrialisation of the economy
Percentage of foodstuff imported	30	40	Strategic dependency of the country on vital imports
Percentage of industrial exports	40	12	Colonial structure of the economy
Percentage of high-technology exported	10–15	1	Technological lag
Percentage of state-funded R&D expenditures	2	0.32	Destruction of intellectual capital

Source: Medvedev 1997: 114.

'structural trap', typical of developing countries. In the context of a general decline in industrial production, the raw material sector appeared to be the only profitable industry capable of generating hard currency revenues. Raw materials production had maintained almost the same level as in the pre-crisis years. In 1995, output was 70 per cent of the 1990 level, with maximum rates in the gas (93 per cent), oil (56 per cent) and rolled iron (61 per cent) industries. Given the large reserves and the low salary rates, Russian natural resources were the only competitive goods on the world markets. In 1995, raw materials accounted for 80 per cent of Russian exports, equal to 20 per cent of GNP (Medvedev 1997).

However, the scientific potential of Russia was exposed to a rapid and apparently inexorable decline. As a result of sharp cuts in the budget, expenditures for research and development fell to 0.32 per cent of GNP in 1993. The number of scientists and researchers also dropped, and the number of research institutes attached to enterprises diminished from a total of 400 in 1990 to 276 in 1994. A massive migration of science workers, either to foreign states or to more profitable and prestigious positions outside research, contributed heavily to the decline of the country's scientific potential (Medvedev 1997).

Many in Russia believed that the state had slipped into a situation of economic insecurity. According to the description provided by economists at the Academy of Sciences, internal and external factors [were] disrupting the normal functioning of social reproduction, destroying the living standard of the population, and, at the same time, provoking a rise in social tension. This condition had come to threaten the very existence of the state (RAN 1994). The risks that the Russian population was facing – famine, cold and epidemics – were as acute as those in a wartime situation. These problems were coupled with the deterioration of the transport and information network, the energy system and the technological and scientific potential of the country (Samsonov 1994).

In concrete political terms, these considerations were translated into a desire to establish dignified living conditions for the population, guarantee social and political security and foster the emergence of a stable system of national values and interests (Lykshin and Svinarenko 1994). In order to achieve these objectives, the state was required to perform a number of tasks to stimulate competitiveness within national industries, provide all the possible guarantees for private economic activity and establish a climate favourable to innovation, investment and the modernisation of the country (Abalkin 1994). A clear role also was identified for foreign policy institutions, upon which Oleg Bogomolov called to avoid the danger of economic and political dependence on foreign countries (Bogomolov 1996). Mutual economic and strategic dependence between Russia and the CIS blocked efforts to re-orient the Russian economy away from the CIS, and many in Russia perceived the reorganisation of these relations as instrumental in countering the state's increasing economic decline.

Interdependence with the CIS countries

In its urge to strengthen relations with Western countries in the early 1990s, Russian foreign policymakers had overlooked developments in the newly independent states. With the continuing deterioration of the internal economic situation, however, the argument that improvement of the domestic economic and political situation of Russia was inconceivable without reintegration with the 'Near Abroad' gained momentum. There was an understanding, shared by many foreign policy analysts and practitioners, that Russia's foreign policy orientation and the definition of its national interests must take into account such components as its 'geographic position, the kind of countries surrounding it, their traditional policy and civilisation orientation' (Narochnitskaya 1992: 137).

The lack of success of policies oriented towards the West reinforced a conviction that CIS cooperation could maintain acceptable rates of growth and stability for the Russian economy. Countries of the former Soviet Union provided Russia with a space in which national producers enjoyed guaranteed access to raw materials, unrestricted entrance to their markets, and unlimited possibilities of cooperation with related enterprises (Faminski 1994). The partial loss of these markets due to the increasingly stratified geopolitical re-orientation of Russia's near neighbours began to be perceived in Russia as a renewed threat to its economic security.

A Russian-based survey published in 1994, for example, demonstrated that, in the hypothetical event of a total collapse of economic links with the former republics, Russia would become the post-Soviet state most capable of achieving self-sufficiency. Should the newly independent states resort to an autarkic regime, Russia would still be able to guarantee 65 per cent of its production, while only 27 per cent of the Kazakh, 15 per cent of the Ukrainian, and four per cent of the Belarusian output would be maintained (Savin 1995). The survey was obviously designed to demonstrate Russia's superiority in the post-Soviet environment, but it inevitably emphasised also the country's dependence on its neighbours.

The break-up of the Soviet Union had induced catastrophic effects for all the national economies. Russia had certainly the most solid economic structure in the region, but the consequences of the abrupt dislocation were none the less experienced, especially in relation to the shrinking of its economic space, diminished access to foreign economic infrastructure and raw materials, loss of ports and increased transportation costs (Silvestrov and Filatov 1994). As a direct result of the highly ineffective trade arrangements put in place in the post-Soviet period between the former Soviet republics (bilateral agreements and barter trade), the shift to world prices starting from 1992, the collapse of the rouble zone, and attempts at trade re-orientation initiated by the former Soviet partners, trade flows had decreased steeply.

In the period of January–June 1992, overall Russian trade turnover was down 30 per cent in comparison with the same period of the previous year, with exports cut by 35 per cent and imports by 24 per cent (Noren and Watson 1992). Over the period 1990–1993, trade among the newly independent states decreased by more than 60 per cent. Exports to the rest of the world dropped from USD 105 billion in 1990 to USD 58 billion in 1993, equal to 46 per cent of the initial figure. Imports fell even further from USD 121 billion to USD 45 billion, equal to 63 per cent of the initial figure. Interstate trade shrank more than trade with the rest of the world; the total was estimated to be 65 per cent over three years (Michalopoulos and Tarr 1994).

In the Soviet years individual republics had often become monopolist manufacturers of specific components and technological equipment, or largely exclusive producers of specific raw materials and semi-finished products. In the mid-1990s, the failure of Russian enterprises to penetrate international markets as obsolete production and non-competitive prices contributed to make their merchandise less appealing for Western buyers, was matched by the conviction that the sheltered environment of the CIS would in any case provide an alternative market (*Finansovye Izvestiya* 29 January 1998; Kolchin 1995).

In addition to this direct influence over the Russian economy, CIS countries played a significant role in controlling, indirectly, Russia's routes to Western markets. After the collapse of the Soviet Union, the majority of the Westward Soviet rail and track routes, pipelines and seaports had been inherited by Ukraine, Belarus and the Baltic states. Russia had been left either with no control over vital transportation lines, or with infrastructures able to provide facilities below international standards.

Russian ports could satisfy only 60 per cent of the capacity required. Of the gas shipped to Europe, 94 per cent was transported through pipelines on Ukrainian territory, and three per cent through Belarusian territory. The Druzhba gas pipeline, for example, crossed Ukrainian territory on its way to European markets, and Ukraine inevitably employed its transit to increase its bargaining power *vis-à-vis* Russia. Ukraine's allegedly arbitrary use of these transport facilities was blamed for causing severe damage to Russian exports, giving rise to prolonged tension between the two Slavic neighbours (RAN 1994: 61).

The gravity of the transit problem forced Moscow to examine alternative solutions, and thus to identify two viable options. Russian companies assumed control over strategic plants on the former Soviet territories either by acquiring the controlling shares of privatised assets, or by diversifying exit routes to foreign markets. However, as the privatisation processes in Russia's neighbouring states were still lengthy and controversial, the latter option was often considered to be the most effective one. On the other hand, Russia actively strove to maintain the energy dependence of some former Soviet republics. Growing energy debts and their inability to drastically re-orient their gas and oil supplies left countries like Ukraine and Belarus exposed to the 'oil whip' and made them more 'inclined' to compromise on other bilateral issues (Smolansky 1995: 75).

Because of the vital role played by the CIS countries in the Russian economy, the establishment of mutually advantageous relations came to be viewed as the top priority for Russian survival strategy. These relations were seen as the 'minimum compensation for the loss of the Soviet Union'. Normalisation of economic and trade relations, and the development of industrial, technical and scientific ties with the former republics, were presented by leading Russian scholars as absolutely essential conditions to guarantee the healthy state of the Russian economy in the short term. In the longer term these relations would preserve and extend existing positions in the CIS emerging markets, and would help Russia to earn its fully-fledged membership of the international community (Kirichenko 1994).

As activity in the CIS stagnated, however, it became increasingly evident that hopes to revive the former Soviet economy within the artificial boundaries of the Commonwealth would not be automatically successful, as had initially been hoped.[5] Frustrated by the inefficiency of the CIS and afraid to compromise their newly-acquired sovereignty, the partners had started to shift away from Moscow's sphere of influence. To counterbalance Russia's overwhelming influence in the region, the former Soviet republics were diversifying their diplomatic efforts through the establishment of new, or the membership of existing, military and economic regional blocs.

Pragmatic nationalism in foreign policy

In the mid-1990s, pragmatic nationalism emerged within Russian foreign policy circles as a reaction to the country's economic decline and the risks associated with loss of control of the CIS markets. In this newly-formulated doctrine, Russian foreign policy was significantly re-oriented from a military and political pre-eminence towards a preoccupation with geo-economics; the country's share in the world economy, the flow of foreign investment and the nation's technological capability came to be viewed as indicators of Russia's Great Power status. Relations with the former Soviet states were restored to a central position within Russian foreign policy agenda as the cornerstone of an attempt to counter the country's economic decline and guarantee its industrial development.

Pragmatic nationalism adopted a post-colonial and economic approach to relations with the CIS, in clear contrast with the imperial and ideological attitude encapsulated in the 'Russian Monroe Doctrine', particularly Andranik Migranyan's claim to Russia's 'special role in the entire geopolitical space of the former USSR'. It was argued that, by embracing a 'Monroe Doctrine', Russia would surrender its option to exercise an *ad hoc* 'rational and pragmatic' distinction between contexts in which Russia's intervention would protect Russian state interests, and situations in which Russia's interests would be best served by a non-interventionist attitude. Moreover, the price of involvement in the domestic problems of the CIS countries would be too high. Russia would probably be drawn into ethnic wars, causing heavy casualties, massive flows of refugees and possible retaliatory attacks upon Russian interests abroad. Finally, a militarist course would impinge on the continuation of democratic reforms, producing, most likely, 'the revival of an authoritarian, besieged, militarised state, with a large degree of central economic planning, and the reintroduction of rationing' (Arbatov 1994: 61–2).

Opposing an approach that stressed military supremacy, pragmatic nationalists proposed a strategy that endorsed leadership rather than control, economic dominance rather than political responsibility. Any project for the restoration of the Soviet Union was rejected as 'pure utopian fantasy', while a pragmatic nationalist policy towards the Near Abroad was to be based on a strategy that '…would be aimed at alleviating the negative consequences of disintegration for Russians especially, that would be relatively cost-effective and stable, that would reduce the likelihood of conflict, and…that would conform to the main strategic goal of bringing about the economic, political and spiritual rebirth and ascendancy of Russia' (CFDP 1997: 14).

Rebuffing the more militant claims from territories now located within the boundaries of the new independent states, pragmatic nationalists recognised that:

> What is needed now is not the reconstruction of the Soviet Union, but, instead, the restoration of some of those beneficial ties. Integration cannot be forced on the countries of the former Soviet Union. Only a rational assessment of and respect for, the needs of each country can lead to the reintegration of the region.
>
> (Travkin 1994: 34)

These aspects of economic security and consolidation of the Russian positions in the 'Near Abroad' become intertwined in the pragmatist vision. A study conducted in the aftermath of the 1996 presidential elections confirmed that an orientation towards a foreign policy aimed at protecting Russian economic interests and restoring relations with the countries of the former Soviet Union was widespread. In a large-scale survey, 94 per cent of respondents identified defence of national economic interests as the top priority for Russian foreign policy. The figure rose to 95 per cent when the interviews were conducted among members of the foreign policy elite. Some 67 per cent of the general public considered the development of relations with the 'Near Abroad' the most important issue; 83 per cent of the foreign policy elite expressed the same opinion. At the same time, 93 per cent of the general public and 97 per cent of the foreign policy elite shared the belief that Russia's internal situation was indeed affecting the country's foreign policy goals.[6]

By the time the survey was conducted, pragmatic nationalism had penetrated official circles of Russian foreign policymaking. A number of documents approved by President Yeltsin in this period reflected this general mood. From the 'Basic Provisions of the Russian Federation Foreign Policy Concept', to the 'Strategic Course of Russia with the State-Members of the

CIS' and the 'Concept of National Security', the importance of domestic and economic issues in setting the agenda for foreign relations was clearly elaborated. An indissoluble link was established between the country's economic well-being and the conditions that greeted Russian agents on the world markets. The government was required to play a more active role in protecting Russian enterprises that were facing, at the same time, a hostile environment on the international arena and the 'unscrupulous' competition of Western corporations on its internal markets (in these documents, CIS markets were considered as internal).

Russian companies were presented as the agents capable of bridging the gap that ideology had created between Russia and its CIS neighbours. Boris Nemtsov, then governor of Nizhny Novgorod, suggested that in order to solve the crisis over the disputed territory of Crimea, Russian business ought to be encouraged to purchase property and business in Sevastopol, thus 'restoring historical justice by capitalist means' (OMRI Daily Digest 20 February 1997).

> If enterprises, hotels, restaurants and cafes are bought by Russian banks, then wages and salaries will be paid in roubles. This in fact will make Sevastopol a *de facto* Russian town.
>
> (Caryl 1998)

Other prominent political advisers positively endorsed this new role for Russian enterprises:

> The force that has the greatest stake in uniting democracy and patriotism is national capital, as it moves out into world markets. It needs a powerful Russia capable of supporting it on an interstate level. It needs a free Russia that does not threaten it with nationalisation or terror.
>
> (*Izvestiya* 6 January 1995)

In the pragmatist doctrine, the conquest of new markets under the banner of Russian capital was viewed as a peaceful invasion that would make Russia great again. At a time when Moscow felt its grip on the countries of the 'Near Abroad' loosen, the rhetoric of national capital gradually replaced the traditionally aggressive nationalistic slogans. This new, civilised Russian nationalism appeared no longer to be interested in the political domination of the countries of its near neighbours. Political or military domination would imply additional costs that Russia was no longer in a position to afford.

The viable alternative proposed by the theorists of national capital was to gain access to the natural resources and the strategic infrastructure of the newly independent states via economic means. The prosperity of Russian business was equated with the prosperity of the state, and economic losses for national companies due to the 'invasion of foreign investors' were presented as a threat to Russian national security. 'We cannot allow', the

1997 Concept of National Security indicated, 'foreign companies to seize control over strategically relevant economic sectors, the military industry, and the natural monopolies.'

The political party *Nash Dom – Rossiya* (NDR, 'Our Home is Russia') was the strongest supporter of this political trend. The then 'party of power' became the channel through which the interests of the export-oriented economic sectors found representation in political institutions. 'Expansion of exports and reasonable protectionism' was one of the slogans echoed at the NDR Party Conference in July 1995 (*Rossiya*, 26–31 July 1995: 3). The party's electoral platform made it clear that NDR considered the raw materials sector and the industries engaged in processing raw materials as the primary sources of economic growth, at least in the short term. The financial basis for those companies would flow from the rapidly growing large banks. The state's role, in their view, would be to secure favourable conditions for those companies which proved able to accumulate the necessary capital and initiate a process of growth (*Segodnya* 6 December 1995).

The party was to seek a 'steady economic development on the basis of national capital' (*Segodnya* 21 July 1995). Finding inspiration in the principle that 'a mighty state means a clear economy', NDR proclaimed the abandonment of liberal policies (*Rossiya* 26–31 July 1995). The liberal stage of reforming the economy, which prepared the way for the modernisation of the country's economy, is already coming to an end and therefore a fundamental change of direction is needed. Instead of financial stabilisation at any price, a new core of reforms providing incentives for the accumulation of national capital is being built' (*Kommersant* 15 August 1995). 'Social state liberalism' was the solution to Russian domestic problems and international challenges. The party's foreign policy aimed at trying to 'provide the most favourable international setting in which this country feels absolutely secure, with its hands free to proceed with economic and social reforms' (International Affairs 1996).

In the promotion of national capital, the party of government coincided with the less belligerent positions of the national patriots, who urged the return of a great Russia, armed this time with the more powerful weapons of the market economy. In Russia's fragmented political space the unifying idea of national capital found fertile ground. 'The idea of a great Russia expresses something more – a need to create a new national ideology that would reflect both the corporate interests of the Russian political leadership and the growing power of Russian national capital' (*Nezavisimaya Gazeta* 16 November 1995).

Big business and foreign policy

Russian business, financial–industrial groups and large corporations were identified within the pragmatic nationalist doctrine as being politically responsible for increasing Russia's economic power and expanding the country's influence abroad. The practice, however, revealed how difficult it was to reconcile the foreign policy preferences of large companies with an official foreign policy line.[7] Engaged in a relentless activity to acquire control over strategic assets in the countries of the former Soviet Union, or preoccupied to consolidate their presence in Western markets, Russian companies developed their own foreign policy agendas.

The coordination of foreign policy between business and state institutions became an almost impossible task because of the inner contradictions of the Russian political and economic arena. First, the nature of the Russian political economy dictated that, while there was a large number of economic subjects potentially interested in foreign policy outcomes, only a few companies had the economic and political resources to pursue an active foreign policy line. The interlocking nature of economic and political elites, patronage networks, size and business turnover, gave Russian companies disparate political weight. Second, the definition of foreign policy interests was hotly contested. Both foreign policy agencies and business corporations presented widely fragmented and often contradictory perceptions of foreign policy interests. The result was a free-for-all strategy in which the most powerful companies tended to follow their own economic interests on foreign markets, often irrespective of directions and instructions issued by state agencies.

The contrasting positions of the energy sector and the military–industrial complex provide the most striking example of how different resource endowments allowed business corporations disparate access to foreign policymaking. The economic wealth of the energy sector, its ability to generate 45 per cent of the country's hard currency revenues and its political connections, were the main determinant of the foreign policy authority that companies like *Gazprom* and *Lukoil* enjoyed. The fact that 'energy diplomacy' was still employed to pressurise political partners and to attempt a *rapprochement* with the former Soviet republics placed oil and gas companies *primus inter pares* to pursue an independent foreign policy (Khiripunov and Matthews 1996). The extraordinary strength of the energy industry created an ambivalent situation whereby individual policies of energy companies were perceived in Eastern Europe and the CIS to be part of a Russian foreign policy strategy. At the same time, however, powerful energy enterprises protected their interests through official state channels. The fact that Rem Vyakhirev, whom the Ukrainian papers nicknamed 'the Godfather of *Gazprom*', tended to accompany then-Prime Minister Viktor Chernomyrdin on almost all his important trips abroad, was read as a clear indicator of this preferential position (Yeremenko 1998).

Lukoil's economic capacity empowered the company to conduct a foreign policy at times in open contrast with that of the Foreign Ministry. In 1994–96 the Foreign Ministry prohibited the participation of Russian companies in projects for the excavation of the Caspian Sea basin until the legal status of the Caspian had been defined. *Lukoil*'s argument, that withdrawing from the projects would cause a remarkable loss for the company, was later embraced also by the prime minister and president, by-passing the official position of the Foreign Ministry (Pappe 1997). Because of this proximity to the *loci* of policymaking, oil and gas companies were often held responsible for Russian foreign policy initiatives. In the vehement anti-Russian campaign run in Bulgaria in the mid-1990s, for example, *Gazprom* was accused of being a tool of Russian imperialism in the Balkans and was urged to sell out its 50 per cent shares in the Topenergy joint venture. As Bulgaria was viewed as key in *Gazprom's* strategy to reach into the Turkish market, the sale of Topenergy shares was to inflict a severe blow to the company's expansion in the region.

At the same time, specific interests of energy companies were clearly recognisable behind the adoption of particular foreign policy directions towards individual countries. Aiming at establishing control over strategic assets located on Belarusian territory, *Gazprom* was probably instrumental in fostering the Russia–Belarus union. At the inauguration of works on the Belarusian stretch of the Yamal–Hamburg pipeline, Rem Vyakhirev praised Belarusian President Alyaksandr Lukashenka as the 'leading integrator in the CIS', and emphasised the importance of the project, which would provide a 'political link between Russia and Belarus' (*Jamestown Monitor* 24 October 1996).

By contrast to the energy sector, the military–industrial complex provides an example of a sector whose very sustainability was dependent on the acquisition of foreign markets. However, it suffered from a relatively low business turnover, which in turn deprived it of significant domestic authority.[8] *Minatom* (the Ministry for Atomic Energy), for example, was one of the most active corporations on foreign markets. Animated by an 'ideology of export', the company was engaged in the foreign trade of nuclear technologies and fuel services to obtain the hard currency urgently required to sustain and modernise its organisation. Because of this reliance on foreign markets, *Minatom* negotiated trade agreements with China, Cuba, India and Iran in open disregard of Foreign Ministry directives. In 1995, a USD 800 million contract was signed with the Atomic Energy Organisation of Iran to complete an unfinished nuclear reactor in Bushehr. The agreement also included the training of specialists and the provision of nuclear-fuel services (*Izvestiya* 8 April 1998). These services were offered to Iran without consulting Russian government agencies, including the Ministry of Foreign Affairs (Baker 1997).

The intense activity of *Minatom* in Asia highlighted the frequent incompatibility between foreign policy objectives as dictated by the state agencies and the foreign policy interests of businesses. *Minatom's* deal with Iran stirred tension between Russia and the United States, especially following July 1998, when the Iranians successfully tested a medium-range ballistic missile, the Shahab-3, considered capable of delivering nuclear warheads. According to Russian and American estimates, as a consequence of Russian nuclear cooperation Iran could be in a position to produce its own bomb within between five and eight years. As a result of the event, America increased pressure on Moscow to freeze projects involving the transfer of dual-use technologies to Iran (*Segodnya* 25 July 1998).

Along the same lines, a number of trade agreements between *Rozvooruzhenie* (the Russian State Company on Export and Import of Military-Technology) and China questioned the consistency between individual companies' economic ambitions and the country's national interests. In a move branded by high government officials as causing 'serious damage' to Russian security, in 1995 the Sukhoi Special Design Bureau sold to China a licence to produce SU-27 warplanes. The agreement *de facto* deprived the Russian aviation industry of a possible USD 1.2 billion on future sales (*Kommersant* 25 May 1996).

Significantly, the traditional military antagonism between Moscow and Beijing had not deterred the Russian military–industrial complex. Despite the fact that the Chinese military doctrine identified Russia as an 'unquestionable enemy' and a 'belligerent force', and more than 60 per cent of Chinese combat-ready forces were deployed to repel a threat from Russia, Russian arms companies were none the less engaged in building up China's military power. Four S-300 surface-to-air missile systems, a submarine originally ordered by the Russian navy, 10 IL-76 military cargo planes, and a number of T-80 tanks were sold to China in 1996 (*Kommersant* 18 July 1996; *Nezavisimoe Voennoe Oboozrenie* 25 July 1996).

Conclusions

Despite the high expectations placed by supporters of pragmatic nationalism upon Russian corporations as foreign policy agents, the practice of Russian business abroad reveals a wide divergence between the policy preferences of individual corporations and the official interpretation of the national interest. As in the enterprises of other advanced industrial countries engaged in foreign activities, Russian companies were interested in maximising their profits by expanding their foreign markets and consolidating their influence over strategic assets in the former Soviet territories.

This implied that some Russian companies were unwilling to become tools of Russian strategies abroad, and some of them were powerful enough to endorse their own foreign policy course, forging alliances (Belarus) or disregarding existing rivalries (China). However, the multiplicity of policy priorities among business enterprises and the disparity of resources and access to policymaking meant that the foreign policy agendas of individual companies frequently conflicted with other companies' interests and with the policy line dictate by state agencies. This notwithstanding, the consensus that emerged around a pragmatic nationalist approach marked a significant shift in Russian foreign policy and a definite step towards its 'normalisation'. Because its Great Power status was to be re-established on the basis of economic rather than military power, relations with the CIS countries were to be restructured. Following the consolidation of the newly independent states, policies towards the CIS were now to be informed by the principles of profit and economic advantage, and were to be aimed at increasing economic power through the acquisition of strategic assets and access to internal markets.

In this perspective, Russian foreign policy in the 1990s was not dissimilar to the foreign policy of many Western countries, in which measures designed to foster a 'corporate expansionism' must be reconciled with the temptation to 'convert the multinationals and their overseas subsidiaries into instruments of...foreign policy' (Gilpin 1975: 139). As Sergei Yastrzhembsky, then spokesman for President Yeltsin, revealed, Russia's leadership had made a conscious choice to actively support Russian business in its foreign activities:

> Recently the government has done quite a bit to find a new approach not only to the interests of the state in foreign trade, but also to those of firms, companies and banks. Before every visit made by the president, wherever there is an opportunity to support a particular project, we definitively do that.
>
> (Caryl 1998)

Notes

1   Annual Address by Russian President Vladimir Putin to the Federal Assembly of the Russian Federation, Moscow, 18 April 2000.
2   For an accurate account of the debate on the definition of the national interests see Light 1996, Valdez 1995, and Aron 1998.
3   An example of this attitude can be found in the June 1997 Statement by the Council on Foreign and Defence Policy: 'In most of the republics, the document says, there was a widely current myth that Russia was "robbing" them, whereas in fact Russia was providing for them' (CFDP 1997: 3).
4   Articles published in these issues had the distinctive feature of a 'call-up' to all the relevant institutions to take part in a joint effort and confront the seemingly irreversible deterioration of the social and economic environment. Economic threats were presented as the consequences of internal instability, rather than as the effects of an unfriendly international environment. The irrevocability of market reforms was never questioned, but a substantial adjustment in the state's role as the major economic actor was urged (*Voprosy Ekonomiki* no. 12, 1994; no. 1, 1995).
5   For an overall evaluation of the CIS perspective see Sakwa and Webber 1999.
6   The elite sample included members of the foreign policy committees of the Duma, editors and foreign policy commentators in the media, senior staff officers, major figures at foreign-policy-related institutes, and persons in economic ministries and privatised enterprises that had foreign trade components (Bashkirova 1998).
7   The general expression 'official foreign policy line' here does not refer to a univocal foreign policy strategy endorsed in the Yeltsin years. On the contrary, it is accepted that the various agencies involved in the making of foreign policy were often engaged in an acrimonious political struggle and that their roles were defined more by the balance of power prevailing at the moment than by a set of codified rules. Shifts of power and alliances caused abrupt changes in the policy line and institutional hierarchies (Malcolm 1996; Parish 1996: 32).
8   In the mid-1990s, foreign trade financed more than 50 per cent of all weapons production by Russian enterprises (*Izvestiya* 19 September 1996).

6 Border security implications for dual enlargement

A comparison of Russia and Ukraine

Frank Morgese

Introduction

In a few years time the European Union (EU) will have a common border in Central Europe with both Russia and Ukraine. The North Atlantic Treaty Organisation (NATO) has already expanded its border to Russian Kaliningrad and to western Ukraine. Though it was NATO that expanded to the east first, the security implications of future EU enlargement have begun to surpass those of NATO enlargement.

The further enlargement of NATO will not negatively affect the security of Ukraine and the Russian Federation. The central purpose of NATO is to protect the sovereignty of individual states. The result has been to draw clear boundaries between those protected by Article V and those outside that protection. These 'outsiders' – Russia and Ukraine – however, both have a special relationship with the alliance according to the NATO–Russia Founding Act and the NATO–Ukraine Charter. NATO has successfully expanded without reviving Cold War divisions in Europe, and the purpose of the alliance is now better defined as providing stability and peace in Europe as opposed to defending members against a re-assertive neo-imperialist Russia. Some argue that this is essentially a case of NATO transitioning from a collective defence organisation to a collective security organisation. Since the attacks of 11 September, NATO's relations with Russia have warmed, and there is talk in Brussels and Moscow of a new rapprochement and accommodation. Russia, for its part, appears to have placed no red lines on the expansion of NATO to the Baltic states. Ukraine has maintained close relations with NATO through the Partnership for Peace (PfP) programme and is bordered by two NATO states, Poland and Hungary. Ukraine has flirted with NATO membership, but most analysts agree that membership is still a long way off. However, given improved NATO–Russia relations and the expansion of the alliance after the next round of enlargement, Ukraine must seriously consider becoming an aspirant and adopting the Membership Action Plan (MAP), or become increasingly marginalised in a diminishing pool of PfP members.

The EU has defined itself as a 'widening' organisation in so far as any 'democratic' country in Europe is a potential candidate for membership.

With the admission of Finland, the EU expanded to the borders of the Russian Federation. The nature of the Finnish–Russian border (history, climate, lack of East–West lines of communication, etc.) has served to mitigate the negative consequences of border security and the political volatility and potential friction of this lengthy EU–Russia contact point. The admission of Poland, Hungary, Slovakia and the Baltic states, on the other hand, will have real and immediate implications for Russia and Ukraine. As opposed to the geo-political consequences, real or imagined, of further NATO enlargement, it is EU enlargement that will have far-reaching consequences on the future alignment of 'European' space.

This chapter will compare and contrast the pros and cons of establishing a NATO and an EU common border with Ukraine and Russia, 'outsider' states of the former Soviet Union that have no immediate prospect of inclusion in NATO or the EU enlargement processes. Specifically, the focus will be the crucial issue of border security, which includes the establishment of new visa regimes, tighter control on trade, migration, refugees, as well as improvement of security measures and regimes over the transiting of illegal narcotics, organised crime and disease – or 'drugs, thugs, and bugs'.

Nato's eastern frontier

NATO enlargement in 1999 brought NATO boundaries to the borders of Russia and Ukraine. Kaliningrad shares a border with Poland, and Ukraine borders both Poland and Hungary. Russia has increasingly viewed NATO enlargement as less threatening. For example, the absence of a credible military threat to northern Russia during the 1990s led Moscow to undertake a broad programme of force reductions and restructuring in the region. Russian threat perceptions of NATO in northern Europe, however, still represent a mixture of traditional and new approaches (Sergounin 1999: 1). The advocates of the new school, which includes President Vladimir Putin, promote the importance of economic, political, scientific and technological, environmental and informational factors to national security.

The traditional or realist approach places emphasis on the strategic importance of the north despite mutual arms reductions efforts and US–NATO–Russia rapprochement. This school holds that the north is still important for the strategic defence of the motherland and that air defence and anti-submarine considerations are still paramount there. Advocates of this view stress that NATO intelligence operations in the area are still targeting Russia. They also point out that the region is home to bases for the diminishing Russian submarine-launched ballistic missile fleet.

In addition to these perceived NATO threats to Russia in the North, the 1999 NATO-led campaign in Kosovo raised concerns in Russia over the new strategic capabilities of tactical, precision-guided weapons. Moscow has tended to acknowledge that tactical (conventional) weapons with precision-guided munitions are taking on strategic relevance. A relatively small number of platforms delivering a relatively small number of weapons (in comparison to the tonnage of World War Two, Vietnam, or even the Gulf War) can have a dramatic political and military effect. NATO's proximity to the Russian border, with access to bases and infrastructure in Poland, the Baltic Sea, the Black Sea and perhaps even in partner countries, could provide NATO with significant advantages in a future conflict with Russia. At the same time, Russian strategic access is becoming more restricted. This was clearly, and embarrassingly, demonstrated when Ukraine, Romania and Hungary denied Russia overflight to reinforce its contingent at Priština Airport in 1999.

Moreover, with the exception of verbal denunciations, Russia has been powerless to stop increasingly intrusive NATO manoeuvres in what Russia considers its 'near abroad'. Under the auspices of the PfP programme and the US bilateral 'In-the-Spirit of PfP' programme, NATO and the United States have conducted a series of ground and maritime exercises along the periphery of the Russian Federation. While these exercises are planned to improve inter-operability between NATO members and partner states, and to demonstrate US and NATO commitment to stability and national sovereignty, Russia has viewed them as provocative and has vehemently protested against them. Two instances in 2000 are particularly notable. In the first, the US 82nd Airborne (Infantry) Division deployed and conducted a strategic parachute drop of a battalion-size task force from the United States to the Yavoriv Military Training Area in western Ukraine. This deployment was scripted as a strategic reinforcement of an on-going peace support operation, as part of the *PEACESHIELD '00* In-the-Spirit-of PfP exercise. Coming soon after the failed Russian attempt to reinforce its airhead in Priština, it represented – to the Russians – a clear example of this new reality. That same year, by coincidence, a US warship was taking part in a port call in Georgia as Russian forces were redeploying from that country. The Russians perceived this as an intentional assertion of US military power in their sphere of influence precisely when they were withdrawing from Georgia.

In addition to these two examples, the United States has also recently conducted combined training on the Baltic coast near Kaliningrad with the Poles, and the US Air Force uses ranges in Slovakia. Ukraine has offered ranges to the US, but to date the US military has not accepted the offer. One of the key issues of concern to the Russians in this 'encroachment' in the 'near abroad' is the Russian concern for air defence. If Ukraine left the current system of integrated air defence with Russia it would greatly complicate the defence of Russia's airspace.

While these apprehensions reflect old Cold War mentalities and insecurities, such views still exist in certain segments of Russian society, especially in the military. Even though Russian threat perceptions of NATO have markedly been reduced as a result of the events of 11 September, just how seriously the Russian elite takes these views was recently demonstrated by the accusation by several retired Russian generals that President Putin was guilty of treason for 'allowing' the US military to base its forces in Central Asia. Reflecting a Cold

War mindset, these officers expressed fear that at some future date these bases might be used by the United States for strikes against Russia. Reacting to NATO's *STRONG RESOLVE 2002* exercise conducted in Poland and Norway, the commander of the Russian Baltic Fleet, Admiral Vladimir Valuyev, stated in an interview with ITAR-TASS: 'It is puzzling that tasks of a totally offensive nature are being resolved off the Russian borders by the NATO strategic exercise, the largest over the past decade' (Nuyakshev 2002).

Since the 1997 publication of its National Security Concept, the Russian leadership has been increasingly emphasising the importance of non-military factors – political, economic and other non-military factors (Yeltsin 1997: 4). The new National Security Concept signed by President Putin on 10 January 2000 reiterates this view (*Nezavisimoe Voennoe Oboozrenie* 14 January 2000). This 'new approach' sees NATO enlargement to the east providing stability along Russia's western border. To wit, Russia has reduced its military forces in the west and military forces based in Kaliningrad are expected to be cut again in 2002 by another 8300 personnel (Nuyakshev 2002). According to the US Joint Staff, Russia also recently requested assistance from NATO to reform its military, and in the Baltic region Valuyev stated that the Baltic Fleet is ready to cooperate on questions of safety at sea and protecting the environment. (Nuyakshev 2002).

Ukraine has already benefited from the eastward expansion of NATO, in that NATO has brought stability to Ukraine's western border. Ukraine has spent the last ten years developing security relationships with its western neighbours. Examples of this cooperation include participation in a combined engineering battalion with Hungary in the region of the Tisza River and in a Polish–Ukrainian Battalion based near the Polish–Ukrainian border that also is active in KFOR. Ukraine also maintains a strong programme of military cooperation with European NATO nations and the United States. As Ukraine's US state partner, the California National Guard – via the State Partnership programme – conducts military-to-military contacts with the Ukrainian Border Troops and other elements of the Ukrainian armed forces. Ukraine does not perceive a military threat coming from the West, and the Russian threat is not military, but both economic and related to criminal cross-border activities.

While a militarised 'Iron Curtain' separating Ukraine and Russia from the rest of Europe currently does not exist, what is coming into being is what some have begun to call a velvet or paper curtain (Moroney 2001: 15). This potential new dividing line between Russia and the West is associated directly with the eastward expansion of the EU and the legal requirements that will ensue and pertain to new member states along the EU's easternmost border.

The EU's future Eastern frontier

On 25 March 2001, Finland started full application of the Schengen *acquis*, or body of laws that abolished the internal borders of signatory states and established a single external border. In Finland, Schengen *de jure* created a 1324-kilometre border between the Russian Federation and the EU. While Ukraine and Belarus do not share a common border with the EU at this time, associate member states such as Poland are under intense pressure to impose more restrictive border security regimes on adjacent non-EU states. The EU and the new border states have for some time been aware of the potential negative consequences of the Schengen *acquis*, particularly as it will apply to Kaliningrad, the Russian–Finnish, Polish–Ukrainian, Polish–Belarusian, Slovak–Ukrainian and Hungarian–Ukrainian borders. Efforts have been underway to ensure the Russian Baltic enclave of Kaliningrad does not become, in the words of the EU's external affairs commissioner, Chris Patten: 'a bone of contention between Russia and the EU' (Traynor 2001).

Anticipating the number of EU states along the Baltic to increase from two to eight in the near future, the EU accepted the Finnish proposal for a Northern Dimension in 1997 at the Luxembourg European Council (Stenlund and Nissinen 1999), which has developed into a comprehensive policy underpinned by an action programme. The Northern Dimension aims to intensify cross-border cooperation between the EU and neighbouring countries and regions in northern Europe. It seeks to create security, stability and sustainable development in the region and improve the environment, and to avoid the creation of new dividing lines in Europe. The Northern Dimension has directed much attention to Russia's Kaliningrad oblast due to the fact that, when the Baltic states and Poland enter the EU, Kaliningrad will be a Russian enclave encircled by member states of the EU. Russians have made references to creating a 'Hong Kong of the Baltic Sea' out of Kaliningrad, but in the foreseeable future Kaliningrad is likely to remain a poverty-ridden, disease infested, polluted and criminal haven in the midst of the enlarged EU. Kaliningrad would thus be a kind of converse Hong Kong. Officials in Brussels even fear that the oblast will become a Trojan horse for illegal immigrants seeking entry into 'Fortress Europe'.

In anticipation of the Nordic countries joining Schengen, Russia and Finland have increased border security cooperation over the past two years. Unlike Kaliningrad's borders with Poland and Lithuania, the Finnish border has long been well protected. This fact, the isolated geography and the climate make the Finnish–Russian frontier an unpopular venue for illegal immigration and other transnational crime. These phenomena tend instead to converge on the Polish border and in the Balkans, where the geography and climate are less hostile and movement is much easier.

The future EU–Ukraine and Belarus borders are of the greatest concern, particularly in light of the EU's desire for a 'hard' border (external borders with strict immigration controls, curbs on asylum seekers, and visa restrictions patrolled and enforced by border police). This area, encompassing Poland's border with Ukraine and Belarus, has been referred to by Germany's interior minister as a 'criminal geographical area'.

Upon Poland's admission to the EU, its eastern border will become the outer border of the EU. Since 1993, Germany has funded material and equipment purchases and helped to enhance security along Poland's borders and assisted Poland's efforts to establish a system for refugee and deportation proceedings. While criminal activity, including car theft, international prostitution, smuggling of illegal drugs and other contraband, are the key targets of this effort, human rights organisations are concerned that the tightening of the borders is too focused on illegal crossings and illegal migrants as opposed to stopping criminal activity. Human rights groups perceive such intensive efforts to establish tight control of the borders as an effort to criminalise migration. Other critics, such as János Vándor, a political science professor at the Budapest Business School, argue that 'the big fish' – smugglers, drug or human traffickers – are rarely caught because they have the money and the means to manipulate the system (Dempsey 2001). Poland supports a 'softer' enforcement of the border – a border open to trade and the legal migration of peoples. In 1998, Poland applied to the European Commission for permission to maintain a non-visa policy with Ukraine as long as possible (*Rzeczpospolita* 1998: 5). To meet its Schengen obligations, however, Poland is reluctantly imposing more restrictive visa regimes on its eastern neighbours and tightening up its border – effectively creating a 'hard border'.

The Schengen *acquis* – creating 'Fortress Europe'

The Schengen *acquis* is named after Schengen, Luxembourg, and came into being in 1985, when France, Germany, Belgium, the Netherlands and Luxembourg met there and agreed on the gradual abolition of checks on their common borders. Five years later, on 19 January 1990, these states signed the Schengen Convention, which is the accord on how to implement the agreement. When it came into effect in 1995, it abolished the internal borders of the signatory states and created a single external border where immigration and customs checks are conducted in accordance with a single set of rules. Signatory states adopted common rules regarding visas, asylum rights and checks at external borders to permit the free movement of persons. Over time, the Schengen area has been extended to include almost every member state, except the United Kingdom and Ireland.

At present, thirteen EU countries have adopted the Schengen *acquis*. In addition, Norway and Iceland, which are not members of the EU, also apply the *acquis* after having concluded a separate cooperation agreement with the Schengen countries. As of 25 March 2001, the Nordic countries (as relates directly to Russia, Finland and non-EU member Norway) began full application of Schengen. In practice, what this means for citizens of the Russian Federation and other non-Schengen states is that regular passport controls are no longer conducted on persons on ferry crossings between Finland and other Schengen countries and on internal flights within 'Schengenland'. Random checks on the borders between Finland, Sweden, and Norway also have been abolished. However, when states accede to the Schengen agreement they are still permitted to carry out border checks for a limited time if public order or national security so require. Persons entering the 'Schengen area', for example at the land border between Finland and Russia, Norway and Russia, at the sea border between Finland and Estonia, and on non-EU flights at airports, will be subject to entry and departure checks as in the past.

The Schengen *acquis* for protecting the external borders of the EU consists of a set of security procedures. These measures begin at the travellers' (immigrant or tourist) point of departure with the issue of a visa. They then include several intermediate steps: document checks by carriers, protection measures in transit countries; the removal of checks at internal borders and replacing them with extensive controls at external borders; a common definition of the rules for crossing external borders; standardisation of rules regarding conditions of entry and visas for short stays; coordination of terrestrial and maritime surveillance of borders outside of traditional crossing points; defining the role of carriers in the fight against illegal immigration; the requirement for all non-EU nationals moving from one country to another to lodge a declaration; the drawing up of rules for asylum seekers (Dublin Convention); the introduction of rights of surveillance and not pursuit; the strengthening of legal provisions for removal/extradition and faster distribution of information on criminals, stolen cars, etc; and the creation of the Schengen Information System (SIS).

Since 1997, the Schengen area has been within the legal and institutional framework of the EU, thus coming under parliamentary and judicial scrutiny and achieving the objective of free movement of persons enshrined in the Single European Act of 1986, while ensuring democratic parliamentary control and giving citizens accessible legal remedies when their rights are challenged (via the European Court of Justice and/or national courts, depending on the area of law). The unclassified elements which make up the *acquis* are available in the Official Journal of the European Communities, an important consideration in that they form part of the legal rules EU 'aspirants' must adopt into their own national legislation (Official Journal of the European Communities, 13 January 2001). These elements, when applied to non-EU members and external borders in Europe, will principally have an impact on the frontier states and regions.

The European Union and Kaliningrad

EU enlargement will directly affect the Russian Federation oblast of Kaliningrad and the region bordering Finland. Kaliningrad is becoming an area of political and economic contention and uncertainty in Europe; it will soon find itself a Russian exclave within the EU when Poland and Lithuania become EU members. Moscow wants the inhabitants of Kaliningrad to retain the right of visa-free travel to Poland and Lithuania, or at a minimum to have access to visa-free corridors to Russia via Lithuania–Belarus and Lithuania–Latvia (Xinhua News Agency 2002). However, EU Commission officials have stated that the rules of Schengen cannot be overridden. Poland and Lithuania strongly rule out 'extra-territorial corridors'. In keeping with directives from Brussels, Poland and Lithuania plan to introduce obligatory visas for Russians beginning 1 July 2003 (Nougayrede 2002: 33). To ease travel outside of Kaliningrad, EU Commissioner for External Relations Chris Patten called on Russia to issue international passports to Kaliningraders, two-thirds of whom do not have such a passport, in part because of the price – USD 30 (Tracevskis 2002).

Kaliningrad is perceived by many West Europeans as a 'cesspool' of crime, poverty, disease and environmental degradation. An EU Commission paper reports that 'Organised crime, trafficking in human beings, drugs, stolen vehicles and illegal migration are all present'. Prostitution and the smuggling of amber, alcohol, cigarettes and gasoline are prevalent. Crime levels in Kaliningrad are 20 per cent higher than the average in Russia. The population of the oblast is 1.3 million, including 18,000 Russian military personnel. More than 30 per cent of the exclave's inhabitant's live below the poverty level. Its shipyards are in ruins, and German tourism – once a hope for revival of the region – is all but non-existent. Rates of AIDS and tuberculosis cases are the highest in Russia. Massive environmental pollution is another prominent feature of the enclave. After St Petersburg, Kaliningrad is the biggest single polluter of the Baltic Sea, due to its high levels of nuclear waste, water and air pollution.

Kaliningrad is very likely to benefit economically from EU enlargement, but, at the same time, it will face changes that will affect the movement of people, goods and energy supplies with the rest of Russia and with its neighbours. Between 10,000 and 12,000 Kaliningraders engage in shuttle trade, with a day's work on average bringing in USD 25 to USD 40 in profit (Holtom 2002). The EU has an ongoing dialogue with Russia, Lithuania and Poland to improve border management and speed up border-crossing procedures. The EU has proposed designing a multi-modal transport strategy and intends to secure funding for priority transport projects; modernising the regional transport infrastructure; assessing the possibility of using Community rules on small border traffic and transit; facilitating visa issuance and managing migration flows efficiently (reducing the cost of passports and of visas) and considering opening member states' consulates and concluding a readmission agreement with Russia.

There are currently three major border crossing points between Kaliningrad and Poland – at Mamonov, at Bagrationovsk and at Krylovo (Tracevskis 2002: 1). A fourth crossing will be developed at Grzechotki (Poland Business Review 2002: 1). The prime ministers of Poland and Russia agreed at the Kaliningrad Summit of Poland, Lithuania and Russia to build a highway from Elbląg to Kaliningrad and to introduce connecting flights from Warsaw to be served by Poland's flag carrier, LOT.

While Kaliningrad is part of the Russian Federation, and responsibility for its future development presently lies with the Russian authorities, the European Commission has had an active assistance programme in the region for over a decade. This is primarily due to the recognition that contemporary developments and problems in Kaliningrad can have an impact on the wider region, both today and in the future. Russian Foreign Minister Igor Ivanov has singled out four problems of the territory – visas, transit, energy and fishing disputes. Energy will continue to be supplied from Russia or Kaliningrad itself. Steps are being taken to resolve the 'fishing problem' by creating agreements with neighbouring countries on quotas for Kaliningrad's fish factories. Given the EU's desire for a hard border to protect the common market, resolving the visa and transit issues is more problematic.

The geographic location of Kaliningrad has made cross-border cooperation and trade/transit facilitation particularly important. Since 1991, the European Union has made a large financial commitment to Kaliningrad, providing roughly EUR 40 million in assistance directly to the region in the Russia National Programme of Technical Assistance to the Commonwealth of Independent States (TACIS), which provides economic assistance to the CIS. Begun by the EC in 1991, the TACIS programme provides grant-financed technical assistance to thirteen countries of Eastern Europe, the South Caucasus and Central Asia (Armenia, Azerbaijan, Belarus, Georgia, Kazakhstan, Kyrgyzstan, Moldova, Mongolia, Russia, Tajikistan, Turkmenistan, Ukraine and Uzbekistan), and is principally directed at enhancing the transition process in these countries. The region has also benefited from other TACIS programmes for Russia and the many regional programmes which TACIS finances.

The Commission has opened a TACIS support office in the city of Kaliningrad. EU support has focused on a number of key sectors to address Russian and EU concerns. Programmes are being implemented to facilitate trade and movement of goods and persons through the development of infrastructure, modernisation of border procedures, and training of enforcement agencies' staff to detect unlawful activities and increase their capacity to collect tax revenue. Currently, there are twenty-three crossing points between Kaliningrad, Poland and Lithuania. In order to ensure the efficient flow of goods across the EU's future external border, investment is needed in physical infrastructure and in processing, including thoroughly upgraded information systems. Under the TACIS Cross Border Cooperation Programme, two border crossings in Kaliningrad received priority funding: Chernyshevskoe/Kybartai-Nesterov (road/rail) and Bagrationovsk/Bezledy (road), on the borders with Lithuania and Poland respectively. These crossing points, identified after a detailed feasibility study, are the major ones located on the Pan-European Transport Network. Work to upgrade the Bagrationovsk/Bezledy project (EUR 3 million) was expected to start in spring of 2002. The Chernyshevskoe/Kybartai-Nesterov upgrade project (EUR 8 million) is expected to begin soon.

As is the case elsewhere in Russia, there is a need for action to combat illegal activities and organised crime, and the Task Force on Organised Crime in the Baltic Sea Region was created to tackle these problems. On the local level cooperation is needed to deal with problems such as car theft. Cooperation could also be directed at improving the independence of the local judiciary, in particular via training and city twinning programmes. TACIS has provided EUR 1 million in funding to assist in fighting organised crime.

Environmental issues are also of great concern to the EU members, and the environment has been a focal point for EU assistance. Like most of the old Soviet empire, there are significant environmental problems in Kaliningrad, problems that have health implications for the oblast's population and go on to affect the larger Baltic region. One particular area of concern is reducing water pollution, and it is recognised that a cleaner Baltic Sea would benefit the whole region. Thus reducing water pollution is a priority objective for regional cooperation efforts. Additionally, more than 400,000 tonnes of domestic and industrial waste are being generated every year in Kaliningrad, only a fraction of which is recycled. As a result of years of this practice, roughly fifteen million tonnes of solid waste have accumulated in municipal landfills. Since there has been no further treatment of these wastes, these dumping sites represent a major source of air, ground, and particularly water pollution. Current EU efforts include a water environmental monitoring and management project (EUR 2 million) dealing with water quality on the borders with Lithuania and Poland, and a waste management project in Kaliningrad's coastal zone (EUR 3 million) designed to alleviate the impact of waste generation on both public health and the environment. There is a European Bank for Reconstruction and Development/Nordic Environment Finance Corporation/Nordic Investment Bank loan for a sewage treatment plant in Kaliningrad city. The EU's LIFE programme has initiated two projects in Kaliningrad, in the areas of urban traffic and eco-tourism. The EU has also financed the establishment of an Environmental Centre for Administration and Technology (ECAT) in Kaliningrad, which was transferred to the local authorities in 1997.

Moreover, the spread of communicable diseases is a serious problem throughout Russia, and particularly so in Kaliningrad. While these problems must be tackled at the federal level, there is a need for preventive action in Kaliningrad itself. TACIS is supporting several initiatives at the local level and in the non-governmental sector to help reform health-care delivery systems and to deal with HIV. Kaliningrad also takes part, as a pilot region, in the Northwest Health Replication Project that seeks to reduce health risks and social disparities across the borders by supporting the reform of the health system in the region. The EU has also supported NGOs in the social and health sector. Under the Cross Border Cooperation Programme (2002–3), Kaliningrad will also receive support for water treatment facilities in the towns of Baltiysk, Svetly, Peimorsts and Yantaroye.

The Finnish–Russian border

The Finnish–Russian border area has been less problematic. President Putin has called it one of the most quiet stretches of Russia's boundaries (ITAR-TASS News Agency 2001: 1). According to the commander of the Frontier Guards in Helsinki, there are annually less than ten serious illegal border crossings from Russia (Brok and Kuprijanko 2001: 1). Legal crossings from St Petersburg and surrounding areas are close to three million annually, chiefly tourists. Even with the large gap in standards of living between Finland and Russia, large migrations of economic refugees have not occurred. Organised traffickers avoid the border because it is very well patrolled. What the Finns fear are the estimated one million third-country refugees living in Russia who are eager to come to the West.

The Finnish chief of the Frontier Guards exercises operational command of the border force. He is assisted by the Frontier Guards Headquarters, a department of the Ministry of the Interior. The Frontier Guards are organised into different districts: four frontier guard districts, three coastguard districts and the Air Patrol Squadron (Brok 2001: 1). In the North Karelian district, the border is controlled daily at different places. In the winter, the border is patrolled daily on skis or snowmobiles, and once every three weeks by helicopter. In the summer, daily ground patrols with dogs and weekly patrols by helicopter provide security. The geography and the climate help with the border control effort. There are no useful roads for vehicles, and the snow and cold work against any serious illegal crossings. The local population living in small villages along the border is also helpful and reports illegal crossers.

Russia is Finland's fourth largest economic partner, and there are a number of well-established regional cooperation programmes between Finland and the northwest regions of Russia. Finland and Karelia traditionally cooperate in areas such as economy, transport, communication, tourism, ecology and culture. In September 2001 in Helsinki, President Putin stated that the two countries planned to open two new border crossing points. He also mentioned a proposal to begin a high-speed rail link between Helsinki and St Petersburg in three to four years. Within the Northern Dimension, concept priority is being given by the EU to cross-border cooperation, border management and cross-border crime. The TACIS cross-border cooperation programme, begun in 1996, has allocated millions of euros for projects along the Russian western border, including some in Finland. The Russian, Finnish and Norwegian border guards and customs services also have very active programmes of cooperation to prevent illegal migration and smuggling. These cooperation programmes may provide a model for application elsewhere; however, the geography, history and climate of this border region are unique and, on the surface, such a model does not appear likely.

The Polish–Ukrainian, Polish–Belarusian border region

Nowhere is Schengen having more of an impact in eliminating internal borders and creating 'hard' external borders on a collision path than on the Polish–Ukrainian border. The same Common Market logic that is turning the EU into a zone of free movement of people, goods, services and capital is creating concern and anxiety among EU members over the potential for uncontrolled waves of economic migrants, refugees and criminals from the East and the Balkans. The greatest future border security concern for the EU is the Polish–Ukrainian border, which sits astride one of the three major smuggling routes into Western Europe. Poland is a candidate on its way to full EU membership within the next five years. Ukraine has declared its intent to become an Associate Member of the EU, but has made little progress to date in reaching that goal. In fact, at the EU Helsinki Summit in 1999, Ukraine saw its aspirations dashed (Zurawski vel Grajewski 2000: 2). The scale of both Poland and Ukraine in size and population will have an effect on the future character of relations between member and non-member states, and EU accession by Poland will have a profound impact on Polish– Ukrainian relations. The effects of this future alignment are already being felt.

Until January 1998, when Poland introduced a new border regime on its eastern frontiers, approximately 3.2 million Ukrainians visited Poland annually (Zurawski vel Grajewski 2000: 4). These visitors came first of all in the capacity of 'trading tourists'. The average Ukrainian visitor spent on average USD 460 per day in Poland compared to the average German (not a trading tourist) who spent USD 36 (Filip 1998). Small-scale individual cross-border trade, therefore, constitutes a key aspect of Polish–Ukrainian relations. At the town of Przemyśl, for example, some 3000 people cross from Ukraine each day to set up cheap bazaars at a soccer stadium (DPA 2000). Poland now has nearly 500,000 migrant workers: cleaners, construction workers and seasonal farm labourers (Dempsey 2001: 20). New regulations have had a significant impact on the eastern border. Delays along the border with Ukraine average two to three hours, and luggage control is very strict (the Russian and Belarusian borders with Poland are even more strictly controlled).

At this time there are no visa requirements for the movement of persons between Ukraine and Poland. This lax visa regime is supported by the Polish public, especially by those living along the eastern frontier where 'trading tourists' are welcome and provide employment for small Polish businesses. However, Poland has been unable to negotiate an exception to Schengen for the Polish–Ukrainian border. Illegal immigration is such a driving issue that the European Commission will likely make no exception. There has even been talk of establishing combined German–Polish border police or 'europatrols' on the eastern border to reinforce the Poles (*New York Times* 2001), but the Poles are reluctant to turn their country into a border post for the exclusive benefit of the EU. A Polish official reacted to this proposal by stating that, if Germans were going to help patrol the Polish border, then perhaps the Spanish border with North Africa should also be patrolled by these 'europatrols'. What the Poles and the Ukrainians must accomplish is to minimise the negative effects of the Schengen border. An open border will not exist, but some recommendations have been made to mitigate the effects of Schengen:

- Add Ukraine to the list of states whose citizens do not need visas to enter EU territory;
- Allow small trans-border movement within the Schengen system;
- Make it easier for those on foot or riding bicycles to cross the border;
- Poland should build new consulates in the border regions and the large cities of Belarus, Ukraine and Russia.

Chances for a EU accommodation on the Schengen provisions are slim, but some benefits will still accrue to Ukraine and Poland. According to Grajewski, Ukrainians, once across the border, will be free to travel beyond Poland to the Atlantic. Poland will witness modernisation and improvements to border security infrastructure in the east, funded by the EU in order to stop illegal migration, international criminal activity and the smuggling of drugs, radioactive material, stolen cars and so on. Also noteworthy is the psychological impact on the millions of Ukrainians who visit Poland and the EU each year. Like East Europeans in the 1970s who visited the West, these Ukrainians will make comparisons and draw conclusions that will accelerate reform at home. The developed West European states will continue to require regular intakes of labour, including seasonal labour. The number of Ukrainian guest workers in Poland does not exceed the number of Poles and Czechs working in Germany, for example. This will favour some type of accommodation between tightening borders and creating workable solutions that prevent the establishment of 'Fortress Europe'.

At present, Poland is trying to combine 'soft' and 'hard' approaches. At the Kukuryki–Kozlowicze border crossing point, they have built a five-kilometre road to allow for the inspection of trucks travelling to and from Poland (Dempsey 2001: 2). The trucks are continually monitored by cameras mounted every hundred yards along the top of the fence. The trucks are then scanned by a drive-in x-ray system. After clearing customs they have no opportunity to stop and become involved in trafficking or any illegal activity. Rather than such a 'hard' border envisioned by the EU – especially, Germany, France and the Netherlands – the Polish government wants a 'green border'. This would consist of checkpoints at twelve-mile intervals, the rest of the border being monitored by air and other surveillance (Castle 2001a). By 2004, there will be ninety-four border posts along the 800-mile Ukrainian and Belarusian borders and 6500 border guards supported by aircraft, helicopters, sensors, dogs and all-terrain vehicles (Fletcher 2002).

The problem of border security for the EU in the east extends beyond the Polish–Ukrainian and Polish–Belarusian borders. Ukraine must also tighten up controls; improve infrastructure and crack down on corruption along its other borders, particularly its northeastern border with Russia. The demarcation of the Russian–Ukrainian border finally took place early in 2002. Starting on 1 January 2002, citizens of Azerbaijan, Armenia, Kazakhstan, Kyrgyzstan, Tajikistan and Uzbekistan were required to obtain visas to enter, leave and travel via Ukraine (Gorobets 2001). Russia was cutting its border troops by 15,000 in 2002, but the forces guarding the Ukrainian border will be enlarged (Xinhua 2001). The imposition of a stricter visa regime in the Schengen zone does not have to be accompanied by a reciprocal visa policy by states remaining outside Schengen. The opposite is true. To attract tourists and to facilitate trade, Ukraine and Belarus should liberalise their visa regimes for EU members. Currently there are too few Ukrainian and Belarusian consulates in EU member states, and the visa process is expensive and overly complicated.

Conclusion

NATO and EU enlargement present quite different challenges for border security. NATO is no longer engaged in the forward defence of Western Europe, and European borders are in most cases protected by civilian police and not military forces. As NATO expands to the east it serves to re-integrate Central and Eastern European countries back into Europe and provides a zone of stability and peace. Likewise it can underpin the security of the former Soviet republics it borders by providing stable and democratic neighbours with defensive military postures. NATO's real challenge will be to continue to balance eastward expansion without threatening those states in Europe remaining outside the alliance – namely Russia, Belarus, Moldova and Ukraine. The recent rapprochement between NATO and Russia and strong ongoing relations with Ukraine leave only Belarus and Moldova outside the fold.

The true border security issues in Europe in the foreseeable future will be tied to the eastward expansion of the EU and how the Schengen states relate to those outside 'Schengenland'. Through initiatives such as the Northern Dimension, TACIS and cooperation programmes with Kaliningrad, along the Finnish–Russian, Polish–Ukrainian and Polish–Belarusian borders the EU is at once is trying to mitigate the effects of Schengen and simultaneously create a new European security zone. Only time will tell if the 'velvet' and 'paper' curtains being created by acts of commission and omission will one day produce a new division in Europe – with what German officials refer to as a 'Belgian Curtain' replacing the Iron Curtain (Hall 2000: 11).

7 Imperialism to realism

The role of the West in Russian foreign policy towards Ukraine

Victor Chudowsky

International relations in the former USSR

No one paradigm or theory can be easily used to summarise the way relations among the states of the former USSR have developed. Neo-liberalism and the democratisation paradigm do not square with reality (Goldgeier and McFaul 1992; Russett *et al.* 1993). Realism assumes security competition among sovereign states; but several states in the former USSR are not sovereign, and realism does not alert us to certain legacies of Russian imperialism and Soviet communism, which are still relevant to understanding the region. However, realism does alert us to the general condition of security anarchy in the region, and the importance of geography. As will be explained, theories on the collapse of empires and the problems of small states located next to large ones are relevant. Within that context this chapter argues that two important variables should be closely examined in trying to explain relations between Russia and the newly independent states: the struggle for sovereignty; and the role of the West. Western support for the sovereignty of nations such as Ukraine and the Baltics has forced Russian foreign policy to move from the imperial paradigm to the realist paradigm. In the imperial paradigm, the focus was on controlling the former republics through centralised institutions such as the Commonwealth of Independent States. In the realist paradigm, Russia accepts the reality of some former republics as sovereign states, in light of Western pressure, but still uses the normal tools of interstate relations – diplomatic, military, economic and political – to influence their behaviour. Despite some continued tensions, the change is a positive one. Any type of future democratic or cooperative security-building in the area of the former USSR can only come about through vigorous Western support for the sovereignty of the newly independent states. To illustrate these points Ukraine is used as an example.

A cursory examination of the map of the space of the former USSR alerts one to the fact that the area consists of one large state, Russia, surrounded by a ring of smaller states, the former republics. This fact alone, leaving aside historical and cultural legacies and economic ties, has important implications. The region's political geography allows us to predict the nature of international relations in the area of the former USSR. Stephen

Walt has examined the question of 'balancing' versus 'bandwagoning' in the behaviour of smaller states in relation to great powers (Walt 1987: 5). In choosing an alliance partner, smaller states 'balance' by choosing the alliance that opposes their main security threat. States balance against their greatest perceived threat, not against the states with the most power. However, there are instances where states 'bandwagon', that is they join in an alliance *with* their greatest perceived enemy. Small states bandwagon because they may want to share in the spoils of their new ally's military victory; out of appeasement, in the hopes that their new ally will attack another state; they want to ally with states with great power and offensive capabilities; they are within close geographical proximity to the great power state; they are weak; they are unlikely to be able to join any other alliance. Practically all of Walt's above conditions are true for the former republics, particularly the latter four. Geography and the distribution of power among states alone forces the former republics to ally with Russia. According to this line of reasoning, the main reason the Baltic countries have not reconciled themselves to a close relationship with Russia is because of the final condition – there is a possibility that they may join NATO.

Further cementing the ties of the former republics with Russia is their experience as part of an empire. Mark Beissinger was among the first to compare in a detailed way the impact of Russian imperialism and communism on the newly independent states with the impact of European colonialism on African and other developing nations. The largest commonality is the imprint of the governing style of the imperial regime onto the new regime. Empires leave legacies across a wide variety of governing institutions that constitute a formidable challenge to reverse (Beissinger 1997). Given this, the legacies of the Soviet Empire are none the less unique. Some are due to the fact that the periphery actually bordered the core (as per Walt's bandwagon conditions). There is also the problem of large numbers of Russians now living as minorities in the newly independent states. As in the African experience, the new state boundaries do not reflect ethnic realities; Soviet 'ethnofederal' boundaries were also purposely drawn to dilute the strength of certain nationalities, and also to set one group against another. Governing structures, as well as attitudes towards society, standards, practices and attitudes towards governing itself are merely leftovers from the previous regime. Societies are largely inert and atomised, as under the Soviet regime, and new elites tend to come from the old communist elite. Bureaucracies have changed little, and presidential administrations have simply replaced the previous republican communist parties in form and function. The Soviet economy integrated the republics; 'new' elites call for a new confederation due to economic necessity. In short, the Soviet imperial experience left very deep imprints upon the societies, economies and political systems of the newly independent states that will make sovereignty and state-building particularly difficult. The newly independent states will be rather weak, and therefore highly vulnerable to Russian pressure (Beissinger 1997: 165).[1]

Therefore any discussion of cooperative security-building and/or of the way the new nations interact with one another takes place against the realities of the pressures which force the smaller nations into dependence on Russia: their geographic location, the legacy of colonialism and the legacy of Soviet rule. Unless another alliance or political arrangement exists which safeguards the security and sovereignty of the new nations, and is both possible and more attractive than dependence on Russia, the status quo of dependence tends to remain.

Russian domestic politics and foreign policy: imperialism to realism

In addition to geography and the legacies of colonialism and communism, there is another powerful factor in relations among the post-Soviet states, and that is Russian foreign policy. Alan Lynch provides a parsimonious and accurate description of post-Soviet Russian foreign policy, describing it as:

> ...a diplomacy which has proved relatively successful in maintaining two important foreign policy objectives that are in potential tension with one another: establishing Russian diplomatic and security hegemony throughout the territory of the former Soviet Union as well as Russia's 'great power' status in international councils while at the same time avoiding a rupture with the G7 states, in the first place with the United States, whose cooperation remains essential to Russia's internal as well as external prospects.

(Lynch 2001: 8)

How has Russia gone about attempting to establish hegemony in the area of the former USSR? In the past decade it has tried two strategies. One, what might be called the 'imperial strategy', has failed, while the second, the 'realist strategy', is a work in progress.

One of the main currents of thinking about the relationship between Russia and the former republics holds that Russia has been an imperial power, meaning it is primarily concerned with 'gathering of lands' or at the very least holding onto them, and constructing highly centralised institutions to administer this empire. In addition, the history of imperial expansion in neighbouring areas has created uncertainty about Russia's 'true' borders and whether 'Russia' and the Russian nation is limited to its current borders or whether it spills over into the former republics.[2] Well into the late 1990s, Russia pursued an imperial strategy towards the former republics by trying to create a highly centralised Commonwealth of Independent States.

The stated policy of the Russian Federation towards the fellow nations of the Commonwealth of Independent States was to have a close military, political and economic alliance with the Russian Federation at the centre, as a regional hegemon. Officially, Russia saw a strengthened CIS as an antidote to NATO expansionism,[3] and used CIS documents not only to object to NATO expansion but to argue for a pan-European security system based on the Organisation for Security and Cooperation in Europe (FBIS 1995b). In addition, Russia saw the CIS as a way to 'protect' the 20–25 million ethnic Russians living in the former republics (FBIS 1995a). The political elite of the Russian Federation in the Yeltsin era was unanimous on the necessity of this policy; the only debate being whether this should be a 'loose hegemony' or a 'tight hegemony' (M Smith 1994).

The 'tight' or 'loose' hegemony argument broke out in Russia almost immediately after the formation of the CIS. As Russia was preoccupied with relations with the West immediately following the break-up of the USSR, its stance towards the former republics was often characterised by a benign, or in many cases malign, neglect. In 1992, Ruslan Khasbulatov (Yeltsin's former hard-line vice president who led the October 1993 parliamentary revolt) and Sergei Stankevich, a Yeltsin advisor, started pressuring former foreign minister Andrei Kozyrev to begin a more coercive policy with respect to the reintegration of former Soviet republics in the CIS. Over time, Kozyrev succumbed more and more to such pressures. Russia's new stance towards the 'Near Abroad' was codified in Yeltsin's September 1995 decree on the CIS and Kozyrev's replacement by Yevgeni Primakov as foreign minister in January 1996. The decree was the clearest statement by the Russian leadership on its goals in the CIS.[4] The main points of the document were:

- the CIS was identified as an area of the Russian Federation's 'vital interests';
- Russia was to prevent CIS states from joining other alliances;
- Russia's national security involved the protection of ethnic Russians in the CIS;
- the goal of the CIS was to create an economic and political alliance with Russia as the 'leading power';
- a 'tight' CIS was seen as a means of preventing separatism within the Russian Federation itself.

In addition the document treats the CIS as a single entity with no internal borders, and external borders protected jointly. So there were calls for a CIS-wide customs union, payments union (to easily convert national currencies to the Russian rouble, with the rouble as a CIS-wide 'reserve' currency), economic union, a strengthened Inter-Parliamentary Assembly, a common 'scientific–technological expanse', 'interstate investment programmes', and a common stock market. Military union involved joint defence manufacturing, joint border patrols and the continued presence of Russian bases on the territories of other CIS states. Intelligence and security forces were asked to 'bar from CIS territory the activities of third-party special services inimical to Russia'. Common positions on issues before the UN and OSCE, as well as a common stance on NATO expansion, were also urged.

If anything is to be emphasised from the above, it is that *the leadership of Russia viewed CIS borders with other nations as Russia's border*. CIS borders were a front line of defence away from Russia's territory, and CIS borders were to be protected by Russians. In addition, it is crucial to remember that the Russian Federation in its current form is also still an empire in which various peoples want autonomy or independence – the Chechens being the prime example. A 'tight' CIS, in Russian thinking, also played the role of an external fence around Russia to prevent various peoples from 'escaping', as the states ringing Russia served as a buffer/fence/*cordon sanitaire* against further separatism. Through the CIS, Russia sought to lock in the status quo as to what nationality gets a truly sovereign state (the Baltics), a dependent state (Belarus, Central Asia, Moldova, Georgia, Ukraine), or no state (Chechnya) in order to prevent a further 'parade of sovereignties' (Rumer 1994).

Second to the security concern was institutionalised multilateral political and policy consultation among the leaderships of the CIS, in the form of the CIS heads-of-government and heads-of-state, the Inter-Parliamentary Assembly, and a set of bureaucratic organs based in Minsk. These bodies would 'coordinate' legislation among states. Institutionalised political cooperation would also have helped Russia with the protection of her 20 million strong diaspora. This should be seen not as an end but as a means to influence politics in the CIS neighbours, through support for dual citizenship, protection against discrimination, support for the Russian language, cultural institutions etc. Documents were also presented at CIS meetings to promote joint children's camps, joint commemorations of World War Two, veterans' benefits, military sports teams, and even commemorations of Soviet cinema. A 'tight' CIS, then, with agreed rules for minority protection, would have given Russia a great deal of leverage over political affairs in the NIS through the diaspora, which it would claim to protect by force if necessary.

The third, and least important (for Russia), concern was economic union. As the largest and most economically self-sufficient state, the primary concern for Russia was protection for domestic industry and markets in the CIS from foreign imports, as well as the ability for her new capitalist class to buy into key industries and enterprises in the 'Near Abroad'. In addition, there were products in the 'Near Abroad' that Russia apparently wanted to buy for roubles instead of hard currency. During the March 1996 CIS Heads of Governments meeting, Russian Prime Minister Viktor Chernomyrdin scolded fellow prime ministers for selling products abroad for hard currency instead of selling them to Russia for roubles, and held the RF–Belarus 'community' as a model for them to follow (*ITAR-TASS* 13 April 1996). Also quite irksome to Russian leaders was the multiplication of new trade ties by the CIS states with countries outside the ex-USSR, and the influx of foreign capital into CIS states other than Russia, often beating Russian capital in the search for raw materials and industrial partnerships.[5]

Ukrainian sovereignty

The definition of sovereignty is not that external authorities do not influence a sovereign state's decisions, only that the state is the ultimate arbiter on that territory and over that population. Russia can pressure Ukraine on various issues – by withholding fuel deliveries, for example. If the Ukrainian government is the sole authority to decide how to deal with such pressure, then Ukraine is sovereign. However, Russian foreign policy towards Ukraine in the immediate post-USSR period was directed at more than simply pressuring the Ukrainian state into various compromises. It also sought *to undermine Ukrainian sovereignty through a variety of means short of violence.* Two related goals of Russian policy were to maintain sole control over the Black Sea Fleet and the city of Sevastopol for Russia; and to draw Ukraine into a tight military, political and economic alliance in the context of the Commonwealth of Independent States. The latter is particularly important because it is Ukraine, more than any other newly independent state, which has blocked the development of a strong CIS.

The Black Sea Fleet

Of all of the issues in Russian–Ukrainian relations, by far the most acrimonious and difficult was the issue of the division of the Black Sea Fleet (BSF). There was also the associated problem of the status of Sevastopol, and indeed the status of the entire Crimean peninsula, as Kiev's hold over the peninsula was at times tenuous. At varying times Russia has claimed sovereignty over the bays of the BSF, its base in Sevastopol, and the whole city of Sevastopol. This of course is in direct contradiction to Ukrainian claims of sovereignty over the same. Russian policy was directed at maintaining this toehold on Ukrainian territory, thus denying Ukrainian sovereignty. Until 1997, Russia maintained an explicit link between the signing of a Friendship and Cooperation Treaty between Ukraine and Russia and the settling of the BSF/Sevastopol issue in Russia's favour, which would have meant exclusive basing rights and control over a sizeable amount of fleet-related infrastructure, and, by extension, much of the city of Sevastopol itself.

Almost from the moment of the collapse of the USSR, the two sides took extreme, almost non-negotiable positions. On 6 December 1991 the Ukrainian parliament passed the Law on the Armed Forces, which called for the establishment of an independent Ukrainian navy, to be constructed by drawing on ships from the Black Sea Fleet. At the December 1991 Minsk CIS summit, it was decided that the fleet would remain under CIS control. However, Ukrainian Defence Minister Konstantin Morozov asserted that *the entire fleet* should be Ukrainian, whereupon Yeltsin countered that the fleet 'was, is, and will remain Russian' (Markus 1995). A 'war of decrees' ensued, with both presidents Kravchuk and Yeltsin claiming ownership of the entire fleet for their respective countries.

Kravchuk and Yeltsin met in Dagomys, Russia, in June 1992 and signed the Dagomys Agreement, the main point of which was that the BSF should indeed be divided. However, the questions of how and when were left open. The subsequent Yalta Agreement of August 1992 established a joint Russian–Ukrainian command, and stated that division of the fleet would begin in 1995. Then, in the controversial Massandra summit of September 1993, the two sides seemed to agree to a formula: there would be an even split, with Ukraine giving many of its ships to Russia and allowing basing in Sevastopol in return for the writing-off of a sizeable portion of Ukraine's USD 5 billion debt to Russia, mostly for energy. By 15 April 1994, the two sides even worked out a formula: of 833 vessels, Ukraine would keep 164. However, RF Defence Minister Pavel Grachev demanded that Sevastopol be the sole base of the BSF, but the Ukrainians would not give in, instead proposing to share the bays at Sevastopol. Grachev stormed out of the meeting (Markus 1995). During this time, relations among sailors in the fleet were worsening. In addition to the flagging controversy, in May 1994 a unit of Russian marines attempted to wrest control of a coastal radar unit manned by Ukrainians by force, but failed.

Expectations that newly-elected Ukrainian president Leonid Kuchma would be more accommodating to Russian demands were short-lived. In the Sochi Agreement of 8 June 1995, the two sides again agreed to disagree; the document confirmed an even split, with Russia buying back a portion with funds owed by Ukraine for energy, so that the final split would be roughly 80 per cent to 20 per cent in Russia's favour. The main additional points of the document were:

- the BSF would be split up to form the BSF of Russia and the Naval Forces of Ukraine, to be deployed separately;
- the main base of the Russian BSF would be located in Sevastopol;
- the division of assets would be on the 'fifty-fifty principle'.

(UPresA News 1996)

However, still to be resolved were the questions of how much the ships were worth, where Ukraine was to base its navy, how much of Sevastopol Russia was to control, how long Russia would lease the base, whether it should be leased at all, and, if so, for what price. However, a November 1995 meeting between Russian and Ukrainian defence ministers Pavel Grachev and Valeri Shmarov settled the peripheral issue of the fleet's coastal infrastructure, which would remain under Ukrainian control, while coastal weaponry would be split (*UPresA News* 1995).[6]

In early 1996 the new RF Foreign Minister Yevgeny Primakov adopted a new Russian policy line on the BSF – there would be no Friendship and Cooperation Treaty, and no visit to Kiev by Yeltsin, until Ukraine allowed Russia exclusive basing rights at Sevastopol (*ITAR-TASS* 31 January 1996). By the autumn of 1996, expectations were raised, only to collapse once again. In early October, meetings between Russian and Ukrainian deputy prime ministers Valeri Serov and Vasyl Durdynets paved the way for discussions between Russian PM Viktor Chernomyrdin and Kuchma on the BSF and a Friendship and Cooperation Treaty, which both Yeltsin and Chernomyrdin stated were linked: no Friendship Treaty without a BSF Agreement first (*Ukrainian Weekly* 1996a). In mid-October, two separate actions set talks back: First, the Russian Duma passed a declaration stating that Sevastopol is a Russian city and called for a halt to division of the fleet. In addition, Moscow's Mayor Yuri Luzhkov and short-tenured National Security Advisor Aleksandr Lebed both declared Sevastopol to be a Russian city. Chernomyrdin and Yeltsin, upon meeting with Kuchma, disavowed the actions; Lebed was fired, and the government declared that the Duma vote was not its policy (*Ukrainian Weekly* 1996b). In retaliation, the Ukrainian parliament passed a resolution banning foreign troops on its territory, and Foreign Minister Hennadi Udovenko raised the possibility of having a third party, such as the United States, mediate the BSF dispute. This forced the Duma to back down on its earlier Sevastopol resolution, and Russian Foreign Minister Primakov issued a statement again reiterating Yeltsin's earlier statement disavowing the Duma resolution (FBIS 1996d).

To complicate matters even more was the unsettled political situation in Sevastopol and Crimea. The majority of the peninsula's residents are ethnic Russians who seemed to have little interest in remaining part of Ukraine. On 23 August 1994, the Sevastopol City Council declared itself a Russian city, an act that the Ukrainian Ministry of Justice declared invalid. Kuchma retaliated by replacing the mayor of Sevastopol (FBIS 1996d). Similarly, the entire Crimean peninsula has also been restive, most notably in early 1994, when Russian nationalist Yuri Meshkov won the Crimean presidency and his 'Russian Block' won a majority in the Crimean parliament. Kuchma again retaliated harshly by replacing the Crimean prime minister (with his own son-in-law, Anatoli Franchuk) and abolishing the post of Crimean president altogether (Lapychak 1995).

In short, Ukraine's hold over the Crimea was characterised by short-term repressive measures to beat back swellings of separatist sentiment. As long as the situation on the peninsula was not violent, the uncertain status quo suited Russian interests, because the issues of the BSF, Sevastopol, the status of Crimea and the protection of the ethnic Russian majority on the peninsula were all tacitly linked. For Russia to sign an agreement to lease the Sevastopol base and share it with a Ukrainian navy, and to sign a Friendship and Cooperation Treaty recognising Ukraine's borders outside of the CIS context,[7] was to cede Sevastopol and Crimea to an independent, sovereign, Ukrainian nation. This, for reasons of security as well as domestic politics, Russia could not bring itself to do. The existing situation, with no treaties and where Ukraine struggles to maintain some semblance of control over Crimea (almost none over Sevastopol, and absolutely none over the Sevastopol naval base) meant a *de facto* lack of full Ukrainian sovereignty over the peninsula, and left open the possibility of direct or indirect Russian control over the peninsula in the future. It also meant permanent exclusive basing rights without bothersome leases or treaties. As late as November 1996, Russia had clearly chosen the latter to be the preferable option, and therefore refrained from signing treaties recognising Ukrainian sovereignty, in particular over the issue of the status of Sevastopol and the basing of Ukrainian ships there (FBIS 1996e).

The Commonwealth of Independent States

The second major goal of Russian foreign policy towards Ukraine was directed at getting Ukraine to become a full member of the CIS. Ukraine is currently an 'associate member', which has no official meaning[8] but in practice means that Ukraine is able to pick and choose of which agreements to be a part. The commonly-mentioned quandary was that Ukraine needed full economic membership of the CIS primarily in order to have free access to the Russian market, while Russia needed Ukraine in the CIS primarily for border and security reasons. However, Russia would not give Ukraine the benefits of economic membership unless Ukraine joined a military/political alliance.[9] Therefore, Russia pressured Ukraine to become a full member of the CIS primarily through economic means, in addition to the aforementioned political means (refusal to sign a BSF and Friendship and Cooperation Treaty).

The primary weapon used by Russia has been access to its market for Ukrainian goods. In the autumn of 1995 Yeltsin signed a decree increasing tariffs on more than 200 types of Ukrainian goods. In January 1996 tariffs were raised again, in particular a huge increase in the tariff on vodka. The latter rise was seen as punishment for Ukraine's delay in joining the CIS Customs Union (*Jamestown Monitor* 26 January 1996). In October 1996, the RF slapped another 20 per cent tariff on all Ukrainian goods imported into Russia, and refused to enter talks demarcating the border between Russia and Ukraine (Perlez 1996). The moves were explicitly linked by Russian Prime Minister Viktor Chernomyrdin to lack of progress by Ukraine in allowing exclusive basing rights for the BSF in Sevastopol (Ivzhenko 1996). The new tariffs also came on the heels of a CIS heads-of-government summit chaired by Chernomyrdin. At the CIS meeting, Ukraine signed only eleven of twenty-seven proposed documents. Chernomyrdin stressed he was 'dissatisfied with the tempo of integration' and stated it was 'high time to work out a vertical management mechanism of integration processes' (*Jamestown Monitor* 23 October 1996).

Perhaps the RF's greatest success has been to draw Ukraine into the unified air defence system of the former USSR. The system was officially set in place at the March 1996 CIS heads-of-state meeting, and the merger came about through the formation of a 'joint industrial–financial group' called 'Granit'. Ukraine's defence plants and research institutes were given key roles in the maintenance and improvement of the system (*ITAR-TASS* 6 March 1996). On the other hand, Russia has failed to get Ukraine to declare itself a military ally of Russia, or even to announce common positions on crucial military issues such as the expansion of NATO. After a 1996 meeting of CIS defence ministers, Ukrainian Defence Minister Oleksandr Kuzmuk refused to sign a CIS statement opposing NATO expansion, and stated that Ukraine had sent a delegation to the meeting only to act as 'observers' (FBIS 1996a). Foreign Minister Udovenko later confirmed the policy of non-cooperation on CIS military matters at an October 1996 foreign minister's meeting (FBIS 1996b).

The role of the West

By the late autumn of 1996, Ukraine and Russia found themselves in a complete deadlock, unable to break ground and sign a Friendship and Cooperation Treaty, something both sides wanted. Russia could not cede Sevastopol and share the base of the BSF with Ukraine; to do so would implicitly recognise Ukrainian sovereignty over the city and also over all of Crimea, and would also recognise such sovereignty outside of the bounds of the CIS. The two sides were also engaged in a harmful trade war, and Ukraine continued to oppose efforts to strengthen the multilateral institutions of the CIS.

However, just a few months later, in the summer of 1997, a treaty was in fact signed, and Russia gave in to virtually all of Ukraine's demands on the fleet and its basing. Russia also recognised Ukrainian sovereignty outside of the context of the CIS. The Ukrainian ability to force its stronger neighbour to give in and sign the treaty was its greatest foreign policy achievement since independence, and it was done by a very shrewd and rational campaign on the part of the Ukrainian elite to forge military and political ties with the West. In short, Ukraine took advantage of the bipolar nature of the distribution of power in Eurasia and 'played the alliance card'. This frightened the Russian government and forced it to adopt a policy towards Ukraine far more respectful of its sovereignty.

It should be noted here that the Ukrainian leadership that took power in 1994 was not necessarily 'pro-Western', and the Westward shift was not due to domestic politics. President Kuchma and the group of advisors and financiers around him were vigorous on the issue of sovereignty, but saw Ukraine more properly aligned with Russia rather than the West. Kuchma himself summed up his feelings on the topic as a candidate:

QUESTION: So, are you in favour of independence?

KUCHMA: With both hands. But this does not mean that I have changed my mind about the need for tight economic cooperation between Ukraine and neighbouring states, in particular members of the CIS, and, I emphasise, first of all with Russia. We can't avoid this – it is primarily Russia, both economically and geopolitically – which is our partner number one.[10]

In 1995, Ukraine's official foreign policy position on the issue of NATO expansion was in fact that of Boris Yeltsin: that NATO expansion plans should be halted, or at least re-examined, or conducted in such a manner that Russia's security interests are taken into account. The Kuchma government's draft governing programme presented to the parliament in October 1996 called cooperation with Russia 'a cornerstone of economic stability'. The government stated the aims of its Russia policy as being to: 'de-politicise' trade and enter into a free trade agreement; sign a Friendship and Cooperation Treaty; come to terms on the 'temporary' presence of the BSF in Sevastopol; demarcate the border between Russian and Ukraine; and receive compensation for nuclear materials delivered to Russia (*ITAR-TASS* 4 October 1996). Kuchma, in a landmark speech before the OSCE in December 1996, stated that Ukraine favoured an 'all-embracing' and 'indivisible' European security system that included Russia, and the strengthening of the OSCE and the 'reform' of NATO. At the time, this was also, of course, Russia's position on the NATO expansion issue (FBIS 1996f).

This may have remained Ukraine's position on NATO expansion were it not for Russia's unyielding position on issues related to Ukrainian sovereignty. Therefore in 1996 the Ukrainian position on NATO expansion began to evolve into one which was far more hostile to Russia's interests; the 'point man' for this policy shift seemed to be National Security Advisor Volodymyr Horbulin, who suddenly took on a more prominent foreign policy role. Horbulin began to use Russia's fear of NATO expansion as a means to extract political concessions from Russia on the issues of sovereignty, the Crimea and the Black Sea Fleet.

The United States and other NATO countries were happy to help in this endeavour. The Clinton administration had been heavily involved in working out the 1994 Trilateral Accord for the delivery of nuclear weapons from Ukraine to Russia, and Ukraine's reimbursement for the undertaking. US officials recognised the tensions in the relationship and the opportunities these tensions presented. For example, then-President Kravchuk went to Washington in May 1993 to discuss plans for the disposal of nuclear weapons in Ukraine, after he had suspended their delivery to Russia over the issue of payment. While he was there, however, a message came from his Ministry of Defence stating that all tactical weapons had been removed from Ukraine by Russian (CIS) forces. The overall effect was to diminish Kravchuk's stature in Washington, making it appear (accurately) that he had no control over tactical nuclear weapons in his country. It was evident that the Russian Federation simply ignored Kravchuk's suspension order and continued to remove the weapons without his knowledge.[11] The behaviour of the Russians also served to poison negotiations over the removal of strategic nuclear weapons from Ukrainian soil, which of course was of great concern to the United States. According to Mitchell Reiss, the negotiations, which lead to the Trilateral Accord were characterised by the 'myriad gratuitous insults and personal slights that Russian negotiators directed to their Ukrainian counterparts', which shocked the American negotiators present (Reiss 1995: 123).

A group of influential American foreign policy figures such as Zbigniew Brzezinski, Frank Carlucci, Henry Kissinger and others at the Center for Strategic and International Studies (CSIS) urged the Clinton administration to view Ukraine as a strategic counterweight to Russian power in the region.[12] Disturbed by the highly volatile political situation in Russia, the Clinton administration agreed with the 'strategic counterweight' argument and also saw Ukraine as an important partner in aiding NATO expansion, routes for transmission of energy resources, and space-related technologies. By the mid-1990s, Ukraine became the third largest recipient of aid from the United States. A special Gore–Kuchma commission was created to raise Ukraine's profile in the United States, and ties between the two defence establishments became quite vigorous. Ukraine also became the most active participant in the Partnership for Peace.

First, in 1996, plans were announced by Horbulin for increased military cooperation with NATO and other countries ringing the Black Sea. This caused Primakov to issue a statement expressing his alarm over the growing presence of Western navies (American, Italian and Turkish) and their joint exercises with states other than Russia. The exercises were viewed as being performed for purposes of 'reconnaissance', and Primakov attributed the increased Western presence to the division of the BSF and the lack of funding for the Russian navy (Interfax 1996). In 1997, Horbulin effectively manipulated this competition to Ukraine's advantage.

The policy shift was cemented by Horbulin's meetings with NATO officials in Brussels, in January 1997. There, he stated that it was Ukraine's intent to 'integrate into European economic, political and security structures', and remarkably, 'normalize relations with Russia through the consolidation of Ukraine's prestige in European structures' (FBIS 1997a). European multilateral organisations, then, would be used by Ukraine to improve relations with Russia – at first glance an odd formulation, in that both countries are not members of the most important of such organisations. Horbulin obviously meant that Ukraine's political gestures towards the West would bring results of some sort with its relations with Russia. In addition, Ukraine sought wider cooperation with NATO, 'which would not be limited by the Partnership for Peace Program', and then went so far as to state that NATO membership for Ukraine should not be ruled out – a statement that he had only a few months earlier publicly scolded Foreign Minister Udovenko for making (FBIS 1997b).

Horbulin's meetings with NATO officials apparently set in motion the Sea Breeze '97 exercises off the coast of Crimea, which took place in the spring of 1997. These exercises brought a fleet of NATO vessels, including American ones, right into the Black Sea. This greatly disturbed the Russian leadership, already upset by NATO expansion. The fear expressed by the Russian leadership was that Ukraine was drifting Westwards; clearly, Russian policy towards Ukraine until that point was proving to be a failure.

Finally, in the summer of 1997 Ukraine's diplomatic overtures to the West came to fruition with the signing, in late May 1997, of the Treaty on

Friendship and Cooperation between Russia and Ukraine, using text developed two years and six cancelled summits earlier. A concerned Yeltsin visited Kiev. 'We respect and honour the territorial integrity of Ukraine', he stated, explicitly recognising Ukraine's borders and control over the Crimea outside the parameters of CIS treaties. As he had been known to do, Yeltsin also made an off-the-cuff statement promising to 'defend Ukraine in extreme situations' even though a military pact was not part of the treaty, nor had this been the topic of any talks (Specter 1997).

In the treaty, the Ukrainian government finally got what it wanted:

- a clear, unambiguous affirmation of Ukrainian sovereignty within its current borders, outside of the context of the CIS;
- a settlement of the Black Sea Fleet issue, whereby a twenty-year lease was signed, and Russia kept approximately 80 per cent of the fleet;
- a write-off of about USD 526 million in energy debt to Russia;
- a write-off (concluded as a side agreement to the Treaty) of USD 450 million of debt for the delivery of tactical nuclear weapons from Ukraine to Russia in 1992 (Interfax 1997b);
- promises of free trade with Russia;
- approximately USD 100 million annually for rent of Sevastopol.

Russia also received much of what it wanted:

- the continued use of Sevastopol as the headquarters of the Black Sea Fleet, as well as most of the fleet itself;
- a reaffirmation of Ukraine's non-nuclear status;
- a statement on Ukraine's part supporting a pan-European security system based on a strengthened OSCE and UN rather than NATO, and a single security system 'from Vancouver to Vladivostok'.

Both countries would benefit from agreed ties in the areas of production of farm equipment, space exploration and the Antonov-70 cargo plane (*RIA-Novosti* 1997; Interfax 1997c).

The treaty was a blow to one of the architects of Russia's CIS policy, and its Minister for CIS Affairs Aman Tuleyev, who stated, correctly, that the treaty recognises the full sovereignty of Ukraine. Tuleyev argued that the treaty was contradictory to the goals of Russia's CIS policy, because it recognised current borders, allowed Ukraine to conduct an independent foreign policy – including the possibility of joining NATO. Also, there is the issue of ethnic Russians as a possible 'fifth column':

> Politically, by signing the Treaty, Moscow will lose large groups in Ukraine of potential supporters of reunification with Russia, most of whom already now regard this document as a betrayal of the 17 million Russians living in Ukraine.

> (Interfax 1997a)

Tellingly, even though Tuleyev was Russia's Minister for CIS Affairs, he was not invited to join the delegation to Kiev to sign the Treaty.

Signed with the treaty was a final agreement on the division of the Black Sea Fleet. While the Ukrainian navy would retain a symbolic presence in Sevastopol, most of the bays of the fleet, along with more than 80 per cent of its ships, went to Russia. A twenty-year lease was signed, for which Russia would pay USD 100 million per year. However, the agreement also stipulated that Ukraine would have the amount deducted each year from its USD 3 billion debt to Russia, USD 526 million of which was for oil and gas. This debt was rescheduled and was to be repaid to Russia within ten years (Interfax 1997c). In addition, USD 450 million was erased from Ukraine's debt as payment for the delivery of tactical nuclear weapons in 1992, something the Ukrainian leadership had been seeking from Russia since 1993 (Interfax 1997b). So financially the agreement was helpful to Ukraine – its debt to Russia was rescheduled and reduced by roughly USD 2.5 billion.

The Friendship and Cooperation Treaty also paved the way for closer cooperation between Russia and Ukraine on military issues. On the very heels of the treaty, and virtually at the same time as the Sea Breeze exercises with NATO, Russian Defence Minister Igor Sergeyev met in Kiev with his counterpart Oleksandr Kuzmuk to sign two agreements. In the first, the two sides agreed not to spy on one another. The second agreement was on defence production, an area of great opportunity for both countries. The two sides also called for joint naval exercises to be held later. The final indication of a turning point in Russian–Ukrainian relations was the highly successful November 1997 visit by Kuchma to the Russian Federation. Instead of being scolded, Kuchma was taken hunting by a tie-less, relaxed and compliant Yeltsin. The two agreed to work out an end to the tariff war between the two countries, and in a speech following the visit Yeltsin clearly and unequivocally recognised Ukrainian sovereignty, specifically its sovereignty over the Crimea, Sevastopol, and its portion of the Black Sea Fleet. He even warned Russian and Ukrainian nationalist 'demagogues' against making inflammatory speeches. The message of Yeltsin's speech was clear: Ukraine is an independent country, and Russia must have close and extremely friendly relations with it. Despite the Soviet-era rhetoric of 'indivisible' friendship between the 'two fraternal peoples', it was nevertheless the first time that Yeltsin clearly, publicly and unequivocally treated Ukraine as a separate nation.

The new businesslike state of relations was also evident in the autumn 1997 Russian–Ukrainian military exercises, military cooperation agreements and the beginning of talks, initiated by Russian Deputy Prime Minister Anatoli Chubais, over the value added tax issue. Kuchma and Chubais came to an agreement on what had been an intractable problem, which basically stemmed from the fact that, until about 1995, both Russia and Ukraine had a 'value added tax' on exports. This was done in order to increase budgets and control the outflow of raw materials and other goods from almost all CIS countries. In 1996, Ukraine unilaterally changed its practice to the more internationally accepted practice of not taxing exports, and instead placing tariffs on imported items, in order to make up for lost funds. The Russians retaliated by also raising tariffs. The tariff wars spread to other products, such as sugar and vodka. Chubais agreed to end the practice of taxing some exports to Ukraine, which although denying the Russian budget some one billion dollars, pleased Russian exporters and improved relations with Ukraine. 'We spoke of love and friendship', said Kuchma after meeting with Chubais (*Kommersant* 1997).

Most notable since 1997 has been a lowering of the level of nationalist and inflammatory rhetoric between the two countries, especially among parliamentarians. There are still immense controversies between Russia and Ukraine, most notably over Ukraine's debt to Russia, energy, Ukrainian privatisation, Ukraine's close relations with NATO. However, these are taking place in an atmosphere of closer relations. Ukraine is still, of course, much smaller and less powerful than Russia, and will always feel pressure from Russia on a number of fronts. However, the recognition of sovereignty and the normalisation of relations have been a big step forward towards security cooperation.

Realism or neo-imperialism?

From approximately 1996 to the ascendancy of Putin, and continuing at the time of writing, Russian foreign policy towards the CIS changed in two fundamental ways. First, its profile was heightened as the Russian leadership became less preoccupied with integration with the West and paid greater attention to the importance of its neighbours. Second, there seems to be a greater willingness to treat some of the newly independent states as sovereign. This is seen as a 'shift to realism' for a number of reasons. First, in this case, Russia has come to view the Ukrainian state apparatus as the primary actor for the conduct of interstate relations, not the CIS, pro-Russian political parties, or the ethnic Russians in Ukraine. Second, Western support for Ukraine, along with Ukrainian intransigence, has made the imperial option impossible. Third, Russia has factored in the reality of the weakness of its own state, so that even if the imperial option was possible, Russia lacks the power to pursue such a policy. State-to-state interaction has replaced interaction through centralised bureaucracies under Moscow's control.

There are numerous reasons for the failure of the CIS to become a centralised apparatus of Russian control over the former republics. First, there was the obvious fundamental conflict between the Russian ideal for the institution and the desire of the leaders of the newly independent states for sovereignty (Olcott *et al.* 1999). During the first heady days of independence, the former republics were primarily concerned with dividing assets and exploring new relationships with countries aside from Russia. Ukraine's steadfast refusal to call itself a full member of the CIS and to refrain from signing the Tashkent collective security treaty provided an example to other states with specific grievances with Russia to follow. Also, as it was in a state of near economic collapse, political turmoil and military weakness for much of the 1990s, Russia did not serve as an example to follow; nor did it have the power or will to create a 'tight' CIS. Its ambitions for the CIS far outweighed its ability to realise them.

Despite the grand rhetoric, in retrospect it sometimes seemed doubtful that Yeltsin and others in the Russian leadership took the creation of centralised CIS institutions very seriously. This is shown by the quiet collapse of CIS armed forces in 1993, and the appointment of Boris Berezovsky as CIS minister (and then his rapid sacking) in 1999. The CIS staff was cut by half in 1999. All of this was done without the consultation of CIS heads-of-state, as required by the CIS charter. Finally, in May 2000 the Ministry for Cooperation with CIS States was abolished. Yeltsin's constant rhetorical touting of the CIS was partly for domestic political purposes. It was used as a political weapon against his communist and nationalist political opponents, who accused him of illegally breaking up the USSR.[13] Thus the CIS was very high on ceremony, with its constant gatherings of heads-of-state and heads-of-government, and its production of over 700 agreements, protocols and statements which in reality had very little impact. President Putin, on the other hand, has completely dominated Russian politics and carries none of the political baggage associated with Yeltsin over the collapse of the USSR; he is not in need of the ceremonial aspects of the CIS for domestic political purposes.

Others have noted this policy shift, but there is still a lack of agreement on its extent. For example, Ilya Prizel traces the politics of Russian foreign policy towards the newly independent states and views it as a shift from the romantic Atlanticism of Kozyrev, where the CIS was largely ignored, to what he calls 'centrism'. Centrism means 'an understanding that Russia has vital economic security interests in the CIS, and that Russia should use its power to mould events in the CIS to its liking.' However, it stops short of imperialism in that it 'does not seek to undertake the expense of actually ruling over the new states, as the oft-postponed union with Belarus indicates' (Prizel 1997: 269–90). This is confirmed by Alla Kassianova's analysis of the evolution of official Russian foreign and security policy doctrines, and other acknowledgements of the greater realism of the Putin presidency in so far as the CIS is concerned (Kassianova 2001). Taras Kuzio, on the other hand, sees little policy shift by the Russians, citing recent interference in Ukrainian elections and the continued delay in border demarcation (Kuzio 2001, 2002).

Dominic Lieven's recent work on the Russian Empire makes it clear that Russia is no longer able to rule the former republics directly. However, Lieven does sees an impulse for the reintroduction of empire coming primarily as the result of competition from the West over influence in the former republics. As Russia sees the former republics gravitate to the West because of the West's economic power, it may try to halt this trend through military and political means, as well as control over oil and gas (Lieven 2000). Like Beissinger, Lieven alerts us to the fact that factors such as geography, post-Soviet language and ethnic politics, the weakness of the newly independent states, and a variety of other factors, will make Russia the leading power in the region, enabling it to practise a kind of neo-imperialism.

None the less, of the countries of the former USSR, the ones which have the most peaceful and normal relations with Russia are those which have formed effective relationships with the West. US and NATO policy has helped shift Russian policy towards some of these countries away from imperialism and towards realism. 'Peaceful and normal' does not mean free of disputes, but rather relations that are conducted through more or less normal diplomatic channels and on the basis of internationally recognised norms. These are the Baltic countries and Ukraine. It must be remembered that at the beginning of the decade there was concern over ethnic tensions in Ukraine and a fear of war and violence over issues such as the Crimea. Tensions were also very high over language laws in the Baltic countries and the treatment of Russians there. These tensions still exist, but are manageable and handled mostly in the context of state-to-state relations, albeit with a good deal of institutional flux.[14] For these countries, political, military and economic support from the West boosted confidence and forced Russia to adopt a more normal approach to addressing bilateral issues – without constant threats to their sovereignty. By using the West to shore up their sovereignty in the face of Russian pressure, these nations have taken an important step forward in the direction of true democratic security building, which can only take place between sovereign nations. By contrast, democratic security building cannot take place in regions where there are separatist movements supported in various degrees by Russia.

Other nations have relationships with Russia that are characterised by lack of sovereignty, inertia and dependence. These include Moldova, Belarus and Tajikistan; the problems here are primarily internal. These nations have decided to bandwagon with Russia, particularly Moldova and Tajikistan which need Russia to address pressing security issues. However, since they lack the leverage of good relations with the West, their security policies will more or less be dictated by Russia.

The success of US and NATO policy towards Ukraine and the Baltics indicates that similar policies should be extended to other countries, in particular to Georgia and Azerbaijan. There are drawbacks, however. Many of these nations cannot be counted upon as strategic counterweights to Russian power in the region because, like Ukraine, they desire a close normal relationship with Russia. Given the changing relationship between Russia and the West, the 'strategic counterweight' arguments may not be as salient. Most of the former republics do not want to be drawn into any conflicts where they are faced with the possibility of allying themselves with the West against Russia. So, while US and NATO policy can increase the chances of peace in the region, it cannot change geography. These nations, even if they achieve true sovereignty, are still small states that border a regional hegemonic power. This fact alone constrains their freedom of action.

Notes

1 Others have also noted the importance of the Soviet legacy in the newly independent states. See also: Motyl 1992, Lapidus *et al.* 1992, Colton and Legvold 1992, and Olcott *et al.* 1999.
2 A succinct explanation of Russian expansionism is found in Odom 1998: 398–407, where Odom interprets Russian security policy towards the CIS as remaining in the tradition of imperial Russia.
3 Former Russian Defence Minister Pavel Grachev called CIS military cooperation 'an alternative to NATO and the foundation for cooperation when NATO expands' (Kangas 1996).
4 The decree is titled 'The Establishment of the Strategic Course of the Russian Federation with Member States of the CIS' (FBIS 1995c; 1995d).
5 Former CIS Minister Aman Tuleyev stated: 'The West stands to gain from economically dismembering the CIS. Integration of poor people does not always work. Integration of rich and poor works better' (FBIS 1996c).
6 Part of the deal also involved the sale of thirty-two Ukrainian SS-19 missiles to Russia, as well as a division of heavy bombers.
7 The CIS charter of March 1992 is the only document to which Russia and Ukraine were signatories, prior to the collapse of the USSR, in which Russia recognises Ukraine as a sovereign nation.
8 There is no mention of 'associate membership' in the CIS charter, nor have what are the rights and duties of an 'associate member' ever been discussed.
9 This is often mentioned by numerous Ukrainian politicians who favour membership of the CIS, and by outside observers such as Peter Van Ham (1994).
10 Lukanov: 83.
11 A detailed account of the story is in Reiss 1995: 95–7.
12 The most influential public arguments were probably those of Zbigniew Brzezinski (1997: 15; 1998: 44).
13 It should be noted that, even at the time of the signing of the Belovezhaya Accords, communists and nationalists were not very strident in their objections; these seemed to rise later when their relationship with Yeltsin was far more tense (McFaul 2001). A good overview of the ferocity of Yeltsin's battles with the communists and nationalists is found in Aron 2001.
14 Russian policy towards Ukraine is still in a state of institutional flux, as primary responsibility for it seems to have landed in the office of President Putin, without a great deal of attention from the Ministry of Foreign Affairs (Bukvoll 2001).

8 The union of Belarus and Russia

The role of NATO and the EU

Clelia Rontoyanni

Introduction

Belarus has been an exception among Central and East European states in not having expressed any interest in accession to either the EU or NATO, even as a long-term prospect.[1] Instead, the Belarusian leadership has chosen a very close relationship with Russia as its primary strategic orientation. This has taken the form of a bilateral integration process, which began with the customs union of 1995, passed through the stages of a Community (treaty of April 1996) and a Union (treaty of April 1997), and resulted in the so-called 'Union-state' established by the treaty of December 1999.

This chapter presents the perspectives of the Belarusian leadership on the Union with Russia on the one hand, and on EU and NATO enlargement on the other. It also examines alternative positions advanced by opposition politicians in order to assess alternative options for the country's foreign policy course. In particular, the chapter highlights the factors that have steered Belarus away from the path of integration with European structures, as pursued by its neighbours. The content of the Russo–Belarusian integration process and the relations of Belarus with the EU and NATO are outlined, with an emphasis on the double function of the latter institutions as both models and external stimuli for the Russia–Belarus Union.

Understanding the choice of Lukashenka and the Belarusian elite

Belarusian President Alyaksandr Lukashenka has used integration with Russia as a major building block of his political reputation, so successfully that Western observers often seem to credit (or charge) him with authorship of Belarus's Russia-centred foreign policy. However, a policy shift away from neutrality (as pursued during the first year of Belarusian independence) and towards alignment with Russia occurred before Lukashenka's coming to office.[2] In 1993, the government of Vyacheslau Kebich came up with the initiative for integration with Russia due to economic considerations. It was hoped that, despite the failure to preserve Soviet-era economic ties on a CIS-wide basis, the Belarusian economy might still be able to benefit from Russian support on a bilateral basis. Unlike the Baltic states or Ukraine, national identity in Belarus, perceived in terms of distinctiveness from Russia, has not formed a motivation powerful enough to persuade Belarusian decision-makers to forsake the option of using Russian props to ease the course of economic transition.

President Lukashenka has continued the policies of his predecessors in minimising potentially unpopular economic reforms, relying on integration with Russia to maintain relative economic and social stability. At the same time, he has given integration with Russia a much stronger ideological underpinning by presenting himself as a champion of Soviet nostalgia and Slavic-Orthodox solidarity. The substantial material rewards that Belarus has derived from its role as Russia's most loyal ally have also proved an important factor accounting for the popularity of integration with Russia. Fuel exports at subsidised prices, combined with Russia's acceptance of barter payments for as much as three quarters of the amounts payable by Belarus, have constituted the principal means of Russian support for the Belarusian economy. The position of Belarus as the highest-ranked CIS country in the United Nations' Human Development Index, for example, has served as evidence of the ostensible success of the Belarusian socio-economic model.[3] Low external debt has been another aspect of the model, much admired, not only by Russian left-wing politicians (communists and their allies in the Duma), but also by what appears to be a sizeable section of the Russian bureaucracy.[4] Market-oriented Belarusian politicians and economic experts have recognised Russian subsidies as a major prop for the Belarusian economy. Still, they have argued that this support has acted as a counter-incentive to conducting economic reforms, thereby making little contribution to the long-term economic recovery of Belarus.[5]

For the time being, public opinion surveys suggest that Lukashenka's relatively high approval ratings have been connected with the integration process and the socio-economic policies that Russian subsidy has made possible (DOS 2000a: 4). Most Belarusians appear to credit the president with ensuring adequate food supplies, paying wages and pensions on time, providing for education and defence, and advancing the interests of Belarus internationally. The 'Belarusian model' has comprised several policy instruments contradicting the prescriptions of liberal economists (e.g.: price controls on food staples; inflationary currency emission; and subsidies to unprofitable enterprises), which also contradict Belarusian treaty obligations to approximate Russian legislative norms and economic conditions.

Perhaps paradoxically, the integration process has also begun to provide the most potent pressures on the Belarusian authorities to proceed with economic reform. Particularly under Vladimir Putin, Russia has pressed the Belarusian authorities to proceed with certain long-delayed reforms, with priority on the privatisation of major enterprises, many of which are targeted by Russian business. Following Lukashenka's re-election to the presidency in

September 2001, steps towards privatisation have been accelerated, but are still stumbling on the Belarusian authorities' insistence upon burdensome conditions for prospective investors (e.g.: employment guarantees; majority control for the state for a probationary period of three to five years). Monetary policy has been an area where Russian requirements (notably the conditions of the Russian Central Bank with respect to monetary union) have prompted reform in Belarus. The incentive of Russian credits to prop up the Belarusian currency led to a tightening of Belarusian currency emission, the elimination of multiple exchange rates in late 2000 and the locking of the two countries' currencies into a fixed exchange rate as of the second quarter of 2001.[6] Belarus received USD 100 million of a Russian credit of USD 250 million during the pre-election period of summer 2001, which was interpreted as tacit support for Lukashenka from his Russian counterpart. Although the sustainability of Russian economic support cannot be taken for granted, its magnitude and the flexibility of economic conditions attached to it render the option of switching to creditors like the IMF rather unattractive to the Belarusian leadership. Regardless of Lukashenka's antipathy to the West and alleged aspirations to the presidency of a Russo–Belarusian state, economic gain represents more than sufficient motivation for any non-nationalist Belarusian leader to persist with the Russia-centred orientation. The programme of Uladzimer Hancharyk, the candidate endorsed by the principal opposition forces in the presidential elections of 2001, contained a commitment to continued integration with Russia coupled with the development of good relations with the West (Belapan 2001: 6).

Belarus faces the dual enlargement: 'Together with Russia in Europe?'

The diplomatic positions of Belarus on the Eastward enlargement of the EU and NATO have been very similar to those of Russia, although the Belarusian leadership has lagged behind President Putin's efforts to improve relations with the Alliance. The official attitude to the pending accession to the EU of several neighbours of Belarus has been neutral or reservedly positive. The Belarusian side has expressed concern over potential negative consequences on trade and cross-border travel. These are expected to affect Belarusian regions bordering Poland after the latter's introduction of visa regulations in accordance with the EU's Schengen agreement. Belarusian policy-makers have also discerned a set of opportunities arising from the country's future position as a state bordering EU territory. These have been reflected in the following objectives, which Belarusian diplomacy has declared with respect to future relations with an enlarged EU: the enhancement of political dialogue; the widening of Belarusian producers' access to the EU export market; the expansion of EU assistance and investment in the Belarusian economy; and participation in various EU-sponsored regional projects in fields such as environmental protection and transport infrastructure.

Following the examples of Russia and Ukraine, Belarusian diplomacy has proclaimed a 'multidirectional' foreign policy. This was not conceived as the 'Ukrainianisation' of Belarusian policy, implying a shift towards Western states and reliance on national-minded forces within the country (Rozanov 1998: 7). The principal aim has been, not to reverse the 'Russia-first' orientation, but to give Belarus its own profile in international affairs, enabling it to become directly involved in European political and economic processes. The first priority in this respect has been to redress the international isolation of Belarus, primarily by improving relations with the West and with the EU in particular (Laptyonok 1999: 45). Belarus had formalised its relations with the EU by concluding an Interim Agreement and a Partnership and Cooperation Agreement (PCA) in 1994. These agreements, alongside EU assistance through the TACIS programme, were suspended in 1997 in condemnation of President Lukashenka's excessive concentration of power in his own hands at the expense of the Parliament and the Constitutional Court, and his use of repressive tactics towards the opposition and the media.[7] Not only opposition politicians, but also what appears to have been an influential section of Belarusian government officials, considered the Lukashenka administration's intransigence towards EU demands to be a serious mistake.[8]

Modest steps forward were made in 1999–2000 (e.g.: conclusion of an agreement raising the Belarusian quota for the duty-free export of textiles to the EU market; the EU revoked visa restrictions for Belarusian officials and increased funds allocated to Belarus), which were linked to the opening of negotiations between the Belarusian president and the opposition. The Belarusian leadership had been hoping that the parliamentary elections of October 2000 would be recognised by the EU, allowing for the reinstatement of the PCA, the full participation of Belarus in the TACIS programme and the reversal of EU member-states' opposition to the Belarusian application for membership in the Council of Europe. However, neither the parliamentary elections nor the presidential elections of September 2001 were considered to have met international standards. After Lukashenka's re-election, the EU began to review the policy of isolation and contemplate broadening its engagement with Belarus. Still, the Belarusian authorities will need to demonstrate a readiness to restore relations with the West by proceeding with political liberalisation (notably, reform of electoral legislation and conditions for the operation of the media, as required by the OSCE). It is doubtful, however, that the Belarusian leadership's interest in improving relations with the West outweighs the concern to maintain a free hand within the country. Concessions to Western criticism are further resisted as a matter of national dignity.[9] Even if Belarus was to display indisputable progress towards OSCE/EU conditions, it has already lost a lot of ground that it would need to make up before its cooperation with the EU reached a level comparable to that of EU–Russia or EU–Ukraine relations.

Compared to Russia or Ukraine, the Belarusian administration has more modest aspirations for the country's role in European affairs and is, therefore, not interested in trying to keep up with its neighbours' rapid development of relations with the EU.[10] The proposal made by British Foreign Secretary Jack Straw for special neighbour status to be given to Belarus, Moldova and Ukraine in conjunction with the impending enlargement of the EU has elicited interest within the Belarusian administration (*Independent*, 16 April 2002). At any rate, the optimal form of relations envisaged by the Belarusian administration does not extend far beyond the bounds of the PCA. This type of agreement, which has also been signed by Russia and other CIS countries, differs from Association ('Europe') agreements, which have constituted the legal framework of relations between the EU and individual Central and East European (non-CIS) states, in containing no reference to the possibility of accession to the EU. President Lukashenka may have defined Belarus as 'a profoundly European country', but, in the view of Belarusian foreign policy planners, a strategy of accession to the EU is not a realistic option for Belarus (*Sovetskaya Belorussiya* 27 July 1999). As an analysis by the Belarusian Foreign Ministry points out:

> Unfortunately, it is evident that the European Union, which represents a universally recognised pole of attraction in the European region, cannot realistically constitute 'a common home' for all European peoples in the medium term.[11]

Therefore they conclude that CIS countries need to emulate the experience of the EU in developing integrative processes among themselves. The CIS as a whole has suffered from chronic discord, which has made agreements signed and implemented by all member-states appear like rare exceptions rather than the norm (Lukashenka 1998: 3–4). As a result, sub-groupings consisting of states with similar agendas have emerged within the CIS: the Central Asian Union (Kazakhstan, Uzbekistan, Kyrgyzstan, Tajikistan); GUUAM (Georgia, Ukraine, Uzbekistan, Azerbaijan, Moldova); the Eurasian Economic Community (Russia, Belarus, Kazakhstan, Kyrgyzstan, Tajikistan); and, finally, the Russia–Belarus Union. Belarusian policy-makers see the Eurasian Economic Community and especially the bilateral union with Russia as the integrationist core of the CIS. They expect that the success of these two formations in creating a common economic space, generating trade and increasing the prosperity of member-states, will encourage other CIS countries to join. In the long term, an integrated post-Soviet region could come to mirror EU structures and constitute an Eastern pillar, eventually merging with the EU into a Europe-wide community (Laptyonok 1999: 44). The Belarusian president, convinced that no CIS country could join Western structures, has repeatedly invited Ukraine to become the third member of the Russia–Belarus Union, dismissing the Ukrainian leadership's 'European choice' (the strategy aimed at accession to the EU) as unfeasible: 'As if it was not understood that nobody in the West is waiting for Ukraine, Belarus, Russia or the others [CIS countries].'[12]

Even for proponents of a European orientation, a strategy geared towards accession to the EU appears unrealistic. Putin's drive to improve Russia's relations with the West, forge closer links with the EU and emulate EU economic and legislative standards has boosted support for a strategy of integration with Europe through Russia among the reform-oriented elite.[13] Gradual integration with Europe by means of economic integration with Russia is supported also by moderate opposition politicians such as Volha Abramava, former Prime Minister Mikhail Chyhir and former Chairman of the National Bank Stanislau Bahdankevich.[14] Apart from the fact that Russia has proved far more successful than Belarus in developing its relations with the EU, Belarusian foreign policy experts believe that such a strategy reflects the expectations of the Belarusian mass public (Sharapo 2000: 65). Survey evidence suggests that Belarusian public opinion is attracted by the higher living standards associated with accession to the EU, but does not wish to see the 'special relationship' with Russia dismantled. In the view of a leading Belarusian analyst, the Belarusian Popular Front (BPF) under Zyanon Paznyak alienated most of the electorate, not due to its advocacy of integration with Western Europe, but due to its anti-Russian rhetoric (Rozanov 1998: 6; Karbalevich 1999: 71, 87). The Belarusian administration's sceptical approach to economic reform and EU policy recommendations, however, represents the main barrier to a successful strategy of integration in Europe with Russia, complicating the development of the bilateral integration process with Russia in the first place.

Still defending the Union's western borders from NATO?

Minsk responded to the first wave of NATO enlargement even more adversely than Russian diplomacy. Belarusian and Russian arguments against NATO's Eastward move were essentially the same, both as a result of a genuine convergence in perceptions of NATO and due to the coordination of the two countries' diplomatic positions as part of the integration process. NATO enlargement was perceived primarily as a breach of trust on the part of the West and of the United States in particular, capitalising on the dismemberment of the Warsaw Treaty Organisation to exercise unbalanced influence throughout the European continent. It was regarded as a contravention of the spirit of the 'Two plus Four' agreements of German reunification and of the treaty on Conventional Forces in Europe (CFE), which implied the preservation of a military balance between NATO and the countries of the former Soviet bloc. The accession of Poland, Hungary and the Czech republic to NATO would end any pretensions to a balance between the military capabilities of NATO and those of its present-day aspiring counterweight, the CIS Collective Security Treaty. This consideration aggravated the Belarusian leadership's resentment of the heavy financial costs entailed by the country's CFE obligations, prodding it to temporarily halt (during the latter part of 1995 and the beginning of 1996) the destruction of weapons inherited from the Soviet Union.

The Belarusian president surpassed even Russia's 'red-browns' in the ferocity of his anti-NATO discourse, describing the Alliance as 'a scary monster staring at Belarus'. His most controversial statements included an expression of regret that Belarus gave up its nuclear weapons and a call for the formation of a Minsk–Moscow–Beijing axis (*Kommersant* 25 September 1998). The exploitation of Cold War stereotypes complemented President Lukashenka's image as a staunch defender of Slavic-Orthodox unity, ostensibly threatened by the West in the form of NATO. Since the expansion of NATO emerged as an inevitable prospect, the Belarusian side has enthusiastically supported the enhancement of the military aspect of integration with Russia. The Belarusian president for long took advantage of tensions in Russia's relations with NATO to emphasise the benefits of the Union-state common defence and to press the point of the contribution of Belarus to Russian security:

> Russians understand perfectly that an attack on Belarus would be primarily an attack on Russia, as was the case in World War One, in World War Two, in all wars, at all times.[15]

In return, he has stressed that Belarus has been:

> Defending both its own interests and those of Russia. And it will keep doing so. Because we [Belarus] have always been a reliable ally for the Russian person and have never in history betrayed him.[16]

During a visit by then Russian Defence Minister Igor Sergeyev to Minsk in October 1998, his Belarusian opposite number reportedly assured him that Russia could – to all intents and purposes – regard Belarus as a Russian military district (*Kommersant* 17 October 1998). In response to criticisms by Russian liberals relating to the costs of integration with Belarus to the Russian economy, Lukashenka has contended that the contribution of Belarus to Russia's security (by means of Russia's lease-free use of the Baranavichy air-defence facility and the Vileyka radio station) is worth more than any economic support Belarus has received from Russia.[17] This argument appears to have been heeded, as by 1999 even politicians from the 'Union of Rightist Forces' had ceased to question the expediency of integration with Belarus on the grounds of economic cost.

Apart from viewing the union with Russia as the epicentre of economic integration in the post-Soviet region, Belarusian diplomacy has portrayed the bilateral union as the nucleus of the CIS Collective Security Treaty and as a putative pole of resistance to a NATO-centric security environment.[18] This corresponds to the joint endeavour of the Russian and Belarusian foreign policy makers to accelerate the emergence of a multi-polar world order, or at least a more pluralistic European security architecture (as opposed to one where decision-making on international security is effectively monopolised by NATO).[19]

NATO's intervention in the Kosovo crisis alarmed the Belarusian leadership, which drew a parallel between Western condemnation of Yugoslavia's human rights record and quasi-dictatorial regime on the one hand, and charges of authoritarianism and civil liberties violations levelled at Belarus on the other. Lukashenka saw himself in the position of Slobodan Milošević, as the target of a US-driven 'demonisation' campaign, presumably intended to justify in the eyes of Western public opinion a future intervention to forcibly remove him from power.[20] As a leading Belarusian parliamentarian said to the author: in view of NATO's new Strategic Concept, which provides for operations beyond the territories of member-states, 'there are no guarantees that Belarus, too, may not become the object of a "humanitarian intervention" '.[21]

As the Belarusian president himself has pointed out, Belarus has not experienced ethnic tensions (nor is there a realistic prospect of this),[22] which renders comparisons with the case of Kosovo inappropriate. As the NATO intervention in Kosovo is appearing increasingly as an exceptional operation rather than the start of a pattern, the Belarusian administration has become rather dismissive of the second wave of NATO enlargement as a direct threat to the country's security.[23] Still, most of the Belarusian elite and public continue to see Russia as a guarantor of Belarusian security, and even Uladzimer Hancharyk, Lukashenka's main rival for the presidency in the September 2001 election, has stressed the significance of collective defence guarantees including protection by Russia's 'nuclear umbrella' (Belapan 2001).

At the same time, the Belarusian stance on NATO has been more pragmatic than Lukashenka's rhetoric would suggest. Indeed, as public concern over NATO has subsided with the end of the campaign against Yugoslavia (DOS 2000b: 1), the Belarusian administration has adopted a markedly conciliatory tone. Belarus returned to the PfP (after suspending its relations with NATO at the same time as Russia in March 1999 in protest against the bombing of Yugoslavia) half a year earlier than Russia. Belarusian diplomacy has expressed reserved satisfaction with its participation in the Euro-Atlantic Partnership Council and a wish to develop 'normal relations' with the Alliance. Belarusian diplomacy even sought to conclude a framework agreement formalising its interaction with the Alliance, conceived as a more modest version of the NATO–Russia Founding Act, but later abandoned the idea as it became clear that NATO wished to reserve such special contractual relations for Russia and Ukraine only. Moderate critics (also within official circles) of the strong anti-NATO line had long contended that it was counterproductive for a small country like Belarus to be aggravating tensions with an all-powerful alliance like NATO, alienating its prosperous member-states, which could provide investment vital to the Belarusian economy.[24]

Russian president Putin's high-profile efforts to upgrade Russia's dialogue and cooperation with NATO (before and after the terrorist attacks of 11 September 2001) have compelled the Belarusian leadership to refrain from any sharp anti-NATO statements. While Belarusian diplomacy thoroughly avoids contradicting the Russian line, no dramatic shift towards cordial relations with NATO could be expected from the Belarusian administration. Belarus has remained rather unenthusiastic about, and even somewhat suspicious of, the PfP, with its participation in the programme being even more limited than that of Russia. Belarusian officials account for this in terms of financial constraints and also on the grounds of the constitutional ban on the deployment of Belarusian troops abroad, which rules out Belarusian participation in international peace support operations, thereby making most PfP activities irrelevant to Belarus.[25] Belarusian forces have, none the less, taken part in some PfP activities (e.g. environmental and other civil emergency exercises) without Russian involvement.

The Russia–Belarus Union: in the image of the EU or NATO? Emulating the EU model

Russian and Belarusian officials have often referred to the EU as the model for the development of the bilateral integration process. This has been relatively accurately reflected in the institutions created by the integration treaties. The treaty 'On the Formation of a Community' (April 1996) established two supranational institutions (whose members are meant to act on behalf of the Community rather than of national governments), the Parliamentary Assembly and the Executive Committee. Like in the European Parliament and the Commission in the earlier stages of the European Community, the Parliamentary Assembly has consisted of delegates appointed by the two countries' national legislatures, and the Executive Committee has been made up of national governments' appointees (usually civil servants). These bodies were, however, clearly subordinated to the authority of the Supreme Council, which was initially made up of the heads-of-state, the heads-of-government, the chairs of national parliaments (two for each member-state, as both Russia and Belarus have bicameral legislatures) and the Chairman of the Executive Committee. The Presidents of Russia and Belarus rotate in the office of Supreme Council chair. Decisions are made by unanimity on the basis of 'one state, one vote'[26] and, in the policy areas of exclusive Union jurisdiction, they are immediately valid without the need for enabling national legislation. The treaty 'On the Union of Belarus and Russia' (April 1997) required that national legislation contradicting Union decisions be amended to ensure conformity (Art. 19) and deprived the Executive Committee chair of membership in the Supreme Council.

The treaty 'On the Formation of a Union State' further weakened the Executive Committee, which was renamed the Permanent Committee. It did so by granting formal status to the Council of Ministers, which took on most of the competence formerly exercised by the Executive Committee: advising the Supreme Council on the creation of new agencies; proposing draft legislation to the Parliament of the Union State (as the Parliamentary Assembly was renamed); preparing the budget of the Union-state; issuing directly applicable decrees and directives. The Permanent Committee was left with a coordinating role, linking the activities of Union-state institutions and national government agencies (Art. 48). In exchange, unlike its Western European counterpart, the Council of Ministers lost its purely intergovernmental composition by including the heads of Union-state agencies (e.g. those of the Borders and Customs Committees) and the Union-state Secretary (a newly created post occupied by Pavel Borodin). The Union-state treaty equally strengthened the Supreme State Council (as the Supreme Council was renamed) by granting its decisions the status of decrees or directives (Art. 35). Further, it defined a sphere of exclusive Union-state competence, which included all aspects of implementing a common economic space (with special emphasis on customs policy and the unification of the two countries' defence industries, energy and transport systems), border policy and the functioning of the regional military force (Art. 17). Other areas of defence policy, the harmonisation of economic and social legislation, and the combating of crime and terrorism, were designated as areas where competence is shared between national and Union-state institutions (Art. 18).

The Union-state treaty provides for a bicameral parliament divided into the Chamber of the Union (upper house) and the Chamber of Representatives (lower house). The upper house, like the former Parliamentary Assembly, is to be formed by an equal number of deputies delegated by the national legislatures of each member-state. The lower house is to be directly elected every four years by the citizens of the two member-states, and to contain seventy-five deputies from Russia and twenty-eight from Belarus, reflecting the unequal size of the two countries' populations (Art. 39). The authority of the Parliament is enhanced by the right to pass immediately valid legislation, adopt the budget and ratify international agreements on behalf of the Union-state (Art. 40).[27]

These changes have yet to take effect, as the first election to the lower house of the Union-state Parliament has not taken place yet due to delays in the national parliaments' adoption of the relevant electoral laws. It appears that, as the drafting of a Union-state Constitutional Act is already under way, elections to the lower chamber of the Union-state Parliament may have to wait until the two countries' electorates have approved the act in a referendum (*Soyuz Belarus-Rossiya* 21 February 2002: 1–2). In turn, the establishment of two new supranational institutions envisaged by the Union-state treaty, an Accounts Chamber and a Court, whose members are to be appointed or approved by the Parliament, has also been delayed. The creation of a supranational Court, whose decisions are to be directly binding on member-states, would be likely to assist the further progress of integration, given that so far there have been no sanctions in case of non-implementation of agreed measures.

The objectives declared in the integration treaties have mirrored the achievements of the European Community/Union to a considerable extent.

An agreement on the establishment of a customs union, which was signed in January 1995 (before the creation of supranational institutions), required the removal of customs controls from the common border and the elimination of all tariffs and quantitative restrictions on bilateral trade. These provisions were implemented as early as June 1996, with temporary restrictions (permitted in emergency situations of extreme budget deficit or shortage of staple goods) being used only in one instance (*Byulleten Mezhdunarodnykh Dogovorov* October 1995: 31–6). Border controls have returned on different occasions on either side of the border, albeit with the purpose of levying customs duties on goods originating from third countries.[28] The formulation of a common customs policy has so far proven an intricate task. Progress towards the bilateral harmonisation of tariffs needs to accommodate relevant negotiations within the Eurasian Economic Community (Sirotsky 2000).

The Community Treaty (April 1996) required the implementation of the four freedoms characteristic of a single market (free movement of goods, services, capital and labour), which were elaborated in the agreement 'On the Creation of Equal Conditions for Economic Actors' and the treaty 'On Equal Rights of Citizens' of December 1998. The latter has proved the least controversial of all integration treaties, its provisions having been implemented by mid-1999. According to the treaty, citizens of Belarus in Russia have access to employment, health care, education at all levels, and various other social services on the same basis as Russian citizens, and vice versa. They equally benefit from full protection granted by national labour legislation in their country of employment. Neither party may impose any restrictions applicable to foreigners on the economic activities of citizens of the other party. The unification of labour and social legislation is to occur according to the principle of maximisation, which requires that common standards be based on those of the state with the most extensive guarantees in each aspect of labour and social provision.[29]

At the same time, operating conditions for private capital in Russia and Belarus have differed substantially. Though Russian companies have gained access to Belarusian state tenders on the same basis as domestic enterprises, their operations in Belarus have continued to be stifled by factors equally relevant to all private business (whether Belarusian or foreign). The integration process has sought to address such problems (e.g.: uneven tax exemptions; varying degrees of state intervention in business operations; different currency export controls) by ongoing negotiations towards the unification of economic legislation and the convergence of national economic and monetary policies. The Belarusian authorities have observed treaty obligations to introduce economic legislation in line with Russian norms very patchily and, in some policy areas where Russian legislation contradicted Belarusian social policy priorities (e.g. fiscal reform), not at all (*Diplomatichesky Vestnik* May 1997: 36, 38; *BMD* March 2000: 77). Since Putin came to office, the Russian government has pressed the issue of

Belarusian adaptation to Russian standards of economic regulation, assigning particular priority to the privatisation of larger Belarusian enterprises.

A series of agreements between the Russian Central Bank and the Belarusian National Bank have focused on the coordination of exchange rate policies as a first step towards the establishment of necessary conditions for monetary union. Efforts in this direction had been thwarted by the non-convertibility of the Belarusian currency, which had been due primarily to the government's frequent resort to inflationary emission to pay pensions and wages.[30] In 2000, the Belarusian authorities re-denominated the national currency, tightened emission and achieved a degree of monetary stability.[31] Belarus subsequently received a large Russian credit of around USD 200 million, intended for the support of the national currency, which was locked into a fixed exchange rate with the Russian rouble in the first half of 2001 (*Izvestiya* 15 November 2000; *Nezavisimaya Gazeta* 3 April 2001). Belarusian negotiators have grudgingly accepted the presence of a single emission centre for a common currency, which at least for a period of three years will be the Russian rouble.[32] The two central banks have elaborated a stringent list of preconditions: full mutual convertibility of the two national currencies; the elimination of non-monetary transactions from both countries' economies; the completion of market reforms and the rule of law in economic activity. They have also been considering ceilings on budget deficit and external debt of 3 and 60 per cent respectively, as specified by the criteria set for participation in the 'Euro-zone' (*Kommersant-Vlast* 13 July 1999: 38). Although these criteria appear somewhat unrealistic, it is planned that the Russian rouble may be introduced in nominal form in the Belarusian economy as of 2005, with the national currency being discarded two or three years later (*Interfax* 27 July 2000).

While the Russia–Belarus Union-state institutionally resembles the EU more than it does a federal state, the repeated failure to implement provisions related to legal harmonisation and economic integration have prompted assessments that the Union exists 'only on paper'. It would be far more accurate to say that implementation has been partial and has lagged behind declared target dates. Initially, these had been based on particularly optimistic expectations, stemming from the consideration that the recent experience of common statehood, participation in a single economy and a stronger sense of shared ethnocultural identity would give Russia and Belarus an advantage compared to the more heterogeneous EC/EU.[33] The experience of Western European integration has demonstrated that reaching agreement on fundamental issues such as monetary policy and achieving effective coordination between national agencies involved in legal harmonisation are time-consuming, cumbersome and often controversy-ridden tasks affecting a multitude of vested bureaucratic and sectional interests. In the case of Russia and Belarus, inadequate administrative capacity and/or resources have posed additional impediments. As an expert working for the Russian government observed:

Many laws of the Russian Federation are also not being implemented. Why should one expect agreements with Belarus to be handled any more effectively? The implementation of laws and international agreements is difficult and this is not a problem faced by Russia alone.[34]

The above difficulties have been exacerbated by the two leaderships' diverging approaches to economic reform. At present, the Belarusian president remains unconvinced of the merits of Putin's policies aimed at integration with the global economy and approximation of EU economic and institutional norms. It is still uncertain whether the Belarusian administration will utilise the post-election period to push through not only the announced programme of privatisation but also a range of other reforms (e.g. deregulation, fiscal reform) required if the bilateral integration process is to move forward.

The Union-state as an alternative to NATO

In the fields of defence and foreign policy, the Russia–Belarus Union has surpassed the levels of integration attained by the EU. In Russia and Belarus, foreign policy coordination and military integration are subject to remarkable little controversy compared to what is the case in Western Europe. Since the conclusion of the inter-ministerial agreement 'On Cooperation and Coordination' (January 1995), the Russian and Belarusian Foreign Ministries have advanced very similar positions on practically all matters of mutual interest. Foreign policy coordination has been conducted both on a day-to-day basis and in terms of longer-term planning. As of 1998, the two Foreign Ministries have introduced 'Programmes of Co-ordinated Actions in the Field of Foreign Policy', whereas joint collegial sessions began in February 2000. In accordance with the Programme documents, Belarusian diplomats receive higher training at the Diplomatic Academy of the Russian MFA and the Moscow State Institute of International Relations.[35]

Coordinated positions have been presented, not only in response to particular developments (e.g.: criticism of NATO enlargement; denunciation of NATO military operations against Iraq and Yugoslavia; condemnation of the terrorist attacks of 11 September 2001), but equally in terms of shared visions of European security and world order. Both countries have advocated the development of a European security architecture centred around the OSCE, as opposed to a NATO-centric system premised on an ongoing enlargement of the Alliance to the East. They have been critical of a world order dominated by a single superpower and the trend towards interference in states' internal affairs on human rights grounds, particularly when this involves the use of military force without sanction from the UN Security Council. Russia and Belarus have supported practically identical positions in international fora such as the UN, the OSCE and the CIS. This is exemplified by Minsk's unreserved support for Russia's 1999 operations in Chechnya and Russian diplomatic efforts at ending the international isolation of Belarus. Moscow has rejected reports of international organisations referring to human rights abuses in Belarus, and has recognised the parliamentary elections of October 2000 and the presidential elections of September 2001 as conforming to international standards. At the same time, as Belarusian officials have pointed out, the two countries retain distinct national interests. In particular, the Belarusian leadership does not see an imitation of Putin's emphasis on close political and economic relations with the EU, NATO and the United States as expedient from the vantage point of the much more limited (in terms of geographical scope and political ambition) Belarusian national interests.[36]

A special relationship in the military sphere became discernible in early 1995, when Belarus granted Russia rent- and tax-free use of the Baranavichy missile-warning station and the Vileyka communications facility for a minimum of 25 years (*Byulleten Mezhdunarodnykh Dogovorov* November 1996: 48–56.). The Baranavichy installation contains the central CIS air-defence administration, and Vileyka constitutes the principal radio control centre for Russia's Navy – including nuclear submarines. As of early 2003, the early warning missile station 'Volga' had still not become operational on the Baranavichy site. Like the Central European member-states of NATO, Belarus does not host military bases occupied by foreign (Russian) troops on a permanent basis and has undertaken, as part of the CFE review of November 1999, not to increase current force levels on its territory.[37] A small number (around a hundred) of Russian Border Troops have been working with their Belarusian counterparts in guarding the borders with Poland, Lithuania and Latvia.[38] On the other hand, according to the October 1998 agreement 'On the Joint Use of Military Infrastructure Objects', the Russian and Belarusian militaries may use all kinds of installations (e.g. command and communications centres, aerodromes, air-defence facilities, bases and depots) in the two countries' border regions for training purposes or on a temporary basis. The modernisation of these facilities is also to be financed in common, whether from the national budgets or from the Union budget.

Inspiration from NATO practices is reflected in a Russo–Belarusian effort to develop rapid reaction forces. During his visit to Minsk in April 2000, President Putin announced the creation of a regional force, combining the whole of the Belarusian armed forces with the Moscow military district.[39] The force is to number up to 300,000 troops (from the two countries' armies, internal and border troops), which would be deployed on the territory of Belarus in the case of an immediate external threat to its security. In the meantime, regional force troops are to remain under national command structures (*Nezavisimaya Gazeta* 18, 19 April 2000). Bilateral command-and-staff exercises relating to the operation of the regional force have been held regularly beginning in October 2000. A reform programme for the Belarusian armed forces has subsequently been introduced, which aims to adapt Belarusian capabilities to the needs of a rapid reaction force – at the same time as gradually reducing troop levels.

Since 1996, when the two countries' air-defence services began joint alert duty, large-scale bilateral exercises have become an annual feature of military integration, beginning with the 'Redoubt 96' exercises. Joint airforce exercises took place in the Tula oblast in March 1997 and in the Moscow military district a year later (*Kommersant* 13 March 1997; *Nezavisimaya Gazeta* 17 April 1998). June 1999 saw the most extensive strategic exercises performed by Russia's Armed Forces since their establishment in 1992. The 'West 99' exercises, which involved all services from five Russian military districts (Leningrad, Moscow, Volga, Urals, North Caucasus) and which were jointly planned and directed by Russian and Belarusian officers, took into account the experience of NATO air-strikes on Yugoslavia in simulating the repulsion of a similar campaign against Belarus and Russia (*Nezavisimaya Gazeta* 23 June 1999; *Krasnaya Zvezda* 23 June 1999). Belarusian airforce and air-defence units participated in the second phases of the exercises, which were partly conducted on the territory of Belarus (*KZ* 25 June 1999). Joint collegial sessions of the two ministries of Defence began in 1998; their main tasks have been to design a common defence policy, an integrated armed forces structure and a weapons procurement programme.

Work towards the development of a common doctrine has resulted in the adoption of the 'Concept of the Common Defence Policy of Belarus and Russia' (1998), the 'Security Concept of the Union of Russia and Belarus' and the 'Concept of the Union's Border Policy' (spring 1999). Common defence orders were placed for the first time in spring 2000. As of 1998, Belarusian officers have been trained in Russian military academies on the same programmes as their Russian colleagues – a privilege unavailable to officers from other member-states of the CIS Collective Security treaty or from any other foreign state.[40] In sum, as former Belarusian Defence Minister Alyaksandar Chumakau has remarked, 'integration has been developing much faster in the military sphere than in other fields' (*Rossiiskaya Gazeta* 24 October 2000).

Conclusions

The dual enlargement has been a crucial factor in the formation of the international environment within which the decision-making elites and mass publics of Belarus and Russia perceive opportunities, challenges and policy alternatives for their countries' prosperity, security and international standing. Belarusian policy-makers saw economic and military integration with Russia as the most feasible external orientation in view of a seemingly compelling trend (often described by the term 'globalisation'), pushing states either to join existing blocs (common markets and/or military alliances) or form new ones. It was not coincidental that the Belarusian leadership's choice in favour of a Russia-centred path was made at the same time as Central European states filed their applications for accession to the EU and NATO. Most Central European countries' quest for the 'return to Europe' negated notions of East Central Europe as an area made up of neutral states, which had been prominent in the early 1990s. The decision to enlarge NATO to the East assisted the fulfilment of the Belarusian leadership's choice by generating a sense of urgency in the minds of Russian policy-makers and by enhancing (Russian) sceptics' appreciation of the strategic advantages of integration with Belarus. Even after the improvement of Russia's relations with the United States and NATO, which has followed the formation of the international anti-terrorist coalition in response to the 11 September attacks, much of the Russian military and foreign policy estab-lishment remains sceptical regarding the longer-term prospects of such a partnership. Against the background of the second wave of NATO enlarge-ment into the former Soviet Union and expanding US influence in Russia's periphery (notably in the Caucasus and Central Asia), the alliance with Belarus is seen at least as an insurance policy.[41]

On the other hand, external actors such as NATO and the EU have barely had a role in directly shaping the process of Russo–Belarusian inte-gration. Any impact these institutions may have had on the process has not been the result of policy planning or diplomatic efforts to stir Russia and Belarus either away from bilateral integration or towards a particular form thereof. The appeal of the EU institutional model, rather than being the product of any EU initiative to promote parallel processes, has been due to the high prestige of the European Union in the eyes of the Belarusian and Russian elites. The EU model has been associated with the growing pros-perity of member-states, a perception that has been reinforced by the powerful gravitational pull the EU has exercised on Central and Eastern European states. If anything, the complexity of the EU enlargement process appears to have led most members of the Belarusian and Russian elites to the conclusion that the capacity of existing supranational struc-tures could not be stretched to the geographical or cultural limits of the European continent – at least in the foreseeable future. The concurrent real-isation of the need for Russia, Belarus and the rest of the CIS to become an integral part of broader economic and political processes, inevitably – for the time being – centred around the EU and NATO, has prompted a strategy of parallel integrative processes combined with growing interaction with the European 'core'. The international isolation of Belarus and the minimal negotiating power that Belarus anticipates it could have *vis-à-vis* either NATO or the EU have consolidated the Belarusian practice of seeking to influence these institutions' policies mostly by relying on Russian advocacy.

NATO cannot be described as a model for the Russia–Belarus Union, for its image in Belarus and, despite Putin's diplomatic efforts, Russia alike remains tainted – both as a result of residual Cold War suspicion and still recent tensions (e.g. over the Kosovo campaign). Nevertheless, Belarusian and Russian decision-makers have regarded the Alliance's unrivalled domi-nance of security in the Euro-Atlantic region as an undisputed – however unwelcome – reality. Again, a mixed strategy of alternative alliance formation and accommodation with the dominant structure seems to have prevailed. The Belarusian leadership has differed from the Putin administration in placing emphasis on viewing the Union-state as an alternative to Russia and the EU as opposed to developing relations directly with these institutions. Recognition of NATO's military superiority has also driven Belarus and Russia to emulate some of the Alliance's features (the emphasis on air power; the move towards professionalisation and rapid reaction forces), even though material constraints inevitably preclude their effective replication. All the same, the objectives of the Russia–Belarus Union-state reflect a vision which could be described as a hybrid of the NATO and EU models, motivated by the rationale: 'If you cannot join them, emulate them (and learn to live with them)'.

Notes

1 Research for this paper was conducted with the support of the UK Economic and Social Research Council, Award nos. R 00429834663, T 026271003.
2 In April 1993, the Belarusian Supreme Soviet voted overwhelmingly in favour of accession to the CIS Collective Security Treaty, which Stanislau Shushkevich (as Chairman of the Supreme Soviet) had refused to sign in October 1992 on the grounds that such a step would contradict the Belarusian constitutional commitment to neutrality.
3 The index includes indicators such as life expectancy and levels of enrolment in education. In 2001, Belarus was in 53rd place, with Russia in 55th and Ukraine in 74th (UNDP 2001: 142).
4 CPRF member and Duma Chairman Gennady Seleznyev has urged the Russian government to learn from the example of Belarus (*Kommersant* 12 March 1997; author's interview with Russian officials, Moscow, June and November–December 1999.
5 Author's interviews, Minsk, November 1999, April 2002.
6 Belarus continues to have the highest inflation in the CIS.
7 When formal relations with the EU were frozen in 1997, the PCA had not entered in force, as the process of its ratification by EU member-states had not been completed. Belarus has continued to receive humanitarian aid from the EU and Belarusian NGOs have benefited from EU funding through the TACIS Civil Society programme.
8 Author's interviews with Belarusian officials, Minsk, November 1999, April 2002.
9 Author's interviews with Western diplomats and Belarusian opposition politicians, Minsk, April 2002.
10 Author's interviews in the Belarusian Foreign Ministry, Minsk, April 2002.
11 Documents provided by the Belarusian Foreign Ministry (spring 2000). This point is made also by Laptyonok 1999: 44.
12 Lukashenka's interview with Yevgeny Revenko on the programme 'Vesti', Russian television network RTR, 24 May 2000; transcript provided by the Belarusian Foreign Ministry.
13 Interview with leading sociologist Aleh Manayeu, Minsk, 10 April 2002
14 Author's interviews with the aforementioned politicians, Minsk, April 2002.
15 From Lukashenka's aforementioned interview, broadcast on RTR (24 May 2000).
16 See note 15.

17 Lukashenka's address to the Russian State Duma on 27 October 1999 (*Rossiiskaya Federatsiya Segodnya*, 10 November 1999: 11).

18 Documents provided by the Belarusian Foreign Ministry, spring 2000.

19 China and the EU are also regarded as prospective regional centres in a multipolar world order.

20 Allegations of a CIS plot to overthrow Lukashenka had surfaced as early as 1997 (*Nezavisimaya Gazeta* 27 July 1997). See also Lukashenka's interview in *Rossiiskaya Federatsiya* 9 August 1999.

21 Author's interview, Minsk, 19 November 1999.

22 Lukashenka's address to the Russian State Duma, 27 October 1999 (*Rossiiskaya Federatsiya Segodnya* 10 November 1999: 9).

23 Author's interviews with Belarusian officials, Minsk, April 2002.

24 Author's interviews with Belarusian officials, Minsk, November 1999. See also Rozanov 1998: 6–7.

25 Author's interviews, Minsk, April 2002.

26 The chair of the Executive Committee had a consultative vote (Community Treaty, Art. 9; Union Treaty, Art. 20).

27 Normative acts passed by the Parliamentary Assembly had the status of 'legislative recommendations', whose function it was to assist the harmonisation of national legislations (Union Treaty, Art. 23).

28 The Russian State Customs Committee announced that it had raised USD 2.5 billion in duties levied on imports from third countries arriving through the 'Belarusian corridor' in the first half of 1999 alone (*NG* 24 May 2000).

29 'Programme of Synchronisation and Coordination of Economic Reforms', *Diplomatichesky Vestnik* May 1997: 38.

30 This produced a disorderly state of affairs characterised by the simultaneous existence of several exchange rates (official rate set by the National Bank; interbank rate used by commercial banks; unofficial and black market rates).

31 This request was granted by the Union State Council of Ministers (*NG* 14 September 2000).

32 This provision is included in the Union State Treaty. The Belarusian National Bank had favoured the Union State Bank with coordinating functions over two national emission centres.

33 Author's interviews with Russian and Belarusian officials, Moscow, June and November–December 1999; Minsk, November 1999.

34 Author's interview, Moscow, 29 November 1999.

35 Art. 17 of the agreement 'On Cooperation and Coordination' of January 1995, (*BMD* August 1995: 35).

36 Interviews at the Belarusian Foreign Ministry, Minsk, April 2002.

37 According to the relevant agreements, the Baranavichy and Vileyka installations do not have the legal status of military bases and may not host in excess of 1450 Russian (military and civilian) personnel.

38 This is provided by the treaty 'On Joint Efforts in the Guarding of the State Border of the Republic of Belarus' (February 1995). The Border Control Committee was established in April 1997 to organise Border Troops activities and assist the formulation of a Union border policy.

39 This formation is provided by Art. 17 of the Union State Treaty.

40 Sixty-one Belarusian officers attended Russian military academies in 1998. This figure had risen to 103 by 2000 (*NG* 19 April 2000).

41 Interviews with leading Russian experts, Foreign Ministry officials and politicians, Moscow, January–February 2002.

Part IV
Security politics in the CIS periphery

9   Security concerns in post-Soviet Moldova

Trevor Waters

Introduction

Conflict in Moldova quickened with the nationalist ferment over matters of language, culture and identity which consumed the Soviet republic in 1989 and surfaced with the secession of Gagauzia and Transnistria in 1990. Civil war, unresolved problems of territorial separatism, ethno-linguistic strife, Romanian irredentism, Great-Russian chauvinism and, most recently, the issue of re-Russification number among the most important security concerns that have plagued the Republic of Moldova since its declaration of independence on 27 August 1991. This chapter examines some of the background factors which generated such problems (some of which may appear to have a characteristic borderland nature, and may, indeed, be typical of borderland states), and reviews the progress that has been made towards their solution.

History and geography

[Moldovans and Romanians have always spoken of 'Moldova', while in the West – until the 1990s – we usually called the territory by its Russian and Latin name 'Moldavia'. 'Dnestr' (or variants 'Dniester', 'Dniestr') is the Russian designation for the river the Moldovans and Romanians known as the 'Nistru'. From the Moldovan/Romanian standpoint the region to the east across the Nistru is, of course, 'Transnistria', which is known, however, in Russian as Pridnestrov'ye, or 'the land on the Dnestr.' The unrecognised separatist state in eastern Moldova is called the Dnestr Moldovan Republic (DMR).]

Founded by the Romanians in 1359, at the height of its power under Ştefan cel Mare (the Great, 1457–1504) the independent Principality of Moldova extended from the Carpathian Mountains and the forests of Bucovina in the west and north to the Danube and Dnestr rivers and the Black Sea. By the mid-sixteenth century, however, Moldova, like the Romanian Principality of Wallachia, had become a vassal state of the Ottoman Porte. Moldova first came under Russian rule in 1812 when Alexander I annexed the eastern half of the principality (a conquest that Romanian historian Nicolae Iorga later decried as 'the rape of Bessarabia') (King 2000: 32),[1] while the subsequent unification of the western half of the principality (which retained the name of Moldova) with Wallachia in 1859 under Prince Alexandru Cuza marked the birth of the modern Romanian state.

Bessarabia (the Russian designation for the territory between the Dnestr and the Prut, derived from an erstwhile Romanian ruling house of Basarab) remained Russian from its liberation from the Turks in 1812 until 1918, when it proclaimed its independence from the collapsing Tsarist Empire as the Democratic Republic of Moldova, and was united with Romania. Bessarabia remained a province of 'Greater Romania' throughout the interwar period, but control of the inter-fluvial region – the 'Bessarabian question' – continued to be a source of tension between Moscow and Bucharest.

The secret protocols of the 1939 Molotov–Ribbentrop Non-Aggression Pact allowed the Soviet Union to annex the eastern half of the Romanian province of Moldova in 1940 and the annexation was confirmed in the 1947 Peace Treaty between the USSR and Romania. In accordance with Stalin's 'divide and rule' nationalities policy, two of the three regions of the annexed territory, Northern Bucovina in the north and Southern Bessarabia in the south, were transferred to Ukraine (and now form Chernivtsi oblast and the southern part of Odessa oblast respectively). A strip of land along the eastern (or left) bank of the Dnestr/Nistru (Transnistria) was detached from Ukraine, however, and added to the central region of the annexed territory to become (in 1940/44) the Moldovan Soviet Socialist Republic (MSSR) and (in 1991) the sovereign Republic of Moldova. Part of the legacy of this shifting borderland between Romania and Russia is that Moldova has never existed as an independent state within its present frontiers, which significantly include territory east of the Dnestr that has never belonged to the Moldovan–Romanian space. Moreover, fragments of the mediaeval Principality of Moldova currently lie in three separate states and constitute the Romanian province of Moldova, parts of Chernivtsi and Odessa oblasts in Ukraine, and the bulk of the territory of the Republic of Moldova (i.e. less Transnistria).

In 1990, the Popular Front of Moldova made strident calls for the reintegration of the 'historic Moldovan lands' of Northern Bucovina and Southern Bessarabia, while Ukraine flatly rejected what it regarded as irredentist pretensions. In November 1994, however, Moldova and Ukraine signed an agreement which stipulated that the two sides have no territorial claims on each other. Moldova is the only former Soviet republic that potentially constitutes an object of foreign irredentism – a fact that has seriously complicated Romanian–Moldovan relations since Moldovan independence.

The sliver of land along the eastern bank of the Dnestr, which constitutes 12 per cent of Moldova's territory and provides the focus for the continuing confrontation, has never been considered part of the traditional Moldovan lands, although it has always contained a sizeable Moldovan population (indeed, the Dnestr river is generally thought to be the eastern border of the Romanian ethno-cultural space). Prior to the Revolution in 1917 the left-bank Dnestr territory belonged to the Tsarist Empire. It subsequently became the western part of the Moldovan Autonomous Soviet Socialist Republic (MASSR, capital Balta, later Tiraspol) – a Moldovan 'homeland' in Ukraine known as 'Bessarabia in miniature' – which the Soviets established in 1924 to put pressure on Romania and buttress their claim to Bessarabia. In Transnistria, then, unlike in western Moldova, Sovietisation, and with it Russification, for instance the use of the Cyrillic alphabet, was enforced for more than seventy years. Indeed, since the region formed a border area until World War Two and was thus ideologically vulnerable, in part because of ethno-linguistic ties with Romania across the Dnestr, Sovietisation was enforced with especial vigilance and vigour. Bright lights burned permanently in Soviet Tiraspol to impress the Bessarabian peasants under the Romanian landlord-capitalist yoke across the river (King 2000: 56)!

When the Romanian army – an ally of Nazi Germany – advanced into the Soviet Union during World War Two it was wholly determined to destroy communism in Transnistria. Excess of zeal in pursuing this aim resulted in brutality and atrocities, which linger in the Transnistrian folk memory, reinforcing fear and suspicion of Romania to this day.

Post-war economic policy sought to develop western Moldova as an agricultural area, while industrialisation – often of a defence-related nature – was concentrated mainly in Transnistria where 17 per cent of the MSSR's total population provided almost 90 per cent of the republic's energy and more than one third of its industrial production (Nedelciuc 1992: 97; Hanne 1998: 10).

Moldovan agricultural development had not, of course, been subject to the Soviet collectivisation disasters of the 1920s and 1930s, and the local peasantry on the west bank adapted well to the relatively painless collectivisation of the post-war period. As was the case throughout the Soviet Union, the peasants were allowed to engage in small-scale private enterprise farming. A successful, entrepreneurial peasant farming outlook and mentality survived better than elsewhere in Soviet territory and forms an important element in the mindset of the population in western Moldova today. Agriculture in Soviet Moldova was, on the whole, efficient, productive and successful – in sharp contrast to most other parts of the Union – and some of the best talent took up agricultural management as a career.

Urbanised and heavily industrialised, Transnistria consists of five *raiony* (or districts) and the city of Tiraspol. It has a mixed population of 40.1 per cent Moldovans (the largest single ethnic group), 28.3 per cent Ukrainians and 25.5 per cent Russians, according to the last USSR census in 1989. Until the 1960s Moldovans made up the absolute majority on the left bank, but their proportion declined as a result of centrally promoted immigration, particularly from the RSFSR, into the cities to man the factories. This population flow has increased in recent years, and many of today's left-bank inhabitants emigrated from remote areas of Russia during the 1980s, including 'President' Igor Smirnov of the self-styled, breakaway 'Dnestr Moldovan Republic' (DMR), who came from Siberia in 1985. Opposite the city of Tiraspol, where the Russians are concentrated and form a majority of the population, on the right bank of the Dnestr is the town of Tighina (Bendery), an important junction, linked by rail and road bridges. Bendery, too, was industrialised and populated by Russian workers following World War Two, and became an enclave of the left bank located on the right bank of the river.

The strategic significance of Moldova

A distinction may be drawn between Moldova's global strategic significance and its regional strategic significance. During the Cold War the territory of Moldova – in peacetime – formed part of the Soviet Union's Odessa Military District. In the event of war it would have been mobilised to provide support for a strategic offensive operation in the South-western Theatre of Military Operations against the Balkans, Greece and Turkey, with the Suez Canal and the North African coast as its second strategic objective. The headquarters for this strategic axis was located in Chişinău (Kishinev). With the end of the Cold War, the collapse of communism and the demise of the Soviet Union, Moldova has lost its global strategic significance. It remains interesting to note, however, that (the now deceased) General Aleksandr Lebed, commander-in-chief of Russian forces in the DMR (1992–95), described the Dnestr area as 'the key to the Balkans', observing that 'if Russia withdraws from this little piece of land, it will lose that key and its influence in the region'.[2]

National defence and civil war

Following the June 1990 declaration on state sovereignty, on 27 August 1991 the Republic of Moldova proclaimed independence and, by September, President Mircea Snegur had already signed the decree that was to lead to the establishment of national armed forces. In addition to the National Army, which is charged with ensuring the military security of the republic, there are also the Frontier Troops of the Ministry of National Security and the Interior Ministry's lightly armed Gendarmerie Forces for the maintenance of public order. The year 1992 witnessed the establishment of the Ministry of Defence, the appointment of the first Moldovan defence minister, and the passing of defence legislation.

Unhappily, the same year also saw the outbreak of a full-scale, local civil war with Transnistrian separatists strongly supported by elements of Russia's highly politicised 14th Army. Whether under the Soviet, Commonwealth of Independent States (CIS), or Russian flag, throughout 1990–91 and subsequently, the 14th Army covertly provided the Transnistrian separatists with weapons, training facilities, manpower, finance, moral and administrative support; occasionally such transfers included whole sub-units from 14th Army. This provided a traumatic baptism of fire for the nascent armed forces of the Republic: some 500 people were killed, many more wounded, while refugees perhaps numbered 100,000, though exact figures remain unclear.[3]

Since late July 1992 the Moldovan Army has been deployed on peacekeeping duties – highly significantly – on the territory of the republic itself. Having failed to secure any UN (or indeed any CIS) involvement in a peacekeeping role, President Snegur was finally constrained by Moscow to accept what was essentially a Russian peacekeeping force. The Yeltsin–Snegur agreement of 21 July 1992 provided for a ceasefire, the creation of a security zone on both sides of the Nistru River and the deployment of a joint Russian–Moldovan–DMR peacekeeping force under the day-to-day supervision of a trilateral Joint Control Commission.[4] Originally the peacekeeping forces comprised six Russian battalions (3600 men), three Moldovan battalions (1200 men),and three DMR battalions (1200 men).

As early as September 1992, Moldova publicly challenged the impartiality of the Russian peacekeepers, charging them with allowing the DMR separatists to maintain men and material in the security zone. The DMR, for its part, was able to continue to create and consolidate the structures of an independent 'state' (government departments, armed forces, border guards, banking system, etc.) under the protection of the peacekeepers.

Politics and ideology

The confrontation on the Dnestr is essentially a political struggle. In Moldovan eyes, the political and ideological forces that underpinned the abortive coup of August 1991 – hard-line communism, Russian nationalism, the military–industrial complex and the determination to preserve the union state – have retained a power base in the heavily militarised region and Russified industrial centres on the left bank. Troops of what has now become the Operational Group of Russian Forces in the Dnestr Region of the Republic of Moldova (OGRF), commanded by Russian officers with a political axe to grind, so the Moldovans say, furthered and continue to further the cause of local Russian or other non-indigenous factions, in a former Soviet republic against the properly constituted state authorities of the newly-independent host country. In short, the Russian military actively supported an armed insurgency whose aim was to establish on the territory of an internationally recognised sovereign state a Soviet-style outpost, the so-called DMR, in a post-Soviet world.

The highly Sovietised population of Transnistria, reinforced by a Russian industrialised workforce, suspicious of the peasant free-market mentality of the right bank, alarmed by the restoration of the Latin alphabet and by the declaration that Moldovan (i.e. Romanian) was to be the official language of the Republic together with Russian, and by the adoption of a version of the

Romanian tricolour as the Moldovan flag, and fearful of the possibility of unification of the new state with Romania, naturally enough saw matters very differently.

On 2 September 1990 Transnistria declared its secession from Moldova. This left-bank refuge for the 'Socialist Choice' enthusiastically hailed the attempted coup in August 1991 while, from the very beginning, western Moldova resolutely defied the putsch, vigorously supported RSFSR President Yeltsin's democratic stand, and resisted peacefully, yet successfully, military attempts to impose the junta's state of emergency.

The DMR subsequently played host to numerous representatives of Russia's red–brown (communist–nationalist) ideological forces, including hundreds of Cossack mercenaries determined to 'defend their blood brothers' and to 'hold the frontier of the Russian state', together with a string of virulently national-istic demagogues like Vladimir Zhirinovsky, Sergei Baburin, Albert Makashov and Viktor Alksnis, the last of whom described the DMR as the base from which the Soviet Union's restoration would begin (Socor 1992a; Bowers 1993: 435–7). Makashov was one of the principal leaders of the Moscow October 1993 insurgency (in which Baburin and Alksnis were also implicated), while Zhirinovsky (leader of the misnamed Russian Liberal Democratic Party which secured an alarmingly high percentage of the vote in Russian elections) spoke of transforming Moldova into a Russian *guberniya*, or province. *Sovetskaya Rossiya* described the DMR as 'an island of Soviet power' and 'a frontier of Russia' (Socor 1993a).

The ethnic factor

The total population of Moldova is 4,335,000, of whom 754,000 live in the capital city, Chişinău. The largest ethnic group, the Moldovans themselves, number 2,798,000 (or 64.5 per cent of the total population). Of the three other major ethnic groups, the 600,000 Ukrainians (13.8 per cent) come second, with 562,000 Russians (13 per cent) in third place, followed by the 153,500 Gagauzi (who constitute 3.5 per cent of the population but who are concentrated in the southern corner of Moldova, along the border with Ukraine). Bulgarians account for two per cent of the total population. Some 70 per cent of Moldova's Russians live in western Moldova, 30 per cent in the DMR. The ethnic mix in the DMR consists of 40.1 per cent Moldovans, 28.3 per cent Ukrainians, 25.5 per cent Russians and various other minor national groups.

The Gagauzi are Turkic-speaking Orthodox Christians whose ancestors fled Ottoman rule in north-east Bulgaria during and after the Russo–Turkish war of 1806–12. There have never, therefore, been any grounds for religious tension between them and the indigenous population. Most of the refugees settled in Bessarabia, which became Russian territory in 1812. Some 140,000 of Moldova's 153,000 Gagauzi are concentrated in south-western Moldova.

The DMR Russians, it must be emphasised, form but a minority in what they regard as their 'little piece of Russia'. Indeed, numerically speaking, they constitute a minority within a minority, for they represent only 30 per cent of Moldova's total Russian population and only 25 per cent of the total population of the left bank. However, given their strong-arm military backing and the *de facto* partition of Moldova, some 170,000 DMR Russians continue to be in a position to constrain severely the social and political choices of the Transnistrian Moldovan and Ukrainian majority ethnic groups, whom they have now effectively isolated from the Moldovan heartland and from the political process in Chişinău.

The DMR Russians never lost an opportunity to play the ethnic card for all that it is worth. Presenting themselves as an unfortunate minority whose human rights were being trampled underfoot by Chişinău's repressive policies of enforced Romanianisation and de-Sovietisation, they fuelled ultra-nationalist sentiments in Russia, and prevailed upon Moscow to adopt a robust posture with regard to the protection of Russian interests abroad. They have, of course, succeeded in securing Moscow's 'protection' with the help of Russian peacekeeping forces and the Operational Group of Russian Forces (OGRF).

It is instructive to recall that in Moldova (as throughout the former Soviet Union), administration, the education system and the media greatly favoured the Russian population. Moldovan and Ukrainian schools and publications were far fewer than proportional representation of their populations would entail. Of Moldova's 600,000 Ukrainians, only 52,000 claim to be fully proficient in Ukrainian, while 220,000 say they no longer know their native tongue. Facilities for Ukrainians in the DMR are very poor, and today most Ukrainians there speak Russian.

For all the inflammatory nationalistic and pan-Slavic rhetoric that still emanates from Tiraspol (and still finds echoes in certain circles in Moscow), and for all the provocative manipulation of the ethnic card and of human rights issues, in general inter-ethnic relations in Moldova at large have not been adversely affected. More than 70 per cent of Moldova's Slavic population resides in western Moldova and does not appear to feel threatened to any significant extent following Moldovan independence. With few exceptions this Slavic majority is strongly in favour of Moldova's territorial integrity and the reintegration of Transnistria, and has not sided with the DMR Russians in any way.

Military and paramilitary forces on both sides, including the combat elements that fought in the 1992 civil war, are ethnically mixed. Casualty figures correctly reflect the ethnic mix of the populations in question and thus provide further grim evidence that the conflict is not an inter-ethnic dispute. On the left bank, for example, Moldovan casualties predominate, followed by Ukrainians and Russians. However, a great many Russians and Ukrainians – some of whom served with distinction – were killed or injured fighting for the Moldovan central government cause. A 'Transnistrian people' as such does not, of course, exist, and the Moldovan civil war has not split the population of Moldova along ethnic lines.

The Russian army in Moldova: support for Transnistrian separatism

Based in Moldova since 1956, the Soviet 14th (Guards) Army, headquartered in Tiraspol, was transferred to the CIS Armed Forces in January 1992. President Yeltsin's decree of 1 April 1992 subsequently placed what remained of the 14th Army under Russian jurisdiction.

Moscow equivocated and prevaricated with respect to the 14th Army's involvement in the 1992 conflict, which culminated in the battle for Bendery that was, in fact, won by the Dnestr insurgents with substantial support from the 14th Army. The Russian army was said to have remained neutral, to have disobeyed orders, to have intervened as a local initiative, to have been ordered to make a show of force, to defend Russian-speaking areas, and to take retaliatory action against Moldova for committing crimes against Russians (Socor 1992b).

By late June 1992, when General Aleksandr Lebed was appointed army commander, Russian combat power in Moldova consisted essentially of one somewhat under-strength and under-equipped division: the 59th Motor Rifle Division. Lebed accused Moldova of being a 'fascist state', said its leaders were 'war criminals', called the defence minister a 'cannibal', referred to Moldovans as 'oxen' and 'sheep', and described his army as 'belonging to the Dnestr people' (*Sovetskaya Rossiya* 7 July 1992; Socor 1993c). Lebed predicted the end of Moldova's independence and its return to a reconstituted Union, and declared that the 14th Army would remain in Moldova indefinitely. Russia's 14th Army continued throughout 1993 and beyond to recruit residents of Moldova's Transnistrian region in violation of international law.

In October 1994, Moldova and Russia concluded an agreement for the withdrawal of the 14th Army from Moldova over a period of three years, which for DMR 'President' Smirnov was 'unacceptable', and for Lebed a 'crime'. However, the withdrawal was to be synchronised with the settlement of the conflict in Transnistria. Moreover, from 1994 onwards Russia has sought to make its *de facto* military base in Transnistria *de jure* – a move that Moldova has so far been able to resist (Gribincea 1998).

Following Russian Defence Minister Grachev's April 1995 directive on the reorganisation of 14th Army and Yeltsin's June decree on removing Lebed from military service, Major-General Valeri Yevnevich was appointed commander-in-chief of the renamed Operational Group of Russian Forces (OGRF) in the Dnestr region of the Republic of Moldova (Waters 1996: 398–401). All members of the OGRF must now hold Russian citizenship. There are hardly any delays over pay.

At the OSCE Istanbul summit in November 1999, Russia again undertook to withdraw the OGRF, including the huge stockpiles of munitions located near Colbasna, by the end of 2002. By the turn of the century the overall strength of OGRF/14th Army had already been reduced from over 9000 in mid-1992 to about 2500 men.

Local autonomy in Gagauz-Yeri

The self-styled Republic of Gagauzia proclaimed its independence from Moldova in August 1990. A 600-strong force of irregulars – the so-called *Bugeac* battalion (who were supported militarily and politically by the DMR separatists) – was formed to protect the interests of the breakaway republic. To this end the paramilitaries seized weapons and conducted occasional armed raids on government installations in southern Moldova. Following delicate and protracted negotiations between Chişinău and Komrat (the capital of the unrecognised republic), Moldova accorded a 'special judicial status' to Gagauz-Yeri (the Gagauz Land) in January 1995. Moldova's creation of an autonomous territorial unit as a form of self-determination for the Gagauzi and a constituent part of the Republic of Moldova – the first move of its kind by an East European state – received praise as a potential model for resolving ethnic disputes in post-communist Europe. A referendum was held to determine which villages would join Gagauz-Yeri. Georgi Tabunshchik, an ethnic Gagauz, was elected to the post of 'bashkan' (or governor), and there were elections to the legislative body for the region.

In June 1995 after the elections, the then Prime Minister Andrei Sangheli declared an end to the conflict between the Gagauz separatists and Moldova. The *Bugeac* battalion was formally disbanded, an amnesty was granted for the handover of weapons, and the paramilitaries were incorporated into the specially created, so-called 'Military Unit 1045' of the Interior Ministry's Gendarmerie Forces.

It was to take some while, as Vasile Uzun, the bashkan's first deputy, emphasised at the time, 'for the rule of law to replace the rule of the gun'.[5] Gagauz-Yeri remains an economically backward area whose agricultural yield is particularly susceptible to Moldova's recurrent droughts. But Moldova has 'solved the Gagauz problem', as the Turkish defence minister put it at the time, in so far, at least, that instability in the region no longer represents a threat to the integrity of the state.

Partnership for peace, neutrality and NATO

On 16 March 1994, Moldova became the twelfth state (and fifth former Soviet republic) to enrol in NATO's Partnership for Peace (PfP) programme (the DMR leadership deplored the fact that Tiraspol had not been consulted). At the signing ceremony in Brussels, President Snegur highlighted his country's policy of neutrality, pointing out that Moldova did not belong to the military structures of the CIS, and elected – unlike most of the earlier signatories – not to raise the possibility of eventual NATO membership. Snegur also said, however, that Moldova's participation in the PfP programme would help to strengthen the territorial integrity, political independence and national security of his country; moreover, the main obstacle to a settlement of the conflict between Moldova and Transnistria was the presence of Russia's 14th Army on Moldovan territory (ITAR-TASS World Service 16 March 1994).

The new Constitution adopted by parliament on 28 July 1994 proclaims Moldova a neutral, sovereign, independent and indivisible state, with equal rights for all minorities. Article 11, in particular, stipulates that 'The Republic of Moldova declares its permanent neutrality [and] does not admit the stationing of foreign military units on its territory'. The provisions of Article 11 are reiterated in the foreign policy concept adopted by parliament in February 1995: 'The Republic of Moldova is pursuing a policy of permanent neutrality, having undertaken not to participate in armed conflicts, in political, military or economic alliances having the aim of preparing for war, not to utilise its territory for the stationing of foreign military bases, and not to possess nuclear weapons, nor to manufacture or test them'.[6] On 5 May 1995 parliament adopted a national security concept, which yet again emphasised that 'Moldova is a demilitarised state and it will not permit the deployment of foreign troops or military bases on its territory and maintains relations of friendship and partnership with all countries' (Interfax 5 May 1995). On 6 June 1995 parliament adopted the military doctrine which 'is determined by foreign and domestic policy, by the constitutional declaration of permanent neutrality, [and] has an exclusively defensive character'.[7]

Moldova has never regarded NATO enlargement in any way as a threat to its security, nor has it raised objections to eventual Romanian or even Ukrainian membership. Chişinău has always insisted that enlargement should not take place to the detriment of Russia, or without taking Russia's interests into account when admitting new members. Indeed, the importance of a special relationship between NATO and Russia, and between NATO and Ukraine, has been underscored. Chişinău has stressed that NATO enlargement must not create tensions or draw new dividing lines in Europe, but should lead to the consolidation of stability and security on the continent. Moreover, an enlarging NATO must provide security guarantees to neutral countries such as Moldova. Chişinău regards cooperation with NATO primarily as a means to support Moldova's efforts to re-establish territorial integrity and to promote the withdrawal of Russian troops. Tiraspol, by contrast, points to NATO 'expansion' as an additional justification both for the region's separatist course and the continued presence of Russian troops in Transnistria.

Moldova and Romania

For nearly half a century of communist dictatorship following annexation, the border was sealed between Soviet Moldova and Romania. Despite the genuine ethno-linguistic links between Romanians and the majority of Moldovans, the Soviets enforced the notion (which is by no means wholly a fiction) of a separate Moldovan 'people' and 'language' (as distinct from Romanians and Romanian). In an address to the Romanian Parliament in February 1991 (on the first official visit to Romania by any leader from

Soviet Moldova since its annexation), the then President Snegur strongly affirmed the common Moldovan–Romanian identity, noting that 'We have the same history and speak the same language', and referred to 'Romanians on both sides of the River Prut'. In June 1991 the Romanian parliament vehemently denounced the Soviet annexation of Bessarabia and Northern Bucovina, describing the territories as 'sacred Romanian lands'. The Romanian foreign minister subsequently referred to the 'evanescence' of Romania's borders with Bessarabia and Northern Bucovina.

Following cultural Romanianisation and the eventual independence of Moldova, there was a general expectation, especially in Romania, though also to some extent in Moldova (despite Chişinău's doctrine of 'two independent Romanian states'), that the two countries should and would unite. The underlying feeling at the time was that the Romanians wanted their country (which they, at least, saw as having been dismembered by the Molotov–Ribbentrop Pact) to be reunited. The Moldovans, however, after their initial, and perhaps injudicious, acquiescence in the idea during their first stirrings of national self-awareness, clearly no longer shared the Romanians' enthusiasm. In January 1993, four senior parliamentarians, all moderate advocates of unification with Romania, were forced to resign their posts (Socor 1993b). Throughout 1993, Moldova continued to distance herself from Romania and abandoned her notion of 'two independent Romanian states'. Throughout the 1990s Moldova has striven to establish a truly independent, multi-ethnic state and there has been no desire to trade a Russian 'big brother' for a Romanian one. Opinion polls consistently revealed that less than ten per cent of Moldova's population support unification with Romania.

In June 1994 Moldova dropped the Romanian national anthem 'Romanian, Awake!' which it had borrowed in 1991, at which time eventual unification with Romania was envisaged. Chişinău repeatedly reproached the Romanian government for its unwillingness to come to terms with the idea of real independence for the Republic of Moldova: Romania should let Moldova 'be master in its own home' and 'strictly respect the right of [Moldova's] people to determine their own future.'

Moldovan–Romanian treaty negotiations started as long ago as 1992. Given the special nature of their historical, ethnic, cultural and linguistic affinities, Moldovan–Romanian relations are very close, yet also rather delicate. A basic bilateral treaty was initialled in Chişinău by Moldovan and Romanian foreign ministers, Nicolae Tabacaru and Petre Roman, in April 2000, and awaits approval by the two countries' presidents and legislatures (Baleanu 2000).

Recent developments: the 'Moldovan Syndrome', the language issue and re-Russification

Recent developments in Moldova give cause for concern. The 'Moldovan Syndrome', as *Novoye Vremya*, the Chişinău Russian-language Democratic

Party newspaper called it at the time, is this: Moldova is the only CIS country to have returned the Communist Party to power (*Novoye Vremya* 27 February 2001). Significantly, the 25 February 2001 parliamentary elections conformed to international standards for democratic elections. With a 69 per cent voter turnout, the Party of Communists of the Republic of Moldova (PCRM) secured seventy-one seats in the 101-member legislature. As Moldova is a parliamentary republic, such a landslide victory did indeed mark a spectacular return of the communists to power. It was the first time this had happened in post-Soviet history. With such a massive majority, Moldova's communists not only became the governing party, but were able to elect their leader, Vladimir Voronin, as president of the Republic and head-of-state, and also have a majority large enough to make changes to the constitution.[8]

Left-wing parties have dominated political developments in Moldova since independence in August 1991. Such parties have their roots either in the former Communist Party of the Moldovan Soviet Socialist Republic, or in the *Unitatea/Yedinstvo* (Unity) movement that emerged in 1989, mainly among Russian speakers who wished to preserve Moldova's relationship with the Soviet Union, and as a reaction to the pro-Romanian and right-wing Popular Front (*Yedinstvo* was, in fact, the Moldovan branch of the all-Union Interfront movement that united political forces inimical to the cultural and linguistic reforms of the late Soviet period).

The centre-right wing of the political spectrum (the successor parties of the Popular Front Movement) has suffered especially from continuous splits, coalition reshuffles and shifting alliances, and is in general characterised by a high degree of fragmentation. Of the seventeen parties/electoral blocs participating in the 2001 elections, fourteen (of which ten had a centre-right political orientation) failed to clear the (new and high) six per cent threshold for parliamentary representation. Some 28 per cent of voters are not repre-sented in parliament and the centre-right electorate effectively made a gift to the communists of some twenty parliamentary seats.

Moldova is the poorest country in Europe (*Economist* 2000; 2001). GDP has fallen to 30 per cent of the pre-independence level. The average wage is about one dollar a day. Some 800,000 pensioners try to subsist on the average pension of about seven dollars per month, though the state has long since been unable to pay pensions and salaries on time. Malnutrition, tuber-culosis and hepatitis are on the rise; life expectancy has been reduced. Roughly 700,000 Moldovans (about one-third of people of working age and one-sixth of the total population) seeking work abroad have in many cases abandoned their children who become 'economic orphans'. Life in general in Moldova, especially in rural areas, is harsh. Such was the background to the February 2001 elections.

Appealing to Soviet nostalgia ('Communists in power – order in the country – welfare in families!'), the PCRM[9] campaigned vigorously for a populist, state-oriented social and economic programme, calling for price controls, broader social guarantees, and for a bigger role for the state in the economy. Granting Russian the status of second state language (language and politics are inextricably linked in Moldova) and considering taking Moldova into the Russia–Belarus Union were also important planks in the PCRM's electoral platform. It seems clear, however, that the communists were swept back into power in a powerful protest vote by an electorate that was frustrated with extreme poverty and with government inaction and lack of reform.

Background to the language issue

Moldova's population of just under 4.5 million includes several ethnic groups but is split largely into Russian and Moldovan/Romanian speakers. Under Gorbachev, *demokratizatsiya* led to demands outside the RSFSR for de-Russification and thus to strengthening the official role and status of the titular republican language. This manifestly challenged the privileged position of local Russians and Russophones in those republics (who were often regarded anyway as occupiers, colonisers or tools of Moscow). There was a backlash among Russophones, especially where jobs were threatened. The ensuing conflict was exploited both by republican nationalists and by communist opponents of reform, thus politicising the language issue. When republics became independent, enshrining the titular language as the official language was closely bound up with the idea of establishing and maintaining full independence. By this time, however, Russian and Russophone minorities had become identified with opposition to democracy and independence. Finding themselves treated as second-class (and probably disloyal) citizens, they turned to Moscow for help. This only served to confirm the suspicion and mistrust of the newly independent states. Issues of language and national identity fuelled the series of conflicts that led to the break-up of the USSR.

Table 9.1 Population of the Republic of Moldova (1989 census)[10]

Ethnic Group	Population	%
Total	4,335,360	100.0
Moldovans	2,794,749	64.5
Ukrainians	600,366	13.8
Russians	562,069	13.0
Gagauzi	153,458	3.5
Bulgarians	88,419	2.0
Jews	65,672	1.5
Roma	11,571	0.3

On 31 August 1989, in a highly charged atmosphere of rallies, strikes and demos, Moldova followed the example of the Baltic republics and passed a law that declared the language of the titular nation to be the official language of the republic. The new language laws also implicitly recognised the identity of Moldovan and Romanian, and restored the Latin alphabet (following their annexation of Moldova in 1940, the Soviets insisted that Moldovan, written in Cyrillic script, was a different language from Romanian in order to promote the idea that Moldovans and Romanians are separate nations). So important was the adoption of the Language Law within the context of the flowering of a non-Soviet, Moldovan national identity, that 31 August, *Limba Noastra* ('Our Language' (Day)), was subsequently declared a national holiday. It is the second most important secular holiday after Independence Day. And 31 August Street, moreover, is one of the main thoroughfares in Chişinău, the Moldovan capital.

Despite the fact that the law provided for Russian to be the language of interethnic communication within Soviet Moldova, 100,000 ethnic Russians went on strike in support of retaining only Russian as the official language. The language reform was also unpopular with the Ukrainians and Gagauzi, who now had to study a third language, Moldovan/Romanian. Indeed, language was the trigger for secession in Transnistria and Gagauzia. Questions of language and national identity remained highly divisive into the mid-1990s. The issue of *what to call the language* (glottonym) was hotly debated prior to the adoption of Moldova's new, post-Soviet Constitution (1994), which defines the state language as 'Moldovan', rather than 'Moldovan (Romanian)' or 'Moldovan which is identical to Romanian', the other options considered. In March and April 1995, thousands of students took to the streets chanting 'Romanian is the official language'.

Russification and political crisis

On 9 January 2002, several thousand people mounted a demonstration in front of Government House in Chişinău in order to protest against the communist regime's introduction of compulsory Russian language study in grade two of primary schools. The protest was organised by the opposition Christian Democratic People's Party (PPCD), whose leader Iurie Roşca called on the demonstrators to oppose the government's enforced 're-Russification' (RFE/RL Balkan Report 11 January 2002) and hailed the protest as a 'wave of national revival'. 'We are Romanians', 'Down with the Bolsheviks!' and 'Don't shove the Russian language down our throats!' chanted the demonstrators, who were mostly younger people and included teachers, parents and students, as well as party political activists.

The anti-Russification protests continued throughout January. Up to forty thousand people (and more when the students returned from vacation) demonstrated in the centre of Chişinău on Grand National Assembly Square, blocking traffic on Ştefan cel Mare Boulevard, the main thoroughfare in the capital. Some 46,000 signatures against the introduction of compulsory Russian were presented to the Ministry of Education. PPCD vice-president Vlad Cubreacov declared that 'the communist regime is a totalitarian one, which serves a linguistic minority, a regime that is no different from the separatist one in Tiraspol' (AP Flux 21 January 2002). Students' Unions, Teachers' Associations and NGOs in other parts of Moldova and, highly significantly, in neighbouring Romania, declared solidarity with the anti-Russification cause. Tensions mounted. The government declared the protests illegal, and on 21 January the Minister of Justice, Ion Morei, temporarily banned the activities of the PPCD, which Council of Europe President Peter Schieder condemned as 'threatening the normal functioning of democracy' (ITAR-TASS 2 February 2002). Chişinău subsequently cancelled the suspension of the activities of the PPCD after the Council of Europe had requested an explanation from Moldova about the decision, which was contrary to basic Articles of the European Convention on Human Rights, and of special concern in view of the forthcoming local elections in Moldova in April (*Basapress* 8 February 2002).

The government decided, on 13 February, to replace curricular texts on Romanian history with a new book on Moldovan history, which re-ignited the general protests against Russification. Although the demonstrations remained peaceful, the protesters now sought the resignation of the government, the parliament and the president, and called for early parliamentary elections. On 15 February, thirty Moldovan NGOs issued a joint statement entitled 'Civic Society Says No', condemning the 'irresponsible actions of the communist authorities, which are aimed at the destruction of the democratic mechanisms on which society is based' (*Basapress* 15 February 2002).

On 17 February, the PPCD called for an anti-government general strike (Interfax 17 February 2002).

The government imposed a moratorium on 21 February on the implementation of the decisions to introduce the Russian language and Moldovan history in school curricula until the end of the academic year (Interfax 21 February 2002). On 22 February, parliament backed down on Russification and voted to cancel the introduction of Russian as a compulsory subject and to delay the scrapping of Romanian history from the school curriculum (Moldovan Radio 22 February 2002). In an address to the nation on state television on 23 February, after yet another day of protests against the government's policy of Russification, President Voronin accused the PPCD leaders, whom he called 'terrorists', of plotting a bloody coup and spreading 'the virus of nationalism' (Interfax 23 February 2002).

On 24 February, an 80,000- strong rally adopted a resolution accusing the communists of suppressing human rights and stifling dissent and calling for civil disobedience. The resolution also called for a complete withdrawal of the Russian military presence from Moldova (*Basapress* 24 February 2002).

Education Minister Ilie Vancea publicly apologised to protesters on 25 February: 'I've made a mistake. I should have been firmer on issues which are sacred to us: our language and history' (*Basapress* 25 February 2002). President Voronin dismissed Ilie Vancea as Education Minister on 26 February (*Basapress* 26 February 2002).

Protests in Chişinău resumed on 26 February despite the latest ruling by the Supreme Court to outlaw the anti-communist demonstrations and rallies. A group of some fifty state television and Radio Moldova journalists issued a statement of protest against the Communist Party's 'reinstatement of Soviet censorship on National Television and Radio'. The journalists also expressed solidarity with the 'popular protests that oppose Russification by force and the deliberate demolition of the democratic system in Moldova' (*Basapress* 26 February 2002).

Conclusion

At the turn of the century there are no immediate external threats to the security of Moldova. The strengthening of the country's independence, which presupposes the continued development of democratic institutions and, most importantly, the yet-to-be-felt emergence of a viable economy, the restoration of Moldova's territorial integrity, together with the withdrawal of the Russian military presence in Transnistria are the major security goals.

It is indeed true, however, that a spectre stalks the land between the Nistru and the Prut. The 2001 elections may have been democratic, but politics in Moldova are far from consensual. How long the demonstrations against Russification continue, and what their outcome will be, remains as yet unclear. But Soviet-nostalgic Moldova is in crisis and likely to remain so for quite some time.

The situation in Transnistria remains very messy. Despite the 1994 accord on Russian military withdrawal, despite the 1997 Moscow Memorandum between Moldova and DMR committing the two sides to existence within a 'common state', despite the 1998 Odessa agreements on demilitarisation and confidence building measures, and despite Russia's commitments at the OSCE Istanbul summit in November 1999 to withdraw its arsenals and troops by the end of 2002, the Russian army remains in Transnistria and the DMR leadership loses no opportunity to consolidate and confirm the structures of an independent state.[11] When Igor Smirnov was re-elected, in December 1996, for another five-year term as DMR 'president', he vowed, 'We will strengthen the independence achieved through such difficulties and defended with blood', and added, 'Transnistria exists in fact; it is a reality'. At the same time Smirnov also said, 'We will categorically insist that the Russian peacekeeping force and formations of the former 14th Brigade remain in the region ... the Russian Army stopped the bloodshed and must stay here' (Interfax 23 December 1996). It was with great military pomp and ceremony that the breakaway republic celebrated its tenth anniversary on Independence Day, 2 September 2000.[12]

It seems highly likely that, for good, old-fashioned geopolitical reasons, Moscow will continue to pursue the policy of equivocation and prevarication that has characterised its military involvement in Transnistria since the creation of an independent Moldovan state in 1991. In one guise or another – OGRF, peacekeepers or military bases – there will almost certainly be a Russian military presence in Moldova as the Dnestr conflict smoulders on for quite some time to come.

Notes

1 Professor King's admirable study is the first and, as yet, the only English-language book to offer a complete account of Moldova and the Moldovans.
2 Interviews with Lebed (*Izvestiya* 26 February 1993; Russian TV 16 March 1993).
3 Moldovan government figures are given in Nedelciuc 1992; for the Transnistrian view see, for example, Babilunga and Bomeshko 1993.
4 *Soglasheniye o printsipakh mirnogo uregulirovaniya konflikta v pridnestrovskom regione respubliki moldova* (Agreement on the principles for a peaceful settlement of the armed conflict in the Transnistrian region of the Republic of Moldova), signed in Moscow on 21 July 1992 by presidents Mircea Snegur and Boris Yeltsin.
5 Author's interview in Komrat, July 1996.
6 *Kontseptsiya vneshney politiki respubliki moldova*, adopted by Parliamentary Resolution No 368-XII, 8 February 1995.
7 See 'General Provisions' section, '*Doctrina militară a Republicii Moldova'*, adopted by Parliamentary Resolution No 482-XIII, 6 June 1995. A summary of the doctrine together with analysis and comment is offered in Waters 1998.
8 Following the 5 July 2000 constitutional reform, the president was no longer to be elected by popular vote, but through a vote of parliament with a three-fifths majority, or sixty-one mandates. The former legislature failed to elect a new president in December 2000 as successor to outgoing Petru Lucinschi, who accordingly dissolved parliament and set the date for early elections on 25 February 2001. On 4 April 2001, parliament elected Vladimir Voronin, leader of the PCRM, as the third president of Moldova. Voronin secured seventy-one votes, his two rivals fifteen and three votes, with eighty-nine of the 101 deputies taking part in the vote. With seventy-one seats in parliament, Moldova's communists also enjoy a so-called constitutional majority: sixty-eight mandates are required to amend the Constitution.
9 The Soviet-era Communist Party of Moldova was banned with the collapse of the Soviet Union. The Party of Communists of the Republic of Moldova was established in 1995. The resurrected communist party was prevented by law from using the designation 'Communist Party of Moldova', hence the rather strange name 'Party of Communists of the Republic of Moldova'.
10 The most recent (Soviet,1989) census still provides the most reliable figures available. In April 2002 the government abandoned plans to conduct a census in October due to the lack of funds. It is worth noting that the Russians are not (albeit by a very small margin) the largest minority in Moldova. However, the Ukrainians, like the other minorities, including the Turkic Gagauzi, are heavily Russified.
11 In June 2000, OSCE Ambassador to Moldova William Hill stated: 'Since the Istanbul document was signed, there has been absolutely no progress on fulfilling the commitments ... The situation, unfortunately, has been frozen'. In late November 2000, Ambassador Hill said that it would be 'very difficult' for Russia

to complete its pullout by the end of 2002 (SIPRI 2001: 558–60). Withdrawal and destruction of a small part of the estimated 40,000 tons of ordnance was indeed accomplished during 2001, but since December 2001 the Tiraspol authorities have obstructed the process by blocking access to the ammunition dumps. Russia doubtless finds it highly convenient merely to look on.

12 Article 11 of the DMR Constitution (adopted following a referendum in December 1995) states that the 'Armed Forces are created for the defence of the sovereignty and independence of the DMR'.

10 Security regime building in the South Caucasus

Tamara Pataraia and David Darchiashvili

Over a decade since independence, the South Caucasian states still face strong external and internal challenges, which directly affect their prestige, sovereignty and national security prospects in a negative way. Internal weakness, manifested in strong ethnic tensions, severe economic problems and political instability, hampered the process of strengthening the statehood and sovereignty of these states. These problems also slowed the pace by which the South Caucasus was able to strengthen its ties to Western European political and security institutions.

The emergence of the post-Soviet independent and sovereign states was closely tied to serious systematic changes that took place in the international arena, as bipolar confrontation faded and the foundations for the emergence of military–political alliances were transformed. For the first time since 1939, small states were able to develop their foreign and security policies in accordance with their national interests, and establish relations with various regional or sub-regional security structures. Modern researchers emphasised that in the new international environment small states 'are not tied to the balancing-bandwagoning dynamics to the same degree as during the Cold War' (Inbar and Sheffer 1997: 49).

The post-communist states of Central and Eastern Europe unconditionally linked their national security strategies with accession into the Euro-Atlantic security structures, namely NATO. Russia aside, amongst the Soviet successor states only the governments of the Baltic countries exhibited surprising political willingness and intellectual determination for independent state-building. For the last ten years they have made significant, coherent and successful steps to achieve the goal, attracted outside support (Van Ham 1995: 61), and demonstrated to the international community that they were ready to exercise a free choice.

By contrast, although the social–political elites of the South Caucasian countries demonstrated their pro-Western stance, external pressure or severe internal problems in the first years of independence resulted in foreign and security policy formation within the Soviet successor, the Commonwealth of Independent States (CIS). Such a decision may be explained by their inadequate statehood and imperial nostalgia for the Russian political establishment.

The South Caucasian states face a dilemma: either to re-orient towards the West or to maintain the primary focus on the North – a choice between democratic and independent development, or the status of a post-Soviet Russian protectorate. By the late 1990s the development vector of the South Caucasian republics began to shift, albeit slowly and incoherently, Westwards. It remains to be seen whether a Westward orientation is sustainable, and whether the specific security complex existing in the region is able to evolve into a security regime with the potential to exclude the use of force in regional states' relations.

Internal and external obstacles to the state-building process, 1991–95

In the first years of independence, domestic and regional policies of the Caucasian political elites were based more on ethno-nationalistic rather than democratic and human rights values. Those policies were unacceptable for ethnic minorities. The ruling elites of the South Caucasus states failed to take into account the ethnic heritage of the Soviet past and were engaged in military confrontation.

Three large-scale conflicts unfolded in the region on ethnic grounds, the Nagorno-Karabakh conflict in Azerbaijan being the most extensive of them. The conflict in Azerbaijan began to escalate in 1988, and culminated in 1992 when the Karabakh autonomous province declared its independence, a move described by Azerbaijan as a territorial claim by Armenia against its sovereign territory. Having accused the Azerbaijani government of pursuing discriminatory policies against Armenian residents of Karabakh, the latter demanded to join the province to Armenia and tried to justify their position by historical facts. However, the history of Azerbaijan interprets these facts differently. The conflicting parties attempted to settle the disagreement by forceful means. After a successful advance the Karabakh army occupied seven Azerbaijani districts around the Karabakh province in February 1994, turning almost one million Azeri into internal displaced persons (IDPs). The conflicting parties signed a ceasefire agreement in Bishkek on 16 May 1994. The balance of forces in the conflict zone has not changed since then, and the Karabakh army is still in control of around 20 per cent of Azerbaijan's territory.

Furthermore, two ethnic conflicts – in Abkhazia and South Ossetia – have broken out in Georgia since 1990, when a new government came into power in Georgia at the first multi-party elections. In the following period, relations between the titular nationality and ethnic minorities became extremely tense. The first armed conflict erupted in the South Ossetian autonomous province. The overthrow of the Georgian government during the 1991–92 coup and Eduard Shevardnadze's inauguration did not ease the situation. Although hostilities ended after Georgia and Russia signed an agreement on 24 June 1992 to deploy Russian-led joint peacekeeping forces (Georgian–Russian–Ossetian) in the region, the status of the province has not yet been settled.

Post-communist societies of the South Caucasus encountered great obstacles in the process of state-building and democratic transition. The weakness of state institutions is one of the main reasons for the escalation of conflicts in the South Caucasus, which was also reflected in their inefficient state management system. The system failed to mobilise political and institutional power, and to impose democratic civil control over the armed forces. The governments of Georgia and Azerbaijan had difficulty controlling their military forces, and thus must take their share of the blame for the development of conflicts. According to an Azerbaijani researcher, Azerbaijan's army exhibited poor training, discipline and organisation in the Karabakh conflict. The army leadership was tainted by corruption and arms trafficking. High-ranking military officials used military resources for their own benefit (Rasizade 2001: 179). That similar processes took place in Georgia has been suggested by a lot of scholars on the basis of witnesses' accounts (Jones 1996: 44; Fairbanks 1995: 29).

The state interests of external powers negatively affected regional stability in the early 1990s in the South Caucasus. As the legal successor to the USSR, Russia successfully used its political and economic influence in the international arena to curb the participation of the international community in the South Caucasus. Russia's policies towards the region did not contribute to state-building and democratisation; indeed, experiencing transition itself, Russia objectively had neither capacity nor subjective interests to help regional countries build their statehood.

The second armed conflict in the territory of Georgia began in the autonomous republic of Abkhazia in August 1992. In September 1993, troops of the Georgian government were defeated by Abkhaz separatist forces. As a result, more than two hundred thousand Georgian IDPs had to flee Abkhazia. Russian peacekeeping forces were deployed in the conflict zone in June 1994 and the situation has been relatively calm since then. UN participation in the conflict settlement is limited: it only has an observer mission in the conflict zone, and is responsible for mediation between the conflicting parties (Darchiashvili 2000: 193).

In summer 1992 the international community made its first formal attempt to intervene in the Karabakh conflict, when the chairman of the Conference on Security and Cooperation in Europe (CSCE) appealed to the presidents of Armenia and Azerbaijan, and the population of Nagorno-Karabakh, on behalf of the Minsk conference on the Karabakh problem, to institute a ceasefire for ninety days prior to the onset of the conference (Moiseev 1997: 66). Moscow wanted the international community to acknowledge its extraordinary role as a guarantor of peace in conflict zones, since 'in the framework of this course Moscow tries to strengthen political positions and secure military–political superiority in the region' (Malisheva 2001: 43).

Many observers believe that active political, financial or military assistance on the part of Russian military–political circles helped to overthrow the Azerbaijani and Georgian governments that came to power at the first multi-party elections in the early 1990s, and instigated separatist movements in these countries (A Cohen 2001: 7). Also, it has been argued that Russia's illegal transfers of conventional and light weapons directly to local interest groups which Russia supported fuelled the conflicts in Nagorno-Karabakh, Abkhazia and South Ossetia. In addition, Russia maintained its military presence in the South Caucasus and kept its troops and military bases in Armenia and Georgia. Although Russian forces pulled out of Azerbaijan, the Karabakh forces, armed and influenced by Russian military circles, are still deployed on occupied territories of Azerbaijan in Nagorno-Karabakh. Russia used political, military and economic leverage to force Azerbaijan and Georgia into joining the CIS in 1993, and continues to control supplies of energy to the South Caucasus regional countries.

Georgia and Azerbaijan both adopted a policy of tight cooperation with Russia in military-strategic issues in 1993, which implied membership of a Russia-led military alliance (Darchiashvili 2000: 194). Such 'bandwagoning' was evidenced by the fact that these countries, along with Armenia, joined the CIS collective security system, which endorsed respective military agreements and regulated the CIS regional security policy under Russia's leadership. Treaties signed in the framework of the CIS were supplemented with bilateral agreements between CIS member states and Russia, which mainly addressed issues of military security. Pragmatism also played a role. Georgian and Azerbaijani political elites both expected Russia to guarantee a more stable environment for their rule, and to help solve at least some of the most urgent national problems.

The Azerbaijani leadership agreed to join the CIS in 1993 in the hope that Russia would help Azerbaijan to win the Karabakh war and cease its military support of its adversary (Polukhov 1997: 19). President Shevardnadze admitted in early October 1995 that he was compelled to sign the agreement legitimising the presence of Russian military bases in Georgia for twenty-five years because of the West's inadequate support to counter Russian pressure. A more pragmatic explanation emphasises that, in the post-September 1993 period, the internal political situation deteriorated in Georgia, and Shevardnadze officially appealed to Russia for help in an attempt to avoid armed confrontation with the opposition. Russia responded by backing the Georgian government and deploying additional troops in places of likely conflict, actually thwarting the danger of a civil war in the country (Darchiashvili 2000: 205–6).

Because of the ongoing war with Azerbaijan over Nagorno-Karabakh, Azerbaijan imposed an economic blockade on Armenia in the early 1990s. Transport links between the two states ceased. The Abkhaz war soon blocked the second railway, which links Armenia to Russia through Georgian territory. Thus Russian aid was viewed as the only way for Armenia to ease the negative effects of the economic blockade. The blockade provided Russia with leverage to maintain its influence in Armenia, and strengthened Yerevan's ability to assist the Karabakh population militarily and economically with Russia's assistance. For this reason the Armenian security policy depends on Russian military–political assistance and, as a result, Armenia's relations with Russia, both bilateral and in the CIS framework, were quickly established. On 29 December 1991, the then presidents of the two countries signed a friendship, cooperation and security treaty. The two governments have worked hard to expand and strengthen bilateral military–political and economic relations since 1992 (Moiseev 1997: 84).

Azerbaijan's security concerns deepened even more after it was disclosed that Russia had secretly transferred armaments to Armenia in 1993–96, while the Armenian Defence Minister Serzh Sarkisian claimed 'over the last two years we have doubled our defence capacity at no cost to the budget' (RFE/RL Caucasus Report, 30 October 1998). Another shipment of Russian military hardware was delivered to Armenia in 1999, including four MiG-29 fighter jets and S-300V surface-to-air missiles. Although Russia denies these transfers, explaining that the armaments are still in Russian possession and are intended for joint use only, other regional countries are strongly concerned with the new shipments, which affect the military–political balance in the region (CIPDD 1999: 2). Georgia was also increasingly dissatisfied with the new format of the cooperation with Russia. There was no positive dynamic in the conflict settlement in Georgia. Russia did not provide any efficient assistance to the Georgian army-building process, while Russian military bases in Georgia posed additional threats and challenges:

> The main concern of the Georgian government is that missions and tasks of the Georgia-based Russian military are unclear and have never been declared openly;
>
> The Georgian government knows little about the exact amount of Russian arms deployed on the territory of Georgia, though both sides have signed an arms control agreement;
>
> The state is unable to gain reliable information on the activities of Russian servicemen at these bases;
>
> According to the Georgian security services, Russian military bases in the South Caucasus are involved in weapons trafficking in the region. According to the official Georgian view, due to lack of control, weapons trafficking in Russian military bases has substantially expanded in scale, so that criminals are able to purchase almost any kind of weapons and equipment, including surface-to-air missiles.1

However, South Caucasian interest in the CIS has waned due to several unfulfilled promises. First, the CIS collective security system was expected to strengthen the defence capability of each South Caucasian country and provide guarantees for the military–political security. Second, the CIS was supposed to facilitate the conflict settlement, which it has not done. Third, the CIS was also supposed to develop economic cooperation between the member states, which again has not materialised in any concrete way.

Poor implementation of the agreements signed in the framework of the CIS collective security treaty increasingly discouraged member states from participating in CIS activities. The efficient implementation of the documents dealing with CIS security issues was called into question, as almost every military cooperation project failed to reach its objectives, while 'many already adopted documents were in fact dead letters' (SIPRI 1997: 120). Implementation of the CIS external border defence agreement, which was signed at the CIS summit on 26 May 1995, for example, proved inefficient. Russia failed to coordinate the border defence and the customs legislation among all of the CIS member states, as most of CIS countries were anxious to control customs incomes and did not want Russian border troops to supervise their import/export operations (Isakova 1998: 43). No serious attempts were made in the CIS framework to resolve conflicts in the South Caucasus, mainly because the member states did not have much interest in settling local conflicts The South Caucasus was also unable to assume the status of energy transport corridor and implement this idea in the framework of the CIS.

The more 'pro-West' of the CIS states – or GUUAM: Georgia, Ukraine, Uzbekistan, Azerbaijan and Moldova (Uzbekistan has since suspended its membership of the organisation) – set as a common goal the development of the Europe–Asia transport corridor and economic cooperation.[2] The statement demonstrated that GUUAM countries lacked belief in the ability of the CIS to satisfy their interests and hopes for cooperation.

Thus, South Caucasian countries gradually grew disillusioned with Russia and the CIS, and more interested in the West, noting that cooperation with Euro-Atlantic structures would best suit their economic and security needs. However, the process is slow and inconsistent. It is hampered by inertia, weak statehood, regional conflicts and uneasiness about Russia.

Developments in regional security regime building, 1996–2002

In the second half of the 1990s, the South Caucasus began to develop into an autonomous regional unity, as Western states increasingly recognised the South Caucasus as a separate region. Initially this recognition was based on the realisation that negative developments in the Caucasus were interrelated and interdependent. In the South Caucasus, as with many geographical regions of the world, conflicts and tensions play a greater role in the regional development than partnership, as ruling elites of newly emerged developing countries usually link national security problems to the threats from neighbouring countries (Ayoob 1995: 57), and concentrate mainly on relations based on envy and mistrust rather than on common interests (Buzan *et al.* 1998: 12). At the same time, neighbouring Russia, Turkey and Iran are also involved in the process and the 'formative dynamics' of the South Caucasus security complex may be considered still in a conflict formation (Buzan *et al.* 1998: 12).

Whilst regional political initiatives to further and enhance South Caucasus cooperation with the West in late 1990s increased, relative stability within the region resulted as hostilities ended, allowing a peaceful state-building process to be initiated. In addition, it became clear by 1996 that prospects for developing common foreign and security policies on the basis of CIS institutional relations were rather limited. Russia appeared unable to ensure a common position of CIS countries with regard even to NATO 'expansion', or to block the PfP programme (Isakova 1998: 56–7).

Two new policies from within the South Caucasus were initiated in 1996 in an effort to secure peace, stability and security in the region. On 28 February 1996, the Georgian president proposed an initiative for a 'Peaceful Caucasus'; the leaders of the Caucasian countries then convened for summit talks in Kislovodsk on 3 June 1996. During the Russia-chaired summit, leaders of Armenia, Azerbaijan and Georgia supported Shevardnadze's initiative and endorsed a 'Declaration of Inter-Ethnic Accord, Peace, Economic and Cultural Cooperation in the Caucasus'. However, strained relations among the signatory countries impeded further progress of the initiative, though attempts to develop regional cooperation and ensure its security did continue. The events of 1996 vindicated a need to view the format of regional peace initiatives in a wider context, and internal confrontation within the region made it impossible for regional actors alone to achieve accord.

The decisions reached at the OSCE summit in Lisbon in December 1996 were of great importance to the South Caucasian states, as they paved the way for the full participation of the CIS countries in European and global processes. By 1996, Russia had formally changed its policy towards the CIS, moving from the conception of a closed security system to recognition that other OSCE member states had a right to join non-CIS regional or subregional structures and implement independent foreign and security policies. OSCE member states unanimously recognised 'the inherent right of each and every participating state to be free to choose or change its security arrangements, including treaties or alliance, as they evolve'. Within the OSCE, no state, organisation or grouping can have any superior responsibility for maintaining peace and stability in the OSCE region, or regard any part of the OSCE accorded greater flexibility in their foreign policy objectives by taking into account globalisation and Western interests and views. As a result, they began to develop bilateral security relations with neighbouring countries and cooperation with European and Transatlantic institutions.

The European Union and NATO are gradually developing policy initiatives towards the South Caucasus, and in doing so are actively transforming security conflict formations into a security regime with the possibility of building a foundation for a security community in the region in the future. This strategy was influenced by the desire to create a stability zone in territories adjacent to Europe, and also by the increasing interest in oil and other energy resources, as well as the communication capabilities of southern regions of the former USSR. Western companies, for example, were the first to become interested in the vast oil reserves discovered in the Azerbaijani sector of the Caspian Sea. For its part the scope of investor interest in the

South Caucasus attracted the strategic interests of other powerful actors – the US and the EU – which consider the region mainly as a potential alternative route for the Europe–Asia transport corridor. The Azerbaijani government and oil companies signed the so-called 'Contract of the Century' on 20 September 1994, to exploit Azerbaijan's oilfields, and its importance was not limited to Azerbaijan. The contract provided conditions and opportunities to attract Western investment into telecommunication and transport projects in order to utilise the regional countries' potential as a Europe–Asia corridor.

The European Union has played one of the most important roles in promoting peace and stability in the South Caucasus region since 1996. Two important interstate projects have been launched by the EU through the TACIS/PHARE programmes, which still retain crucial meaning for South Caucasus development as all of the three South Caucasian countries are involved in these projects. TRACECA – the Europe–Caucasus–Central Asia Transport Corridor – formally ratified in 1998, encourages mutual coopera- tion between South Caucasus states in support of the development of transport arteries through the Caucasus. INOGATE (Interstate Oil and Gas Transport to Europe) is designed to modernise energy infrastructure and develop multiple routes for energy exports.

In January 1997, the European Parliament approved the EU's strategy for relations with the South Caucasian republics. The document defined the region as a sphere of the EU's interest. EU representatives later explained that this document was adopted due to the growing Western interest in Caspian Sea oil and gas resources (Komisina 2001). Western strategy and interest could not co-exist with Russia's desire to maintain exclusive influence in the region. Although the attitudes of various Western political and security structures towards this role were not consistent, in general the West was well aware that the South Caucasus was neither part of Russia nor a sphere of exclusive Russian influence.

On 22 April 1996, the South Caucasian republics and the European Union signed the Agreements on Partnership and Cooperation in Luxembourg, which came into force on 1 July 1999. According to the Agreements, three monitoring committees have been set up for each of the South Caucasus states: the Cooperation Council, the Cooperation Committee and the Par- liamentary Cooperation Committee. Also in 1996 the European Parliament created a commission for relations with the South Caucasian republics, which provided an opportunity for developing coordination and cooperation be- tween regional countries. This demonstrated a new sub-regional approach on the part of the EU towards independent states of the former USSR, and particularly the South Caucasus through developing a special strategy for the region.

At a meeting of the EU–South Caucasus Cooperation Council in October 2001, the EU called upon the South Caucasian countries to strengthen and develop regional cooperation. From the EU side it was underlined that, in view of the need to effectively combat international terrorism, the strategic importance of the South Caucasus for European security and stability has increased further (Centre for European Integration Studies 2001).

Admission of all the South Caucasian republics to the Council of Europe – albeit late in the day and at different times between 1999 and 2001 – also had a positive impact on the development of political relationships in the region. Membership in the Council of Europe undoubtedly increased the responsibility of the South Caucasian political elites for the democratisation of their countries. Participation in the Parliamentary Assembly of the Council of Europe provided these states with an additional opportunity to expand ties with European structures and develop regional cooperation.

In addition, prospects for developing relationship between South Caucasian countries and their neighbours were partly connected with the activities envisaged under the framework of the Black Sea Economic Cooperation (BSEC) as well (BSEC 1997: 13). The BSEC forum was transformed into a regional organisation in 1999 with the goal of implementing economic targets, but does not focus on conflict resolution processes or the promotion of new security initiatives. Even the establishment of the BLACK-SEAFOR naval unit, in the framework of BSEC, did not signal the inclusion of military–political aspects among the priorities of the organisation, because the unit's activities were limited to search-and-rescue missions The BSEC forum provides a good opportunity for South Caucasian states to maintain dialogue and contacts in a broader regional framework. At the same time, the fact that most BSEC member states face severe economic problems, as well as other internal types of challenge, negatively affects the efficiency of the activities conducted under the framework of the organisation. Moreover, the regional interests of strong powers as members (Russia, Turkey Greece) often contradict each other, hampering the success of cooperative approaches.

With regard to the OSCE's contribution to the regional cooperation of South Caucasian countries, the implementation of the principles of military–political treaties adopted in the framework of the OSCE treaties may help defuse the atmosphere of mistrust in the region. Between 1996 and 1999, OSCE member states worked to adapt the Treaty on Conventional Forces in Europe (CFE). Results of this work were particularly beneficial to Azerbaijan and Georgia. Together with other OSCE member states (e.g. Moldova) these countries officially refused to grant Russia part of their national quotas on conventional armaments as stipulated by the treaty, and the OSCE collectively backed this position (CIPDD 1999).

Within the framework of the OSCE and with the help of Western democratic countries, it became possible to begin the process of removing Russian military bases from Georgian territory. The OSCE provided its principal and official support to Georgia's position in the process and this undoubtedly contributed to reducing the security dilemma and additional tension among regional states. Although obligations in the framework of the OSCE have only political significance and do not entail any legal liabilities, it is important that the Final Act of the OSCE Summit of 1999 provides for monitoring and assessment of the withdrawal process and creating grounds for implementation of the agreement in the future.

The process of CFE negotiations had implications for the further development of regional initiatives. During the CFE talks, Azerbaijan and Georgia managed to reach common ground with Ukraine and Moldova with regard to their strategic concerns, and created 'GUAM'.[3] However, without a collective security system and guarantees for peace and stability, the development of regional economic projects within the GUUAM framework will be difficult; Azerbaijan's proposal to create a GUUAM peacekeeping battalion – GUUAMBAT – and prospects of its participation in pipeline defence have been the main themes of the security agenda (Liklikadze 2000). According to independent experts, the subsequent meetings on defence-related cooperation scheduled for Tusovets were postponed because, in addition to the political and economic problems of GUUAM member states, some countries grew rather cautious about the military aspects of GUUAM cooperation.

Additionally, Armenia's specific geopolitical situation has undermined the role of GUUAM in the development of a South Caucasian security system. Armenia is currently not a GUUAM member, and is thus excluded from economic projects oriented towards the South Caucasus. The Armenia–Azerbaijan conflict prevented Armenia from participating in the development of GUUAM cooperation. Despite existing obstacles, Armenian President Robert Kocharian gave assurances that Armenia was interested in GUUAM and was willing to take part in South Caucasian economic projects (Malisheva 2001: 48.). Kocharian has stated that Armenian policy is aimed at preventing new dividing lines and confrontation in the region (Department for Information and Publication 2001: 9). Thus the GUUAM initiative, which was conceived within the framework of the OSCE and encouraged by economic projects and as the focus of US interest (the US Congress allocated USD 37 million to GUUAM countries – most of which was earmarked for Armenia in 2001), may finally contribute to the development of the South Caucasian security regime.

Lessons learned from the implementation of sub-regional Agreements on Arms Control and Confidence and Security Building Measures – such as the General Framework Agreement for Bosnia and Herzegovina – The Dayton Agreement, 1995 (SIPRI 1998: 536) or the Florence Agreement on Sub-Regional Arms Control, 1996 (SIPRI 1997: 517–24) can prove useful for the South Caucasus, as there is a possibility to establish measures for sub-regional stability in the OSCE format. The leadership of the South Caucasian states has already indicated that they have such interests. It must be mentioned that the initiative of a regional security pact was voiced for the first time at the OSCE summit in November 1999.

At the OSCE Istanbul summit (18–19 November 1999), the presidents of the South Caucasian republics gave assurances that their countries were ready to expand regional cooperation, in particular to adopt a Caucasian stability pact. During the summit Azerbaijan President Heidar Aliev proposed the idea of a South Caucasian stability and security pact, which would secure withdrawal of foreign troops from the region (*Sakartvelos Respublika* 18 January 2000). The Armenian president also backed the idea of a new security regime but with a different approach and in the framework of the European security system (Malisheva 2001: 47).

In January 2000, under a Turkish initiative, a new concept of Caucasian stability was developed. Given the importance of the region, Caucasian stability is a task of common European significance and, therefore, regional countries and Russia, together with the EU, US and Turkey, should create a new security and cooperation system (*Sakartvelos Respublika* 18 January 2000: 2). The idea of a Caucasian stability, security and cooperation pact is still on the agenda and its successful implementation will depend on the degree of interest of the Euro-Atlantic security structures in the near future.

Projects implemented in the South Caucasus under the aegis of the OSCE aiming to contribute to the peace process in the region are also important. Apart from so-called human dimension activities (monitoring of human rights and democracy), the OSCE is also carrying out programmes on mediation in the talks on the Karabakh and South Ossetian conflicts. Conflicting parties are supportive of the format of the talks because the experience of recent years has shown that no country can resolve the conflicts alone: '…that is why the active participation of other countries and Euro-Atlantic structures is crucial for the issue' (*Sakartvelos Respublika* 18 January 2000: 2).

It must also be mentioned that the support of the OSCE has helped ease tensions between Russia and Georgia. The OSCE continues to monitor the Chechen and Ingush sectors of the Russian–Georgian border. It helped improve relations between Russia and Georgia when another crisis unfolded in November 2001, when Russian military aircraft bombed Georgian frontier areas neighbouring Chechnya. As Georgia is unable to defend its airspace efficiently, it was OSCE observers who alerted the international community to the violation of Georgian borders and to the bombing, providing respective evidence.[4] The international community's timely response helped alleviate the Russian–Georgian tensions, proving once again that OSCE framework does possess efficient tools for developing peace and stability in the Caucasus.

In the framework of the NATO PfP programme, all South Caucasian countries are given absolutely equal opportunities to develop their co-operation with North Atlantic security institutions. A 'Caucasian Working Group' was created in the framework of the Euro-Atlantic Partnership Council (EAPC) in 1999, which was supposed to facilitate the development of a common sub-regional cooperation policy.

Azerbaijan and Georgia have intensified their activities in individual cooperation programmes within the PfP framework since 1997, and the cooperation appears set to expand. Their cooperation with NATO evolved into an essentially new stage after these South Caucasian countries joined the Planning and Review Process (PARP) in the framework of the PfP programme. In the PARP presentation document, Azerbaijan and Georgia stated their willingness to participate in peacekeeping operations under NATO auspices. Twenty-three Georgian peacekeepers left Georgia for Turkey on 23 March 1999 for a one-month military training course there (*Dilis Gazeti* 6 March 1999). With Turkish assistance, Azerbaijani and Georgian peacekeeping units were incorporated into the Turkish peacekeeping battalion, and were deployed in Kosovo in the German zone (Liklikadze 2000). The process is ongoing and Georgian peacekeepers continue to fulfil their peacekeeping mission in KFOR in rotation.

Armenia's participation in PfP activities was initially more formal (Department for Information and Publication 2001: 12). Armenia has been reluctant to join PARP (although at the time of writing the Armenia authorities have warmed to the idea), and its armed forces had not participated in any joint training or exercises in the framework of the PfP prior to 2002. Armenia took part in only one PfP activity in 2001, whilst Azerbaijan and Georgia participated in over 140 such activities (Muradian 2001: 131). However, in recent times Armenia has expressed greater interest, and this is a positive tendency. While visiting the South Caucasian republics in September 2001, NATO Secretary-General Lord Robertson persuaded his Armenian partners to create a special battalion to take part in NATO exercises. At Lord Robertson's request, Greek colleagues will assist Armenia in establishing a special unit for participation in PFP exercises. Armenia is also set to host the 'Cooperative Best Effort' military exercise of NATO partner states in 2002.

Past developments demonstrated that participation in NATO programmes was very important for the weak and unprofessional defence structures of Azerbaijan and Georgia. Some positive developments are already evident in the defence systems of these countries. The experience of recent years vindicated beliefs that these activities can play a significant role in strengthening defence capabilities. First of all, they contribute to the education and professionalism of the militaries of partner states, to democratic control over the armed forces, and to the internal stability of the countries. Cooperation between NATO and South Caucasian republics is also important for promoting democratic values in these societies. In addition, government officials get an opportunity to learn Western approaches, and to gain experience of crisis management, civil–military dialogue and civil democratic control over the armed forces. No other regional security institution can provide a framework for such large-scale efforts. That is why participation in the programme is even more important for regional countries, which had to build their security systems in times of war and under rather unfavourable conditions.

The development of cooperation with NATO can facilitate integration of the regional countries with the North Atlantic space. Efficient participation of South Caucasian countries in NATO programmes will boost regional cooperation and encourage regional countries to participate more actively in the development of a cooperative European security system. It should also be noted that NATO plays an important political role in defending the interests of

South Caucasian republics. The interests of Azerbaijan and Georgia were taken into account during adaptation of the CFE Treaty, not only due to these countries' initiatives, but also because Russia and NATO reached an agreement on restrictions of the treaty. Under this agreement, the treaty signed in Istanbul in November 1999 was supplemented with a document that banned any increase in the territory of Eastern European signatory countries, while NATO undertook to refrain from permanent deployment of its forces on the territory of new members.[5] For its part, Russia pledged to withdraw its surplus forces from the region. This aspect was especially important, as it helped agree the current balance of forces in the South Caucasus.

Moreover, the South Caucasian countries have developed bilateral cooperation on security issues with NATO member states on the basis of their participation in NATO programmes, which have contributed to military reforms and allowed them to begin the transition to a Western-style army building. The process facilitates integration of South Caucasian states with Euro-Atlantic security structures and is aimed at either beginning and/or implementing security sector reforms in South Caucasian countries. Whilst the intensity of bilateral cooperation with NATO members is different for each South Caucasian republic, this cooperation is limited to the NATO interests and objectives as outlined in NATO programmes.

For this reason, assistance programmes do not contradict NATO common policy, and they correspond with agreements signed in the framework of the OSCE. Respectively, they do not tend to undermine the balance of forces in the region. Although Western countries take care of the technical equipment of the South Caucasian countries' armed forces, this assistance does not provide for supplies of armaments or military hardware to partner states. In this case, OSCE and NATO guarantee that the forms of stability building and military assistance in the region will be transparent and acceptable for all parties.

The military assistance programmes of these countries have always aimed to improve the professionalism and foreign language skills of the Georgian servicemen. Besides this, there were various kinds of military–technical or material supplies (e.g. uniforms, food). Foreign advisors also help Georgia develop conceptual defence documents. The International Security Advisory Board (ISAB), for example, has already elaborated recommendations for the Georgian government on the development of Georgia's National Security Concept, which was approved by the National Security Council. Donor countries pay special attention to Georgian border defence. Georgian border troops were created mainly with the help of the US, and they have been guarding the country's borders independently since 1999, when Russian border guards withdrew from Georgia.[6]

Turkey, Azerbaijan and Georgia have displayed growing interest in joint security cooperation. Turkey, a NATO member, and Georgia and Azerbaijan agreed on 3 January 2002 to prepare a security cooperation accord, which should be consistent with the global anti-terrorism war and define means to fight other forms of organised crime. The level and efficiency of US assistance in the South Caucasus has become especially distinctive since 11 September 2001, but additional tensions and confrontation between Armenia and Azerbaijan still attract the attention of the US administration on a different level (*Yeni Yuzil* 22 January 2002). In the post-11 September period, all three South Caucasian states allied with the international anti-terrorism coalition (its importance was vindicated by US Defense Secretary Donald Rumsfeld's visits to all three South Caucasian states in December 2001), and US military assistance programmes in South Caucasian countries increased remarkably in 2002. The scale of security assistance to Georgia is especially noteworthy. One of the main objectives of the programme is to help the Georgian Special Forces combat terrorism in the country; about two hundred American Green Berets are equipping and training four Georgian rapid-deployment battalions, totalling 2000 soldiers.

Conclusions

Recent tendencies in the South Caucasus revealed that the US, NATO and the EU have become especially interested in the region after 11 September 2001. The fact that all South Caucasian republics allied with the US-led anti-terrorism coalition and welcomed the West's efforts to achieve peace and stability in the region, which mainly aim to strengthen control over uncontrolled territories, suggests that the idea of regional cooperation will work not only in theory but also in practice. At the same time this tendency will succeed only if all regional forces of the Euro-Atlantic space participate in the process and the interests of each are taken into consideration. The OSCE format has great potential in this respect.

In order not to waste the unique opportunity to build not an 'imperial' but a democratic cooperative security system in the region, the South Caucasian republics have to overcome many obstacles. The West is actively trying to help transform the conflict-prone region into a 'security community' so that regional countries will no longer hold grudges or display suspicions towards each other, but rather will defend their interests within the framework of cooperation and confidence-building. However, not every interested actor appears ready for the task.

So far Russia has failed to fulfil all its obligations in the framework of the OSCE with regard to the South Caucasus. It is still unclear whether Russia will withdraw its troops from Georgia. At the same time, Georgian–Russian relations have been strained due to unresolved conflicts in both countries (Chechnya, Abkhazia). The political and military establishments of the two countries continue to blame each other. Georgia accuses Russia of supporting Abkhaz separatism, while Moscow blames Georgia for loyal approaches towards Chechen guerrillas and cooperation with them. Russia also does not make a secret of its strongly suspicious attitude towards the prospects of military cooperation between South Caucasian states on the one hand, and Turkey and the US on the other.

Russia is not alone in such a stance. Tensions between Armenia and Turkey are so deep that these countries are unable even to establish diplomatic relations with each other. Turkey has exceptional relations with ethnically kindred Azerbaijan and, quite logically, this factor has a strong impact on Armenian–Turkish relations. The Armenian leadership wants to find a solution to the problem of Nagorno-Karabakh on the basis of the principle of self-determination.[7] In return Azerbaijan has accused Armenia of carrying out aggression against its territorial integrity.[8]

However, the Karabakh conflict is not the only reason that accounts for the Armenia–Azerbaijan confrontation, though, unless it is settled, prospects for cooperation between Armenia and Azerbaijan, and respectively the development of the security community in the South Caucasus, will remain gloomy. One key factor is that the atrocities committed against Turkey's Armenian community in 1915 are still alive in the historical memory of the Armenian nation. The government of Armenia views these events as a Turkish policy of genocide, and is striving, with support of the Armenian Diaspora, to persuade the international community to recognise the genocide of Armenians. Turkey vehemently denies any responsibility for the sins of the Ottoman Empire and, simultaneously, is very concerned with the deployment of Russian missiles on Armenian territory.

Prospects of Iran's participation in the South Caucasian peace process are ambivalent and vague. Iran and Azerbaijan have been at odds with each other over disputed territories in the Caspian Sea. At the same time, the US still regards Iran as a rogue state. Richard Kozlarich, the US ambassador to Azerbaijan, once officially warned that all American companies would withdraw from the international consortium if Iran received a share in the project to develop Azerbaijan's oilfields (Polukhov 1997: 27). Against such a background, insinuations about the rise of two rival blocs (Russia–Armenia–Iran on the one hand, and GUUAM, supported by Turkey and the US, on the other) and prospects of their likely encounter in the South Caucasus continue. There is still some logic in the fear that transits of Caspian Sea energy resources may impede efforts to build up stability in the region due to the conflicting interests of some regional countries.

It also cannot be ruled out that the Georgian leadership may renew strategic rapprochement with Russia. Although today the West provides unprecedented support to the real independence of Georgia by trying to free the Georgian security system from Russian influence, the process is far from complete. Russian border troops left Georgia in 1999; the same year, Georgia withdrew from the CIS collective security treaty. Reforms advised by NATO experts are under way in the Georgian armed forces. Shevardnadze has stated that membership of the European Union is one of the country's main priorities. On the other hand, Russia maintains its influence in breakaway Abkhazia and South Ossetia. The Russian influence is also strong in the Armenian-dominated Javakheti region of Georgia, as well as in the Adjaria Autonomous Republic. In the past, Shevardnadze had said that the Russian–Georgian partnership did not mean only the deployment of military bases; Georgia also expected Russia to help restore its territorial integrity (*Sakartvelos Respublika* 8 April 1997). If tomorrow the Russian political elite succeeds in resolving the social and political problems of Russia and offers Georgia real help to regain its breakaway territories, the number of supporters of the Russian protectorate may increase in the Georgian government. Shevardnadze himself has frequently tended to ally with Russian military–political circles in order to consolidate his government. Besides, Georgian society retains a potential for anti-democratic and orthodox fundamentalism, which can contribute to the reinforcement of the pro-Russian political vector.

Georgia, along with as Armenia and Azerbaijan, has undertaken no more than the first steps towards consolidated democracy and a civil society. Georgia, along with Armenia and Azerbaijan, is characterised by corruption and lack of confidence in the government. When speaking about integration with the European Union, it should be emphasised that this process is a serious challenge to South Caucasian political elites. Yet they must first prove to the international community that the South Caucasus is an inseparable part of Europe and that South Caucasian countries might become members of the European Union together with other European nations. As long as they have yet to prove it, there are no grounds to believe that a cooperative security system can be completed in the South Caucasus in the near future. It seems possible, and even reasonable, that the development of the region may not depend directly on membership of the European Union or NATO, and the peace process will continue anyway with the help of various countries and international organisations, including the EU and NATO. But the region will surely never progress, if democracy fails and the protectorate is revived.

Notes

1   Statement made by the head of the Georgian Parliamentary Committee of Defence and Security, Giorgi Baramidze, on the international conference 'Crisis Management Strategy in Georgia' (CIPDD 2001).
2   Statement of the Presidents of Azerbaijan, Georgia, Moldova, Ukraine and Uzbekistan at the NATO/EAPC Summit in Washington, 24 April 1999. Source: official website of GUUAM (www.guuam.org).
3   The first official document of the GUAM, a joint communiqué, was signed by the member states at the summit of the Council of Europe in Strasbourg on October 10, 1997. They stated their common interest in developing bilateral and regional cooperation, European and regional security, political and economic contacts. Uzbekistan joined the GUAM in 1999, when it became GUUAM.
4   'We registered the air strike at Georgia. It was carried out from Russian territory': Statement of Ambassador. Michelle Lakomb, the OSCE envoy to Georgia, in an interview with Georgian national TV on 28 November 2001.
5   Final Act Of The Conference of the States Parties to the Treaty On Conventional Forces in Europe, CFE.DOC/2/99, 19 November 1999.

6   Statement of Georgian President Eduard Shevardnadze, joint press conference with the US Secretary of Defense William Cohen, 1 August 1999, Tbilisi; *Droni* 18–21 July 1999; *Resonanci* 18 July 1999.
7   Lisbon Document 1996, Annex 2, A Statement of the Armenian delegation at an OSCE summit in 1996.
8   Azerbaijani President Heidar Aliev's speech at the ceremony to admit Azerbaijan to the Council of Europe on 25 January 2000.

11 Western approaches to security cooperation with Central Asian states

Advancing the Euro-Atlantic security order in Eurasia

Jennifer D. P. Moroney

America encourages and expects governments everywhere to help remove the terrorist parasites that threaten their own countries and the peace of the world. If governments need training or resources to meet this commitment, America will help.

President George W Bush, 11 March 2002

America will have a continuing interest and presence in Central Asia of a kind that we could not have dreamed of before.

US Secretary of State Colin Powell, 6 February 2002[1]

Introduction

Although the US, Russia, China and, to a lesser extent, other influential states and institutions such as NATO and the European Union (EU) have been conducting their own economic, political and military 'campaigns' in Central Asia for the past decade (Russia, of course, for much longer), this region has only been given considerable Western media attention since 11 September 2001. However, Russia and the US have been vying for leverage over this crucial region for the past decade for a myriad of reasons, albeit to a lesser extent, not least due to the presence there of relatively large oil and gas reserves. In an environment increasingly marked by extreme political and economic uncertainty, both the West and Russia have sought to maximise political, economic and military leverage in Central Asia.

Russia views this region as firmly within its sphere of influence and interest and as a bulwark to instability coming from the south, specifically from Afghanistan, Iran and, potentially, India and Pakistan. Russia has strongly supported the development of closer relations with the Central Asian republics on an economic, political and military level through the Commonwealth of Independent States (CIS) organisation, specifically by including them in the CIS security framework, the CIS Collective Security Treaty and through other mechanisms, such as the Shanghai Cooperation Organisation (SCO).[2]

The West and particularly the US, also have vested strategic interests in Central Asia, given the region's proximity to Afghanistan to the south and

China to the east. What has helped it to increase its access and influence in this region is the fact that the US has been conducting bilateral and multilateral military exercises with the Central Asian republics of Kazakhstan, Kyrgyzstan and Uzbekistan since 1996. US forces were already eminently familiar with the terrain, personnel and facilities in these three countries prior to 9/11, which, although it did not necessarily lead to the opening up of military bases to US troops, none the less certainly contributed to the ease with which US forces moved into Uzbekistan and Kyrgyzstan. However, while the US and NATO have reaped many benefits from this seven-year cooperation programme in Central Asia, the US has not been as successful in promoting democratic norms and respect for human rights, or political and economic reforms in these countries.

Central Asia in the security vacuum

For the first five years following the break-up of the Soviet Union, the Central Asian republics were not a priority for Western security assistance and engagement. This was primarily due to their geopolitical location, viewed as being firmly within Russia's sphere of influence. As a result, the US Government (USG) and NATO were not very interested in this region, even given its untapped oil and gas reserves. The US provided no substantial economic aid packages to Central Asia. The US and NATO were focused on assisting the western Newly Independent States (NIS), particularly Ukraine and Moldova. The Caucasian states (Georgia, Azerbaijan and Armenia) were also higher on the priority list in comparison with Central Asia. The Central Asian republics had no 'Western card' (unlike Ukraine, for example) by which to attempt to leverage Russia's influence in the political, economic, energy or military sphere. Moreover, NATO was not attempting to increase involvement in Central Asia, given the region's proximity to Russia and assured Russian objections to US/NATO military or political outreach to these states. Therefore there was no Western security option for these states, which serves to explain their relatively tight security cooperation with Russia within the CIS framework.

It should come as no surprise that the Central Asia region, a crossroads for a myriad of influences, including Slav, Middle Eastern and Chinese, is experiencing extreme instability along ethnic, religious and other lines. Non-traditional or 'soft-security' (non-military) threats to border security, such as the transit of terrorists and narcotics, are among the primary security concerns for the West, Russia and China, as well as for the Central Asian republics. These threats are not region-specific and carry the risk of conflict spill-over into the Caucasus, Ukraine, Moldova, Southern Europe and even further westwards.

These security issues were only really brought to the forefront of US engagement in Eurasia in the mid-1990s. US security interests in the region – primarily the transfer of small arms, terrorism, narcotics trafficking and energy infrastructure protection – became much clearer in 1998. The transformation of the Islamic Movement of Uzbekistan (IMU) from terrorism to insurgency tactics, and its degree of sophistication and soldiering, encouraged the US Department of Defense to focus resources on Special Forces exercises in the region. US Special Operations forces began engaging in Kyrgyzstan and Uzbekistan in 2000 (more modestly in Kyrgyzstan than Uzbekistan) because of the desire to prevent these countries replicating the fate of Chechnya. In other words, if left to their own devices, the USG feared that the Kyrgyz and Uzbek governments would adopt the same tactics as Russia if they were not shown alternative methods for dealing with such insurgencies.

Central Asian interests in closer Western ties

An interesting question regarding what Central Asian states would like from the US and NATO would be: do Central Asian states view the increase in security cooperation with the West, including training, equipment and expert-level advice, as a means by which to implement a Western-oriented approach to democratic security building? Moreover, do the US and NATO view security cooperation activities with Central Asia as a means by which to reinforce Western-oriented approaches to democratic security building over the longer term? Just what are the key factors driving this relationship?

To begin with, outright political support for the US after the 9/11 attacks has played a huge role in increasing US financial and technical assistance to this region. All five Central Asian states – Uzbekistan, Kyrgyzstan, Kazakhstan, Turkmenistan and Tajikistan – officially and publicly denounced the terrorist attack against the US, but offered varying degrees of support and territorial access. For example, Kyrgyzstan and Tajikistan initially agreed to provide the US access to their airspace for humanitarian purposes. However, Uzbekistan, which has the largest Muslim population in Central Asia, along with the most extremist militant groups, went further by offering the US and its allies the ability to station ground forces and equipment at one of its air bases. Kyrgyzstan also offered the use of Manas airport as a base for the US and the Coalition. These bases have enabled the US and the International Security Assistance Force (ISAF) to launch offensive air strikes against the Taliban in Afghanistan. None the less, a closer look at Uzbekistan in particular provides an interesting perspective on the correlation between security assistance and democracy building, which is worth noting.

Prior to 9/11, Uzbekistan refused to implement necessary political and economic reforms, while ignoring US criticisms regarding its poor human rights record. Because of Uzbekistan's poor performance on these issues, Uzbekistan has been largely ineligible for Western financial assistance. However, because the US is relying on Uzbekistan in the war on terrorism, human rights violations do not necessarily preclude Uzbekistan from receiving considerable financial support and other training necessary to build a strong coalition of those willing to fight against terrorism. However, recent developments seem to indicate that US security assistance will be tied to a certain degree to Uzbekistan's human rights record. But how closely is a matter for debate. What is clear is that human rights abuses continue – for example, in the management of refugees and the treatment of detainees and POWs. Nevertheless, presidents Islam Karimov and George W Bush signed a five-point 'Strategic Partnership' agreement on 12 March 2002, which calls for the US to 'regard with grave concern any external threat' to Uzbekistan, while committing the former Soviet state to 'intensify the democratic transition of its society politically and economically'. In general, this agreement was intended to increase cooperation on economic, legal, humanitarian and nuclear proliferation matters. US Secretary of State Colin Powell signed an agreement to buy land for a new US embassy in Tashkent and the US Export–Import Bank granted Uzbekistan an additional USD 55 million credit guarantee (Milbank 2002).

The twenty-page agreement accords President Karimov a vague US pledge to support Uzbekistan against any external threat, which is accompanied by promises of military training and hardware. In exchange, Karimov committed in writing to a long list of economic and political reforms, such as establishing a multiparty system, ensuring free and fair elections and independence of the media. Additional promises include reforming the judiciary and carrying out the free market economic programme that the World Bank and the International Monetary Fund have been pressing in Uzbekistan for several years (Diehl 2002).

Although it is clear that Uzbekistan has much to gain from its new-found strategic partnership with the US, it also has much to lose. For example, a large military build-up in Uzbekistan over an extended period of time could certainly serve to exacerbate regional tensions, between Uzbekistan and other Central Asian republics on one hand and between Uzbekistan and Russia on the other. Regional tensions could cause the states to lose complete control over their already porous borders, making them a virtual free-for-all for the passage of illegal narcotics, 'weapons of mass destruction' (WMD) and terrorists. Moreover, Uzbekistan is already seen by its neighbours as a regional hegemon, and a heightened status for Uzbekistan in terms of political and military cooperation with the West will only serve to reinforce this view in the eyes of Uzbekistan's smaller neighbours.

It is clear that the US is using Uzbekistan as a 'bridgehead for the defence of the US strategic interests in central and Southern Asia', writes Martha Olcott (Torbakov 2002). Uzbekistan hopes that this new-found 'alliance' with the US will first and foremost help the state to defeat two increasingly powerful extremist groups operating within its territory – the IMU and the *Hizb-ut-Tahrir*. Second, a longer-term military presence should help the Uzbek government increase its sovereignty and territorial integrity *vis-à-vis* Russia. Third, Uzbekistan hopes to reap considerable financial gains as a result of its cooperation with the US. President Karimov has viewed Uzbekistan's support for the war on terrorism as a means by which to benefit economically without having to push economic or human rights reforms. Up to now Karimov has used both the IMU and terrorism in a broader sense as an excuse to crack down on the political opposition.

The benefits for those countries in Central Asia that support the US in the war on terrorism are seen to outweigh the potential drawbacks (e.g. negative reaction from Russia or diminished regional cooperation). Perhaps Karimov is banking on a deepening of cooperation between the US/NATO and Russia in coming months, which would greatly heighten Uzbekistan's security situation by reducing the likelihood that Putin would be successful in employing economic and political leverage over Uzbekistan.

US/NATO interests in Central Asia

Central Asia belongs to a broader CIS region in which personal contact is extremely important. The military is a key component in the furthering of positive and fruitful contact. After the terrorists attacks on the US, the military could not have simply moved in on Uzbek territory in the way that they did and have expected things to go as smoothly. US regional engagement programmes in Central Asia, and especially in Uzbekistan, emerged as a case in which continued cooperation, at least for the short term, appeared to have reaped a considerable strategic benefit, allowing vastly different political cultures to align their interests against the specific goal of countering terrorist activities.

With this understanding in mind, NATO and the US seek to achieve several political and military objectives in the Central Asian region. These include, but are not limited to the following:

- increasing operational access to personnel and facilities in partner countries;
- increasing opportunities for information gathering;
- promoting positive, sustained political–military interaction with the USG;
- building a coalition of the willing;
- promoting defence reform and restructuring;
- promoting partner defence self-sufficiency;
- promoting human rights and the adoption of Western models and international norms;
- countering negative political and military influence in this region of other influential actors;
- promoting regional cooperation;
- promoting interoperability between US/NATO and Central Asian militaries.

More specifically, through military exercises, the following objectives in Central Asia are advanced: US forces are privy to a relatively high level of familiarity with partner country practices, facilities and equipment; inter-operability with US and allied forces is increased each time an exercise takes place as Central Asian forces learn more about NATO doctrine and military practices; counterparts discuss human rights practices in all exchanges; US combat abilities are sharpened; mutual trust and sustained political–military interaction, not only with US counterparts but also between Uzbek, Kazakh and Kyrgyz forces, is improved.

It is hoped that this sustained interaction will help these countries to improve their coordinated efforts to deal with the transnational security threats common to the entire region, such as terrorism and Islamic insurgencies, drug and human trafficking and the transiting of WMD from East/South Asia through Central Asia to Eastern and Western Europe. All the while, Central Asian participants are meant to be moving closer to the adoption of Western practices and doctrine and away from Russian variants on certain issues.

The US *Regional Cooperation* exercise series has exposed Central Asian states to rules of engagement, the rule of law and the doctrine of international organisations. This exercise programme emulated the Baltic Battalion (*BALTBAT*). The idea was based on the assumption that states in close geographical proximity to one another that also share similar transnational security threats would be willing to work together in a concerted effort to address these security threats. However, the US quickly found that Central Asia was *not* the Baltics in this regard. Whereas the Baltic states were driven to regional cooperation by the prospects of NATO and EU membership, this was not true for Central Asia. Their inherent rivalry and distrust of one another made multilateral exercises and initiatives very difficult.

Additionally, the gathering of information is no doubt an important focus of the war on terrorism and highlights the need for closer relationship with countries in the region where terrorist organisations are known to be operating. It is interesting to note that Tashkent was the former command post of the USSR's Turkestan regional command and a collection point for electronic eavesdropping on China and the Indian Ocean. Many of the former Soviet surveillance stations in Uzbekistan are now used by the state authorities. Much of this electronic information gathered about terrorism has been shared with the US. Additionally, because the Uzbek leadership continues to maintain a firm security apparatus over its citizens, information on suspected terrorists or sympathisers in Uzbekistan has already been gathered. There is, however, a troubling realisation about the means by which information is gathered in Uzbekistan and other FSU countries. For example, Uzbek security officials have been accused of torturing suspects (and, therefore, intelligence obtained through interrogations is certainly questionable), so there is thus an inherent dilemma between the gathering of intelligence Uzbek-style and the promotion of human rights and democratic norms, another key US goal in the region.

Will the US's new-found partnership with Central Asia and particularly Uzbekistan encourage the US to turn a blind eye to human rights abuses and totalitarian tendencies in the region? While the US Department of Defense has been involved in military security cooperation with several of the Central Asian republics to promote contact between the armies, the US State Department has been pressing Central Asian leaders to liberalise their governments by fostering democratic norms and practices. The engagement policy has not been without risk. As the US Government was pushing non-democratic leaders into accepting a more democratic model for governing their states, it was also working with patronage-riddled military and non-military police forces whose political, military and cultural loyalties continue to be uncertain.

The State Department acknowledged again in early March 2002, in its human rights report, that new Western allies in Central Asia – from Pakistan to Uzbekistan to Yemen – have poor human rights records. The report also cited Russia for its brutal war in Chechnya, with military sweeps that have resulted in disappearances, torture and execution (Slevin 2002). However, senior administration officials recognised that the partnerships the US is developing will hopefully eventually lead to improved civil liberties in these countries. Assistant Secretary of State Lorne Craner stated that an improved human rights performance is an 'important by-product of our alliance with them' (Slevin 2002). While human rights discussions are an integral component of US engagement, the important question is: to what extent are such programmes having any visible impact? Does the need for immediate access to this region cause US policymakers to play down known human rights and democracy abuses?

Uzbekistan has received USD 160 million in US foreign aid in 2002, which essentially tripled US foreign aid to this country. It will be interesting to see whether relations between the US and Uzbekistan on a security level will continue to intensify, regardless of President Karimov's record on human rights and other necessary reforms. In the past, it is important to note that failure to institute required political and economic reforms has precluded US security assistance to other FSU countries, such as Tajikistan. But Uzbekistan appears to be a 'special case' at the moment.

Mechanisms available to US/NATO for security assistance to Central Asia

US security cooperation or engagement programmes such as the Warsaw Initiative Fund (which funds the US component of the Partnership for Peace programme) and the Cooperative Threat Reduction's (CTR) defence and military contacts programme have played a pivotal role in securing US operational access for Operation *Enduring Freedom* (OEF).CTR, which funds many of the US Department of Defense's (DoD) peacetime military activities with the countries of the former Soviet Union, has provided the DoD with direct access to various levels of military and political decision-makers in Central Asia. It has also facilitated the building of strong professional and personal relationships between US officials and their counterparts in these countries.

Similarly, the Warsaw Initiative programme for Central and Eastern Europe and the FSU has assisted in the training and development of military capabilities in Central Asian states. Warsaw Initiative activities include English- language training, funded through the International Military Education and Training (IMET) programme, as well as non-lethal training and equipment transfers through Foreign Military Financing (FMF). The Warsaw Initiative also includes other training activities, such as courses at the George C. Marshall Centre in Garmisch-Partinken, Germany, which focus on helping these countries to reform and restructure their defence establishments, encouraging civilian control of their militaries, professionalising their armed forces and instituting practices which will help to improve their human rights and democracy records.

Moreover, other USG interagency programmes, a border security initiative called the Export Control and Related Border Security (EXBS) programme, executed by the US Customs Service, aim to secure and stabilise the extremely porous external and internal borders of the Central Asian republics. The initiative focuses in part on enhancing national and regional interoperability (e.g., by supplying surveillance and radio equipment) and involves the border guards and customs services, as well as the respective ministries of defence and general staffs of the partner countries.

Because the militaries of Central Asia are predominantly composed of ground troops, the focus of CTR and the Warsaw Initiative activities in this region have been on land forces, with the US Army and Special Forces, including Joint/Combined Exchange Training (JCET) activities, taking the lead. In recent years, an active exercise schedule has been completed in Kazakhstan, Kyrgyzstan and Uzbekistan, with the bilateral *Balance* exercise series. These exercises include *Balances Ultra, Umbra, Umpire* and *Unity*, held annually with US Special Forces, and they focus on small-unit tactical operations in urban, desert and mountain environments. A multilateral exercise series, *CENTRASBAT/Regional Cooperation*, involves these same three countries. Particularly in Uzbekistan, these exercises have proven invaluable for helping the Tashkent government to counter security threats such as the IMU, as well as establishing and fostering close working relationships between the US and Uzbek militaries. In addition, Kyrgyzstan, which shares a strategically important border with China, has provided the US access to build a new airforce base on its territory. Although Tajikistan did not previously participate in formal security cooperation, consultative talks between the DoD and the Tajik Ministry of Defence in early 2001 explored possible ways to develop bilateral security cooperation and arguably eased subsequent US efforts to use Tajikistan for overflights and basing.

The rationale for US–Central Asia cooperation is rooted in a complicated list of security concerns. On one level, the US sought to replace the affinity for Russia held by Central Asia's decision-makers, particularly President Karimov of Uzbekistan, and to create more reliable allies in the Caspian Sea region. However, more immediately, the US sought to assist Central Asian states, particularly Uzbekistan and Kyrgyzstan, in their endeavours to resist the IMU and to ensure their cooperation in programmes to prevent the spread of WMD – two goals which have become much more urgent since 11 September 2001.

Maintaining a 'foot in the door' in Central Asia: comparing the US and NATO models

Central Asia has not always been high on the list of priorities of the US and, especially, of NATO. Western FSU republics such as Ukraine have received much greater attention. While the US and NATO have been encouraging the western CIS to focus resources on defence reform and restructuring, civil–military relations, peacekeeping, force professionalisation and interoperability with NATO, with the goal of bringing them into the European security order, Central Asia has received virtually none of this encouragement and very little security assistance by comparison. However, this does not mean that Western policymakers overlooked Central Asia entirely from the mid-1990s until present day. On the contrary, US–Central Asian security cooperation has been much more focused on the conducting of such bilateral and multilateral exercises as *Balance* and the 'in the spirit of PfP' *CENTRASBAT/Regional Cooperation* series. Moreover, because Central Asia was seen as a 'threat-driven security environment', 'getting-to-know-you' familiarisation activities had to be pushed through quickly in order to deal with the threat at hand – primarily Islamic insurgencies such as the IMU and, to a lesser extent, *Hizb-ut-Tahrir*. This could lead to the conclusion that US cooperation with Central Asia is strategy-driven; at least the argument can be made that engagement is more focused, because of the threat-driven security environment in this rather volatile region.

However, NATO's approach to Central Asia (and the Caucasus) has met with some constraints and more serious challenges along the way. The main reason why NATO has been less successful at engaging these countries is because NATO advocates a specific model for its engagement with partner countries in Eurasia which is focused on improving regional cooperation. Although this model has been successful for the most part in promoting regional cooperation in Eastern Europe and even in the Western FSU through PfP, the application of this model to a region in which deep distrust and years of war characterise the current state of relations is a challenge, to say the very least.

Another challenge for NATO in its efforts to bring the Central Asian states into the European security order revolves around the issue of providing training and equipment to build capacity in these countries, in an effort to improve their defence self-sufficiency. NATO is often a slow mover in terms of planning and executing security assistance programmes and, more often than not, it does not have the money to provide such assistance. However, NATO's 'tools', which include PfP to improve interoperability, confidence-building and regional cooperation, and the Planning and Review Process (PARP) to assist in defence reform and restructuring, are certainly noteworthy, beneficial methods of engagement. For the most part, participation in PfP has not been a political or military issue for the Central Asian states, although the financial burden often precludes their participation, as NATO requires the partners to contribute towards the exercises. PARP, on the other hand, requires partners to disclose information on the state's range of defence and military capabilities, along with detailed answers about the force structure and the defence budget, an approach that is viewed as extremely intrusive from the old Soviet mindset. Moreover, defence budgets and force structure issues during Soviet times were (and in most cases, still are) classified.

Other FSU NATO partners (such as Ukraine) have participated in PARP, disclosed 'sensitive' information, acknowledged the importance of improving regional cooperation, information sharing and interoperability and defence reform, and as a result have moved closer to Western security structures in the process. In theory, if the Central Asian states follow a similar path to Ukraine, then it is likely that they will move closer to NATO. However, the challenge for NATO in this particular region is to ensure that the mechanisms for building partnerships in Central Asia are appropriate to the needs of these countries in this threat-driven security environment. To be sure, Uzbekistan and Kazakhstan joined PARP after 9/11, which is a significant step forward.[3] But the partnership could be more relevant for the needs of these states. Elements of the partnership in PfP could include, for example, some focused exercises to improve energy infrastructure, military support to civilian authorities in a crisis, and regional cooperation to counter the transnational border security threats which all of the Central Asian states face. In short, NATO activities with these countries must evolve in order to be relevant to the security needs of these states. Otherwise NATO runs the risk of being seen as an ineffective multilateral engagement tool for this region, encouraging these states to seek only bilateral security assistance from the US and other key allies, who are seen as more in tune with their needs from a security perspective.

Vying for strategic influence in Central Asia and the Caucasus

The extent to which the US and NATO allies will be successful in drawing closer to the Central Asia republics will naturally depend to a considerable degree on Russia's reaction. Two major issues influence Russia's policy towards Central Asia: the response of the Russian bureaucracy to a continued US and allied military presence in the region after the war in Afghanistan is over; and the 'new pragmatism' of Russian President Putin, especially in the context of his apparent desire to strengthen ties with the West in the war on terrorism.

Following a request from the US to station troops on a temporary basis in Central Asia, the response from the Russian executive branch was not initially favourable. Russian Defence Minister Sergei Ivanov originally strongly objected to the presence of US troops in Central Asia, but Putin overruled the MOD on the understanding that the deployment would last only for the duration of the military operation in Afghanistan. US forces are now stationed at the Uzbek base at Khanabad and at the Kyrgyz base at Manas airport in Bishkek (400 miles from Afghanistan); both bases are in relative close proximity to Afghanistan. Khanabad will house more than 1000 US personnel and Manas will be home to over 3000 personnel and about thirty American and allied aircraft by June 2002. Six US Marine FA-18s and six French Mirage 2000s will be based there for air combat operations, and other US allies will base five KC-135 tankers and four C-130 transport aircraft to re-supply troops and fly humanitarian aid operations to Afghanistan. The US has concluded a one-year status-of-forces agreement with Kyrgyzstan, which gives the US broad military authority to use the airport for combat and combat support operations so as to carry out Operation*Enduring Freedom*. The US has agreed to 'compensate' the Kyrgyz government by paying landing fees and costs – which is standard US policy for use of a foreign commercial airport (Loeb 2002).

While the intensity of the Afghan campaign has slowed, the resources going into Manas tell a rather different story, which may be seen as a commitment to a ground presence in Kyrgyzstan for the foreseeable future. The broader political and strategic relationship with the Central Asian republics also reflects US interests in a region rich in oil and gas reserves. However, this presence, at least for the short term, reflects a need to demonstrate to allies and partners the commitment of Washington to re-engage its military should terrorism re-emerge as a major threat to stability in this region.

However, the prospect of a longer-term US military presence on the ground has the tendency to raise eyebrows, not only in Russia but also in China, which borders both Kyrgyzstan and Tajikistan to the east. China has been seeking to expand its influence in this region and, together with Russia, has led the charge to establish the Shanghai Cooperation Organisation, which includes several Central Asian republics, to counter the spread of Islamic extremism and terrorism (Loeb 2002).

This new US presence in Central Asia is significant, since the insertion of US troops in the FSU has long been feared by Moscow. President Putin and the Director of Russia's Federal Border Service, Konstantin Totsky, have stated that they do not see why the US should remain after the hostilities die down in Central Asia (Loeb 2002). However, Russia's policy towards the continued presence of US troops on FSU territory is inconsistent and vague. For example, Putin accepted a US military presence in Uzbekistan and Kyrgyzstan, and even appears willing to accept the membership of the Baltics states in NATO, although this 'relaxed' policy does not include the acceptance of the deployment of NATO's military assets on Baltic territory.

On the other hand, Putin has shown much more resistance with respect to Georgia, as President Eduard Shevardnadze has threatened to invite US troops to help deal with the breakaway republic of Abkhazia (such troops would be likely to support Shevardnadze's attempts to eject Russian peace-keepers from Abkhazia), and to help train and equip Georgian forces to deal with terrorist movements (i.e., Chechens) in Georgia's Pankisi Gorge region. This region lies within Georgian territory, but the government in Tbilisi is too weak to patrol the rugged terrain or arrest the rebels operating there. Russian Defence Minister Ivanov described the Pankisi Gorge as a 'mini Afghanistan on Russia's doorstep', a statement in line with Russia's past tactics which have pressed Tbilisi either to crush the rebels or drive them back to Georgia (Tyler 2002). Not surprisingly, Russia has come out against this US 'train and equip' programme, preferring that Georgian forces push the rebels out of Georgia and back into Chechnya (*Washington Post* 27, 28 February 2002).

The US programme in Georgia included a shipment last year of ten UH-1H Huey helicopters and now includes a contingent of about forty US Special Forces military personnel on the ground. Up to 150 military trainers could be sent to help prepare Georgian soldiers to re-establish control over the Pankisi region. It is interesting to note that the US is giving Georgia USD 64 million, three times Georgia's entire military budget (cited by Former US Assistant Secretary of State for Intelligence Tobi Gati, PBS 2002). Perhaps even more interesting, the introduction of US trainers and US equipment fundamentally changes the equation for the Georgian government because Georgia can now face the Russians with greater confidence and claim that they will have the capability of maintaining their security, which is a new development.

US officials have not stated an explicit goal of training Georgian forces to capture suspected terrorists, though this objective is most likely to be on the Bush administration's agenda to further the war on terrorism. Georgian officials would naturally like the US to provide military hardware such as tanks, munitions, artillery and armoured vehicles before their troops are sent to Pankisi, but it is as yet unclear whether the US will oblige.

Russia's reaction to US military presence in Georgia has ranged from fear that the US is seeking a stronger foothold in the Caucasus (i.e., Russia's backdoor) to some satisfaction at the official linking by the US of the Chechen rebels in Georgia to *al Qa'idah*. Putin's objections to a US presence in Georgia and the other Caucasian states are beginning to wane, though it is difficult to tell whether this will be an enduring policy. However, the recognition of the Chechen rebels as 'terrorists' with an *al Qa'idah* connection is a big win for Russia. The sending of a US mission to Georgia represents a belief by the Bush administration that Arab fighters connected to *al Qa'idah* have joined Chechen rebel forces to battle the Russian army, an assertion made by Putin months ago, but doubted until now in the US. A high-ranking US defence official recently stated that 'we have a clear connection between Chechens and *al Qa'idah*. They clearly fall under the potential targets of the global war on terrorism' (Kozaryn 2002).

But while Putin is known to be seeking more Western recognition, he is facing resistance from hardliners in his government, particularly from the Ministry of Defence, who opposed Putin's decision to back the US-led war on terrorism and especially his decision not to oppose the establishment of US military bases on the territory of the former Soviet Union. Still, Russia's attitude toward Western, and particularly US, involvement in the FSU, and specifically in Central Asia and the Caucasus, is changing, albeit slowly. The broader context of closer relations between Russia and US/NATO in the war on terrorism has spurred this change. However, a US military presence in Central Asia is only a first step. Russia's response to US military involvement in Central Asia and the Caucasus over the short term will continue to be a major factor in the West's ability to influence the strategic direction of this region. Moreover, Russia's response will determine the extent to which the US and its allies can help these countries to deal with border security issues, including countering the spread of WMD and the trafficking of narcotics and small arms and the proliferation of terrorist networks in this region.

Advancing the European security order in Central Asia

The evolution of US security ties with the Central Asian states must be viewed through the prism of developments in US/NATO–Russia relations. A US/NATO–Russia rapprochement will directly impact US relations with the Central Asian states, as well as Russia's approach to the region it formerly controlled. Keeping this perspective in mind, Central Asian and US/NATO policymakers should consider the following strategic options.[4]

Central Asian states will be more successful in their strategy with the US and with NATO and the EU if they focus attention on the following:

* improve transparency and accountability;
* work with Western institutions and agencies to improve the criminal justice systems;
* take steps to bring in new legislation which clearly identifies corruption, money laundering and narcotics trafficking as crimes;
* demonstrate a firm willingness to improve regional cooperation, particularly in the spheres of border security and information sharing;
* recognise that US security assistance is not the 'be all and end all', and that building a strong cooperative partnership with NATO and the EU now is equally as critical, particularly for being part of an established 'process' for bringing partner countries closer to the West.

Moreover, US and NATO policymakers should consider elements of the following approach:

- follow a multifaceted foreign policy approach by tying economic packages and military assistance to improvements in human rights/democratic records;
- distribute economic aid packages in tranches, perhaps through US government agencies and NGOs operating in these countries;
- avoid a large-scale military build-up in Central Asia after the war in Afghanistan begins to subside, but maintain a visible presence through a continuation of military and civilian contact programmes;
- consider working closer with other regional organisations such as GUAM or other sub-regional security organisations, where possible, to promote regional cooperation and a stronger coalition of Western-oriented partners;
- link US military presence to the broader desire to eradicate all terrorist networks in the region, including the Chechen rebels;
- promote Western solutions to transnational problems in the region (e.g., border security, dealing with terrorists, etc.) to counter the Russian approach (i.e., as adopted in Chechnya);
- clearly specify goals for engagement beyond the short term, from the intensification of political and military relations to capability building training;
- consider hosting an annual border security exercise in Central Asia, which would bring together the five states and relevant government agencies (border guards, MOD, customs officials, etc.) to ensure that NATO remains important to this group of important partner countries in the war on terrorism.

The USG and its allies must have clearly defined short- and long-term objectives in place in order to determine the level of success of the engagement programme with Central Asia and the broader CIS region. Such a strategy should include longer-term objectives for security cooperation; shorter-term milestones to measure progress along the way; and an assurance that all activities conducted have a place in the broader strategy, which above all should be linked to the success of each of its partners in Central Asia in advancing democratic norms and practices.

Success may be measured by analysing the responses to these questions:

1   Are the frequency, tone and results of dialogue between US/NATO and Central Asian counterparts better or worse than a year ago?
2   To what extent has Western operational access to persons and facilities increased?
3   To what extent is a true coalition of democratically-minded partners being built?
4   To what extent has regional cooperation been encouraged as a crucial component of improving security and stability in the region, promoting Western norms and objectives?

5   Is the sovereignty and defence self-sufficiency of these nation-states improving?
6   To what extent are these countries turning to the West in an effort to improve their security situation?
7   Is there tangible evidence of positive trends in human rights and the adoption of accepted norms regarding democratic accountability and the rule of law?

Conclusions

It is not enough for the US and NATO to have a 'foot in the door', particularly in regions such as Central Asia. The West needs to have an overall strategy with measurable objectives and goals in place in order to achieve its specific objectives and to leverage available resources to the fullest extent. A crucial component of this strategy should be to emphasise the importance of a continuing *presence* in this region, which might not include the establishment of numerous bases. But at the moment the West does not appear to have a longer-term strategy towards Central Asia beyond the short-term goals of using the region as a springboard to Afghanistan and reducing the proliferation of terrorist organisations in the region. In formulating a longer-term strategy, the US and its allies need to recognise that Central Asia is a region in which all actors are constantly looking over their shoulders at other actors, within their own country and within the region. They look at these other countries, and even at their own people, sometimes as enemies and sometimes in the context of keeping them firmly under control. They are also, most importantly, looking at Russia. Although the era of Russian military control is over, Russia will continue to have a strong economic and political influence over this region and will continue to regard these countries and their fate as a critical component of Russian security.

On one hand, the current attention devoted to the strategic importance of Central Asia (and the Caucasus) is likely to greatly increase the region's political, military and economic ties with the West, while at the same time diverting attention away from the western FSU and from the potential role of sub-regional organisations, such as GUAM, in the promotion of security in the region. Some of our traditionally stronger partners in the FSU have not made a concerted bid to support the war on terrorism, perhaps because they feel somewhat removed, at least in a geopolitical sense. For example, referring to the efforts of the Allies in the war on terrorism, Ukraine President Leonid Kuchma stated in November 2001, 'they'll do perfectly without us' (Torbakov 2002). Such apathy towards this transnational security threat, which affects all coalition partners, is problematic to say the least. Meanwhile, Moldova appears to be realigning with Russia, as Moscow and Chişinău signed a friendship treaty in November 2001, which recognised their 'strategic partnership' and accepted Moscow as the main arbitrator in the Transnistran dispute. Certainly the support offered to date by the Central Asian leaders far surpasses the level of support offered by other actors in the region.

On the other hand, the likelihood of bringing these states of Central Asia fully into the European security order is bleak, due to geopolitical realities and their internal political and economic situations. However, it should be clear that, although the Central Asian states, like the western FSU, are not likely to join NATO at any time in the near future, the US is attempting to establish a framework for increasing the ties between Central Asia/Caucasus and the West, which will probably be similar to the support offered to the western FSU in the late 1990s. On both counts, if the West had chosen not to develop closer ties with these countries, this inaction could be seen as a *de facto* acceptance of the region being firmly in Russia's sphere of influence. The US has chosen to forge ahead with the deepening of security engagement programmes with Central Asia over the past seven years, even at the risk of alarming Russia. Clearly, this programme has reaped tremendous benefits for the West in the war on terrorism. The existing activities have been effective in advancing mutual goals and objectives in the region. However, it is equally clear that the US and her allies lack a longer-term strategy for this region.

Faced with considerable threats to sovereignty and security on a multitude of levels, Central Asian leaders will continue to seek external assistance as they lack the capability to deal with crises on their own. The internal weaknesses of these states render them extremely vulnerable to outside encroachments, especially from Russia. Although Russia itself is rather weak, it is far stronger than all of the states in Central Asia combined, and, while its direct influence over their domestic affairs has decreased in recent years, Russia is still the dominating military, political and economic force in the region. Therefore it is in the interests of the US and its allies to work actively with countries in this region to increase the likelihood that Western methods for dealing with instabilities are adopted.

The extremely high profile of the war on terrorism since 11 September has encouraged the West, and particularly the US, to increase its security assistance to Central Asia and the Caucasus, primarily to deal with domestic terrorism and other insurgencies and to improve external border security. The US has sought to support these countries in their efforts to counter the trafficking of WMD, illegal narcotics and immigrants. However, the nature of US security assistance and other security-related activities in Central Asia makes it difficult for the US to have a balanced foreign policy which also includes rejecting countries with poor human rights and domestic reform records. European NATO countries have declared themselves in favour of this balanced approach to engagement with Central Asia and the Caucasus, primarily because they recognise the importance of linking military and economic assistance with domestic political and economic reform. By adopting elements of the approach advocated by NATO allies, the US will be much more successful in helping to bring these states into the European security order in the longer term.

Notes

1 Secretary of State Powell, testifying before the House International Relations Committee, 6 February 2002.
2 Formally known as the 'Shanghai Five', which includes Russia, China, Kyrgyzstan, Tajikistan and Kazakhstan, changing its name after the accession of Uzbekistan in 2001.
3 Interview with NATO official in the Defense Planning and Operations Division, NATO Headquarters, Brussels Belgium, May 2002.
4 See also Hill 2001.

Part V
Security dynamics

12 Conclusions

Security dynamics and the 'post-Soviet bloc'

Graeme P. Herd

Part I: The 'Soviet bloc'

The concept of a 'Soviet bloc' had relevance and purchase in the Cold War era. It conjured and combined concepts and power-relations constructed in the eighteenth and nineteenth centuries, while centring on the ideology of Russia as a Great Power, a centralised monarchical autocracy, a multi-ethnic land empire with a Eurasian presence but European centre of geopolitical gravity. In the twentieth century, this imperial tradition of a Russo–Soviet empire was transformed by Stalin during and after the Great Patriotic War (1941–45). As Dominic Lieven noted: 'arguably, the single most fatal blow dealt by Stalin to the Russo–Soviet empire was his annexation of the Baltic republics, Western Ukraine and Moldova in 1944–45' (Lieven 1999: 15) This empire was founded not simply on the incorporation of an 'inner empire' consisting of the Baltic states, Western Ukraine and Moldova in 1944–45, but also on the creation of an 'outer empire' through the installation of communist regimes in Central and Eastern Europe (CEE) between 1945 and 1948.

At the height of the Cold War, Western policymakers perceived a divided Europe straddled by a hegemonic Soviet Union at the head of an 'anti-imperialist' camp, integrating and controlling a bloc of satellite states in CEE over whose foreign and security policies it dominated and determined. The Stalinisation process drew strength from the pervasive presence of a Soviet army re-legitimised by its victory in the Great Patriotic War, and supported by the disillusionment of the old and, in some cases, compromised elites, contrasted by the elan and ideological certainties offered by energetic, organised and disciplined communist parties. Stalin had adopted a 'revolutionary imperial' paradigm in which his 'fusion of Marxist internationalism with tsarist imperialism could only reinforce this tendency in place well before World War II, to equate the advance of world revolution with the expanding influence of the Soviet state' (Gaddis 1997: 29).

Europe was divided between great power blocs, both East and West, each with their sphere of influence within a bi-polar international environment. As Nikolai Novikov, the Soviet Ambassador to Washington, noted in his evaluation of the Marshall Plan: 'a careful analysis of the Marshall Plan shows that ultimately it comes down to forming a West European bloc as a tool of US foreign policy'. In the West, the North Atlantic Treaty Organisation (NATO) and a nascent EU 'marshalled' Western democracies into military and economic alliances. In CEE, although Soviet control was never as uniform, homogenised or consistent, as the myth of a 'monolithic bloc' might suggest, the creation of the Warsaw Treaty Organisation (WTO) alliance (May 1955) and COMECON bound CEE militarily and economically to the Soviet Union. This provided the Soviet Union with a secure platform from which to project power globally and promote communist victories in China, North Korea and North Vietnam. The Soviet Union was the core of the 'Soviet bloc' – if not of the communist bloc after the split from Belgrade and Beijing. It became, to paraphrase Article VI of the Soviet Constitution, the guiding hand, and played the leading role in the formation and implementation of foreign and security policy in CEE. Communist party elites and key constituencies and interest groups within the Soviet Union held and exercised power, but as more recent Cold War reassessments have emphasised, although ideological stereotypes and established doctrines predominated, Soviet foreign and security policy decision-making process did allow for debate and differences of emphasis over the means to agreed ends.

Despite Albania's isolationism, and Yugoslavia's determination to retain its ideological autonomy in the politics of its alternative path to socialism (the 'Third Way') and its embrace of non-alignment as a security strategy, the Communist – if not the Soviet bloc – was strengthened by the Stalin-isation of CEE. Romania's ambivalent relationship with the WTO, the turbulence created by the Berlin Blockade (1948–1949), the East Berlin riots (1953), the Budapest and Warsaw Uprisings (1956), the Berlin Crisis (1958–62), Prague Spring (1968) and Polish unrest in the early 1970s did not seriously threaten Soviet hegemony at a fundamental level. Arguably, these 'counter-revolutions' in CEE only served to make more explicit the Brezhnev Doctrine of limited sovereignty as WTO armies suppressed by force the uprisings in Budapest and Prague. The exercise of the Brezhnev Doctrine in CEE upheld Soviet strategic parity with the West and also reinforced Soviet control, power and legitimacy within the borders of the Soviet Union. Indeed, in the historiography of the Cold War, the 'New Left' revisionists cite Western containment policy as a key factor in underpinning rather than undermining Soviet totalitarianism (Burns 1986: xx).

The Soviet Union was a key international actor. As a member of the UN's Security Council, a global nuclear power, a key source of ideological and polit-ical competition and economic power, it gave meaning to our understanding of the international system. The Cold War paradigm became the predominant framework or prism through which we conceived the distribution and practice of power on the international stage. The Soviet 'second world' (the 'East') offered an alternative model of development for those 'third world' states (the 'South'), and challenged the foundations for capitalist economies and democra-cies in the 'first world' (the 'West'). The Soviet bloc constituted a fundamental first-order governing dynamic in global security politics for the second half of the twentieth century, a role that appeared to be totally and universally undermined and discarded by the turbulent period of 1989–1991.

With the sudden and staggered collapse of the Soviet satellite states in CEE in 1989, and then the Soviet Union itself in 1991, the expectation amongst most scholars, analysts and practitioners was that the newly emergent – in some cases re-emergent – independent states would move from authoritarian state-building towards democratising their political systems, economies and foreign and security policies. As *Chapter 1* notes, democratic peace theory predicted that tensions and cleavages within and between the states in the region would gradually diminish, as all undertook a gradual strategic reorientation Westwards and reintegrated into a globalised economy. As a result, the cooperative capacities of former Soviet states have been adopted by researchers as a litmus test of the ability of these states to respect and uphold sovereignty and international law and become integrated in the international system.

The adherents of democratisation predicted that as a result tensions and cleavages within and between the states would gradually diminish, as all undertook a gradual strategic re-orientation westwards and reintegrated into a globalised economy. Democratic states shared the same norms and values and as a result enjoyed the efficiency of inter-democratic bargaining and conflict resolution. It was also argued that democratic states choose their wars more wisely than non-democratic states, have larger economies, form stronger alliances, and make better and more consensual decisions. When they do go to war they have higher levels of public support and can count on greater support from their militaries. The accountability and transparency within democratic states and in their oversight of the military reduces corruption in the defence sector and increases public legitimacy. For these reasons it was widely supposed that stability in post-Soviet political developments would increase as states in the region democratised. The only contested issue was the speed at which the process would occur, with an acknowledgement that variable-speed democratic transitions and consolidations were likely. Broadly speaking, the Baltic states were expected to undertake the transition first and move furthest fastest, whilst the five Central Asian ships of state would take up the rear of this Westward-steaming convoy.

Francis Fukuyama was the first to suggest that 1989 represented the triumph of market capitalism and liberal democratic ideology over all possible alternatives (Fukuyama 1989). The ideological dialectic that had shaped the international system, the struggle before 1945 between communism, capitalism and fascism, had been reduced after 1945 to competition between capitalism and communism. In the post-Cold War world, 'market-democracy' was set to become the modernisation project of choice for all states. The future of the international system was to be characterised by the gradual democratisation and consolidation of market-democratic institutions, policies, value and culture. Liberal institutionalism – internationally generated norms, procedures and institutions for the enforcement of mutually agreed legal frameworks –

would ultimately lead to the replacement of international anarchy with the international rule of law (Fukuyama 1992). The 'West was Best', and the twenty-first century offered more of the same; the 'End of History' paradigm was upon us, the triumph of Western-style modernity was set to create one universal world civilisation.

By 1993, Samuel Huntington, analysing the same events as Fukuyama, agreed that 1989–91 represented the demise of the Cold War international system, but offered a radically divergent interpretation of its implications (Huntington 1993). He argued that, as a consequence of the breakdown of the Cold War order, the future was not one of 'democratic peace' and cooperation within a single global system, but rather one of continual and protracted wars between 'civilisational blocs'. Seven civilisations spanned the globe, each at its heart characterised by alternative belief systems and the values they encapsulated. Western Christianity, Slavic Orthodoxy, Islam, Buddhism, Hinduism, Confucianism and 'possibly African' civilisations were now unconstrained by rigid bi-polar stability. Although the Soviet Union had been a superpower with foreign and security policy objectives that were global in reach, with the collapse of the Soviet bloc Russia's status had been downgraded to that of a major power. It had regional security interests – particularly in the deep South – and a civilisational resonance as the core state of Slavic Orthodoxy (Huntington 1996a). Where these civilisations brushed up against each other, Huntington argued, cultural fault-lines could be identified, and it was along these fault-lines that future wars were most likely to be located. This left hanging the question of where the cultural faultiness would to fall in the Caucasus and Central Asia: was Ukraine to be divided? These quibbles aside, a 'Clash of Civilisations' paradigm emerged to challenge that of the 'End of History'.

Both of these mutually exclusive paradigms have been subjected to powerful attack; neither were assumed to have sufficient explanatory power to account for the full range of dynamics that drove and characterised the international system, nor indeed the complexity of international relations in the post-soviet bloc. Geoffrey Hosking, for example, accounted for the collapse of the Soviet Union primarily in terms of a struggle for privilege within the *nomenklatura* patronage system, which ultimately resulted in Soviet elites declaring independence from the centre in order to consolidate their own power bases. He asks: 'does the Russian Federation remain a neo-nomenklatura fiefdom, fought over by rival networks which control industry, commerce, media?' (Hosking 1999: 222). Other scholars have directly questioned the paradigms of Huntington and Fukuyama, particularly their failure to appreciate the extent to which a rapidly globalising world challenges the hegemony of the state as the agent of modernisation. The Traditional Security Dilemma has been replaced, over the last 30 years, by a New Security Dilemma (Cerney 2000). Here, fragmentation and radicalisation and their associated insecurities are not bounded by identifiable state, civilisational or cultural frames of reference, but rather by socio-economic conditions, questions of identity and autonomy, alienation and the struggle for social power.

Consequently, states are challenged by social forces that act globally and pursue multiple and competing objectives within different timeframes and utilising a range of divergent means (Herd and Weber 2001).

Russian perspectives on the endurance, sustainability and desirability of Russian hegemony are equally contradictory and partial, conceived as they were in the context of vanishing supremacies, diminished possibilities and a pervasive post-imperial identity crisis. Broadly, three schools of thought are said to have dominated foreign and security policy debates within the Russian Federation. The first – the liberal-Atlanticist school – rejected manifest destiny, the necessity of maintaining a militarised economy and the resurfacing pre-Soviet Russian Orthodox and communist–nationalist messianic strains in Russian political culture – the disparate and complex cornerstones of Eurasianist thought within Russia. Rather than integrating around a shared idea of Russian historical development, which stressed the uniqueness of Russia as a distinct civilisation and perceived the West as 'denationalising Atlanticism', the liberal-Atlanticists wanted Russia to emerge as a prosperous, 'normal', democratic country, to become (again) a pillar of Western culture and civilisation. The centrists dominated the space, if not exactly between the Eurasianist and liberal-Atlanticist schools, then at least at the third corner of Russia's foreign and security policy triangle. Centrists perceived Russia's orientation as Western, lacking as it did natural allies in Asia. However, good relations with the West would be undermined by NATO 'expansion', a process which avoided recognition of Russia as a Great Power with legitimate political, economic and diaspora-related state interests its 'Near Abroad' (Prizel 1998: 239–99).

What, then, has been the experience of the former Soviet bloc, from the Baltic region through to Central Asia? How might we best understand the condition of security, stability and interstate relations in former Soviet space? To what extent have these states developed cooperative foreign and security policies towards their immediate neighbours? What is the nature of the relationship and interplay between internal and external aspects of democratic security building? How might we characterise the main security dynamics in shaping interstate bilateral and multilateral relations in post-Soviet space?

Part II: The Baltic states

Part II examined issues relating to the foreign and security policies of the three Baltic states. All three states are united in their strategic reorientation Westwards and their efforts to become integrated within European and Euro-Atlantic institutions. The Baltic states left one Union into which they had been forcibly integrated during the Soviet period, and have attempted to overcome obstacles and challenges to become integrated into another – albeit radically different – the European Union. Their shared experience of occupation and of being independent sovereign nations in the Interwar period, their coordinated break from the Soviet Union, and their aligned strategic reorientation Westwards in the face of Russian opposition and insecurity have all combined to promote the perception that the Baltic states constitute a single sub-regional geopolitical bloc.

Can this most economically developed and democratised, stable and 'European' of the former Soviet sub-regions be perceived in terms of shared foreign and security identity, goals and objectives? At a superficial level, this perception is uncontested as the Baltic states demonstrably have more in common with each other than they do with the rump of the former Soviet bloc. However, as Adam Grissom in *Chapter 2* notes, the commonalties forged in foreign and security policy through the late 1980s and 1990s are challenged by the November 2002 Prague Summit in a number of ways. The Prague Summit represents a symbolic Rubicon; accession into NATO is the achievement of the primary foreign and security goals of all three Baltic states. Integration into the Euro-Atlantic security community brings with it the duties and responsibilities of membership. These requirements will be long-term and, in the context of the 'global war against terror', are fast evolving and becoming more burdensome (defence expenditure, human capacity) as NATO attempts to match the reality of its April 1999 Strategic Concept – a collective security organisation with a collective defence core – with the reality of potential member-state capacity, not to mention the growing trans-Atlantic drift in technological capability, shared strategic culture and political will so apparent amongst existing member states.

Formal NATO accession, as well as highlighting the requirements of membership, also places an emphasis on secondary foreign and security policy objectives, such as EU accession, stabilising inter-societal relations, combating organised crime and illegal migration, and the requirements of Schengen border regimes. This 'soft security' agenda is more complex, and harder for the Baltic states to address, shaped as it is by the interplay of supranational EU and member-state policy formation and the antagonistic push and pull of intergovernmental and federal dynamics, second-echelon EU enlargement debates and the contested direction and purpose of ESDP. Moreover, once accession to NATO and the EU has been achieved, it is highly likely that – just as happened after Iberian Peninsula integration or the formation of the Benelux bloc – the constituent parts will follow their own occasionally divergent interests; and accession will lead to a greater fragmentation of the Baltic states in foreign and security matters. This, in turn, will reduce the collective geopolitical weight of the Baltic bloc as a whole, but increase the bargaining power and influence of individual states in new informal alliances and partnerships within the EU and NATO.

It is clear that an undercurrent of divergent policy goals, sources of insecurity and integration policies has existed through the 1990s and was visible to the discerning analyst in the pre-accession period. Whether we examine inter-Baltic institutional collaboration in the economic (free-trade agreement) or political (Baltic Assembly) spheres, trilateral cooperation has been weak and largely ineffective, subsumed to the primary strategic goal of EU and NATO integration – worthwhile in so far as it demonstrates cooperative capacity and so serves this larger end. In *Chapter 3*, Mel Huang carries forward the broad analysis of the previous chapter by focusing on intra-Baltic foreign policy cooperation within the military–security sector. This sector is widely perceived as the jewel in the crown of intra-Baltic cooperation – the most active, interoperable (personnel, materiel, infrastructure) and effective example of practical and meaningful cooperation. However, as this analysis argues, even *BALTBAT* – the flagship of military cooperative efforts – has achieved little in substantive (albeit much in public relations) terms. Despite the volume and quality of intra-Baltic military cooperation diminishing over the longer term after NATO accession, NATO will remain the lynchpin of Baltic security in the long term.

Through the 1990s a number of paradoxes and dilemmas punctuated and helped characterise the complex nature of security relations in the region: the greater Russian opposition to membership, the greater the Baltic domestic pressure and Western acceptance of integration; Russian acquiescence and acceptance of the process reduced the necessity; Baltic integration would consolidate Russia's isolation; sovereignty and independence could only be secured through integration into a supranational union. As Vladimir Putin's Russia has gradually begun to accept the reality of NATO enlargement in the Baltic region, the issue of EU integration has risen in strategic importance. In *Chapter 4*, Ingmar Oldberg identifies pressures that shape Russia's Baltic policy through the 1990s and into the new century – in particular the geo-economic considerations that have arisen in line with closer EU cooperation and the prospect of Baltic EU membership.

The unresolved tension between the different foreign and security policy camps within the Russian Federation is mirrored in the highly contested debate that characterised the ends to which economic levers of influence are deployed by the Russian Federation. It also illustrates the extent to which former Soviet republics were able to reorient their foreign and security policy after 1991, despite the high degree of economic centralisation that characterised the Soviet political economy and geography. Indeed, this Russo–Baltic case study underlines the limits of economic pressure when deployed to attain politico–military or societal security goals. Russia's determination to remove Baltic NATO integration from the European security agenda necessitated acquiescence to closer Baltic EU integration, and hence the reduced dependence upon the Russian economy. Russian economic sanctions through the reduction or redirection of energy exports and transit trade harmed Russia's own economic interests and those of her 'compatriots' in the Baltic states, who wee employed in port and rail transport networks.

The focus on Kaliningrad and the interrelated requirements of Schengen border regimes demonstrates the extent and all-encompassing nature of the Russo–EU policy agenda and the necessity of compromise and accommodation. It is increasingly clear that a correlation is emerging between Russia's economic development – its ability to modernise its economy, state and society – and its relations with its largest trading partner, the EU. The manner in which the EU and Russia compromise over the numerous points of potential and actual disagreement will prove a precedent for Russia's ability to be integrated into the wider world.

Part III: The Slavic republics – a core CIS?

Part III turns our attention to what might be considered the core of the Commonwealth of Independent States (CIS) – the three 'Slavic republics', Russia, Ukraine and Belarus. As Rosaria Puglisi observes in *Chapter 5*, the geo-economic dynamic in Russian foreign and security policy through the 1990s reached its apotheosis after the August 1998 meltdown, and was ultimately reflected in the 2000 Russian Foreign Policy Concept. The rise of the centrists or pragmatic nationalists to predominance in the mid-1990s, and the impact that the influence of Russian business elites on Russian foreign and security policy formation had on interstate relations within the former Soviet bloc, characterises a key security dynamic. Essentially, an emphasis on economic links, transit trade and energy diplomacy provided Russia with the means to both address domestic reform (an agenda largely shaped by the deterioration of an economy caught within a 'structural trap') and enhance the state's international status.

Russia's initial post-Soviet security strategy had been to adopt the line of least resistance and fall back upon economic networks and patterns of relations that had been created in the Soviet period. This inevitably placed an emphasis on the importance of maintaining intra-CIS economic trade. Whilst this reinforced dependency relationships in the short term and increased the likelihood that CIS states would accommodate Russia on bilateral points of dispute, in the process it sheltered Russian business from the realities of the market and global economic competition. As a result, Russia, alongside the majority of CIS states, was largely untouched by integration into the global political economy in the 1990s. The political and security costs of such a strategy outweighed the benefits and, by the mid-1990s, Russia had begun to pursue the same goals by different means – what could be seen as the 'outsourcing' of foreign economic relations to the foreign policy preferences of big business.

The limits to financial/industrial group domination of Russian foreign policy were evident. Big business generally lacked the resources to pursue independent foreign policies, little common ground could be found between competing companies, particularly those in the energy sector and the military–industrial complex, and, whereas the state attempted to project power and maximise interests, companies were more interested in market share and maximising profits – at times mutually incompatible goals. The rise in importance of economic factors in Russian foreign policy was evidence of the normalisation of Russian foreign policy in an age of globalisation. Economic factors have shaped relations within the former Soviet bloc, and it is not unnatural to conclude that Russia, as the largest former Soviet republic in terms of territory, population, economic wealth and military power, has proved the main dynamic within this complex.

However, as Frank Morgese demonstrates in *Chapter 6*, external factors have also aligned and highlighted disparities in the foreign and security politics of states in the former Soviet bloc. Whilst the previous section identifies and assesses security implications of EU membership to first-echelon states, this chapter compares and contrasts the impact of NATO and EU enlargement on both Russia and Ukraine. Through the 1990s, the NATO enlargement process in general and the deployment of NATO during the Kosovo campaign of 1999 in particular explicitly demonstrated Russian military weakness, an army the revolution in military affairs has largely bypassed at a time when Russian strategic access over former Soviet satellite states in CEE has been denied. Whilst NATO military manoeuvres in Ukraine, the Baltic states and Poland have heightened Russian military sensitivities, EU enlargement projects a much more complex and sophisticated security agenda for both Russia and Ukraine.

The extent to which the Russo–Finnish/EU/Schengen border regime can be replicated along the Russo–Baltic and Ukrainian–Polish border is open to question. Such enlargement of the Euro-Atlantic security community into – for the first time – former Soviet territory will place additional strains on Ukraine's foreign and security policy of non-alignment and 'equidistance' between and Russia and NATO. What might be the effect of further NATO enlargement on Russo–Ukrainian relations?

In order to address this question Victor Chudowsky in *Chapter 7* evaluates the tensions and pressures that shaped Russia's relations with Ukraine in the post-Soviet period, and argues that through the 1990s Russia adopted an imperialist and hegemonic strategy towards Ukraine. The CIS became the main vehicle of Russian leadership in foreign and security policy within CIS-space, allowing Russia to influence both politico–military and economic relations between the former republics – particularly Ukraine – and helping to stabilise the territory of the Federation itself through the protection of Russians living beyond Russia. Russian control of the Black Sea Fleet and the city of Sevastopol, and Russia's applied pressure to bring Ukraine to accept full CIS membership ('tight cooperation') are all illustrative of Russian efforts to achieve this central strategic goal.

It is into this equation that we attempt to calculate the role of the West, or, more accurately, the US, in shaping Russo–Ukrainian relations. Bill Clinton's second term as president (1996–2000) viewed Ukraine as a 'pivot state' within the region and a 'strategic counterweight' to Russian power. This policy entailed the increase of US–Ukrainian military aid and the widening of Ukrainian security cooperation with Euro-Atlantic security structures and initiatives. It has become clear that, whilst the West has shaped Russo– Ukrainian relations, there are limits to Ukraine's ability to become integrated in Western security structures and, perhaps more importantly, those limits are as much a product of Western policy as they are of

Ukrainian internal weakness and inability to satisfy the integration criteria. If Ukraine does become integrated in the EU or NATO without Russia, then two important security consequences would appear to follow. Russia would be more isolated from the Euro-Atlantic security order, and Ukraine would cease to act as a counterweight to Russia with the CIS.

Dual enlargement has had a profound and growing impact on Russo–Ukrainian relations. It would appear that the same cannot be said for Belarusian–Russian relations, as both states – Belarus in even more categorical terms than Russia – have expressed the desire not to be integrated into NATO, and Belarus's reaction to the prospect of Baltic and Polish EU accession is lukewarm. Rather, Belarus has identified Russia as its primary strategic partner, and signed a Union Treaty with the intention of full integration into a single state. In *Chapter 8*, Clelia Rontoyanni brings the analysis of interstate relations within the Slavic core of the former Soviet bloc to a close by providing a clearly argued assessment of the paradoxical role of dual enlargement on Belarusian–Russian relations.

She argues that the 'Russia first' foreign policy of Belarus, based on the strategic goal of full integration, provides Russia with a means of reforming Belarus – particularly the 'Soviet model' economy – ahead and in the name of union. At the same time, Belarus has attempted to end its isolation within the international system by formalising relations with the EU whilst seeking closer integration with the CIS. Indeed, Belarus promotes the EU as an example of an effective integrative model that the CIS could well emulate. Belarus and Russia have attained full foreign and security policy integration, particularly in terms of military-to-military coordination. NATO enlargement Eastwards – its speed and implications – provides Belarus with the context and strategic rationale for integration with Russia, whilst the EU provides the institutional model. President Lukashenka's falling popularity in 2003 (under 20%) has highlighted the extent to which the rhetoric of union and cooperation with Russia matches the reality of a rather frosty relationship; it has exposed the degree to which Lukashenka has hitherto used the Belarus–Russia relationship instrumentally for domestic political advantage and the consolidation of his pre-eminent position within the state.

This parallel integrative process has yet to gain currency within the CIS outside the confines of the Belarus–Russia Union; Ukraine, for example, has not expressed an interest in such integration, and Moldova, although it pays lip service to the ideal, is incapable of realising such integration. However, for its proponents the reintegration of the Slavic core might be perceived as the first step to a wider reintegration of former Soviet territory and the emergence of a post-Soviet bloc in international relations. To what extent is this a viable option for the future? Does Slavic reintegration have a greater resonance outside of Moscow and Minsk, or are other security dynamics more compelling and less directed within the other CIS states?

Part IV: The CIS periphery – Moldova, South Caucasus and Central Asia

Part IV proceeds to direct our focus towards the periphery of the CIS, with an evaluation of the foreign and security policy of a non-aligned Moldova, an analysis of Georgian foreign policy within the complex context of security relations in the south Caucasus, and an introduction to an emergent dynamic that increasingly will shape the security environment in Central Asia – namely, US bilateral and multilateral relations with states considered hitherto to fall within Russia's sphere of influence. This final section allows us to compare and contrast foreign and security policy characteristics over the whole of what was the Soviet bloc.

In *Chapter 9*, Trevor Waters characterises the security politics of Moldova, a borderland state with just under 4.5 million inhabitants. Moldova is one of Europe's smallest and poorest states, but in the Soviet period the Moldovian SSR held a strategic significance as the key to the Balkans. In the post-Soviet period, Moldova has been fragmented by language, culture and identity as tensions between pro-Russian separatist movements and pro-Romanian unification groups on its territory have stalled transition and reform. Moldova is formally neutral, but its ability to exercise its own foreign and security policies has been severely constrained by the self-styled breakaway Dnestr Moldovan Republic (DMR), a highly Sovietised outpost in the post-Soviet world. Russia's policy of equivocation and prevarication has allowed Moscow to support Transnistrian separatism through the Russian peacekeeping forces and Operational Group of Russian Forces (OGRF). The recent election of a communist regime to power in Chişinău has sparked a push to re-Russify and a corresponding backlash through the formation of an anti-Russification movement. Moldova appears to be caught in a series of transition traps, with little prospect of stabilising its internal security, and beset by a growing raft of transnational sources of insecurity, such as illegal migration, drugs and prostitution networks, and small arms smuggling.

Georgia's independent state-building project and attempts to develop a coherent foreign and security policy have also been similarly constrained by a turbulent post-Soviet environment. In *Chapter 10*, Tamara Pataraia and David Darchiashvili posit the choice between reorientation Westwards or the maintenance of a primary focus to the North – between democratic and independent development and post-Soviet Russian protectorate status. Separatist movements in South Ossetia and Abkhazia, a civil war between Armenia and Azerbaijan, and Russia's exercise of political and economic influence to exclude the participation of external actors in the South Caucasus have all undermined democratic security building in the region. It is clear that – as with the case of Moldova – the CIS has proved remarkably weak as a tool of reintegration. Indeed, its very ineffectiveness has prompted closer and stronger links with Euro-Atlantic security institutions in the 1990s. In this respect, NATO and PfP activities have proved highly visible in the post-9/11 international environment, but it remains to be seen whether Russia's strategic realignment with the West – post-9/11 – translates into the security politics of the South Caucasus and Central Asia. Will Georgia be able to pursue a policy of strategic rapprochement with Russia whilst strengthening cooperative security links with the West?

Chapter 11 brings this section to a close, as Jennifer Moroney charts the growth of US security assistance to Central Asia and the Caucasus – a process that increased dramatically following the events of 11 September, but which began in the mid-1990s with bilateral and multilateral military exercises. Although the CIS has provided Russia with a leadership role in foreign and security policy-making in the region, the importance of energy infrastructure protection coupled with the potential spillover effects of transnational security threats (terrorism, illegal migration and organised criminal activities) helped define and clarify US security interests in the region.

In the zero sum equations of post-Cold War security politics, an increase in US interest in the region could only be achieved if Russia was gradually forced out of her traditional sphere of influence. However, the attacks of 11 September and the global war against terror provided the ideological legitimacy and strategic rationale to increase aid to Central Asian governments. US access to military infrastructure and intelligence-sharing in return for economic assistance and support took place irrespective of Central Asian efforts to democratise their foreign and security policies. However, in identifying Uzbekistan as the key strategic partner or 'bridgehead', the US has countered the traditional role of Russia in the region and tilted the struggle for regional hegemony between Uzbekistan and Kazakhstan in Uzbekistan's favour. Pre-existing regional rivalries have also rendered cooperative security exercises largely impotent, despite the wide range of mechanisms available to the US and NATO to deliver security assistance and increase cooperation.

Whilst all states in the former Soviet bloc continue to face challenges and obstacles to stability and security, the nature of these obstacles and the challenges that they pose to external actors differ radically. In Central Asia and the South Caucasus, the West faces a dilemma – how to balance the interests of security with support for democracy. Should the West support authoritarian regimes facing radical Islamic opposition, or face strongly anti-Western Islamic regimes? In the Baltic states, attempts to integrate into NATO and the EU are subject to stringent criteria that demand political capital be spent by the elites to persuade the publics that benefits outweigh costs. In Russia, President Putin's ability to undertake strategic realignment has been facilitated by fundamental and deep-seated disparities within the Euro-Atlantic security community. These differences allow Russia to draw closer to European NATO through adaptive acquiescence in the Baltic region, all the while maintaining a semblance of strategic parity with the US through arms control negotiations and coalition partnership in Central Asia. A paradox emerges: the very weakness of the concept of a 'global war against terror' becomes its greatest strength; the inherent ambiguities and ambivalence embodied by this 'war' provide Russia with an ideological pretext for foreign policy change through strategic realignment, whilst the fractures within the Euro-Atlantic security community allow for differentiated realignment with the West. This strategic stance will shape Russia's relations with Belarus, Moldova and Ukraine.

Foreign and security policies within the periphery of the former Soviet bloc are fragmented and divergent, where separate integrative dynamics shape and inform the respective regional security agendas in the Baltic states and Central Asia. As a result, the role of Russia as a bridge, an overarching and unifying dynamic, is increasingly diminished. Paradoxically, the weaker is Russian power projection at the periphery, the greater its normative power at the CIS centre – Belarus, Ukraine and Moldova. These states, with little likelihood of integration with the West and riven by internal structural weaknesses, will fall back on traditional hierarchies sustained by new inequalities in wealth and power.

In the months following 11 September 2001, many of the underlying systemic trends have become much more visible, as has our understanding of their influence on international relations. The primacy of the US in the international system is most obviously demonstrated by its huge technology and weapons advantage over its nearest rivals, and to a large extent it sets the international security agenda. The September 2002 US National Security Strategy notes that the US does not fear being conquered by other states but rather – paradoxically – failed or collapsed states and the 'nexus of tyrants and terrorists' pose the greatest threat to its stability. The Strategy explicitly asserts that the US will not permit other individual states or coalitions of states to challenge its global hegemony in the future and expresses the willingness of the US to act alone or within 'coalitions of the willing' to defend its interests and protect its citizens. It is clear that the abandonment of containment and deterrence for the doctrine of pre-emption is set to shape security politics in the new century. How, though, might such changes transform the Euro-Atlantic security order, and what are the implications for the former Soviet bloc?

Within the context of the 'global war on terror' and the increase of US bilateral links with key strategic partners in the region, it is likely that Eurasian states will seek to counterbalance US influence through increasing use of international organisations such as the OSCE and UN (and perhaps NATO's PfP), as well as organisations that are restricted to former Soviet space such as the CIS (through informal networks), and Eurasian organisations such as the Shanghai Cooperative Organization (SCO). At the same time, Russia will increasingly seek to operationalise its strategic realignment with the CIS, over which it has hegemony, and is likely to adopt the preemption doctrines of its strategic partner – the US. The continued instability in the Middle East and Central Asia – the post-Saddam regime appointed after operation 'Iraqi Freedom' is completed, the continued efforts to reconstruct Afghanistan, and Iran's status within an 'axis of evil' – will prompt regional powers such as Iran, Iraq, China, Japan and Turkey to continue attempts to increase their influence over former Soviet space.

The dual enlargement process in the West will complicate the role of regional powers to the South. At the November 2002 NATO Prague Summit the accession of seven new member states by 2004 was agreed, including the three Baltic states. The December 2002 Copenhagen EU Summit also adopted a 'big bang' approach to the first round of EU enlargement, and ten new EU member states – including the three Baltic states – will be integrated into the EU in 2004/2005. These processes will further fragment the coherence of what was the former Soviet bloc, whilst at the same time reinforcing ties between Russia, Ukraine and Belarus, the Slavic core of what was once the Russian empire and Soviet bloc.

Looking to the future, how might demographic change, natural resources and the environment, science and technology, the global economy and globalisation, national and international governance and future conflict affect the security of individuals, societies, states, and sub-regions within and between the former Soviet bloc and the global international system? Although the evolution and impact of these key global trends and dynamics are difficult for the student of post-Soviet security politics international relations to discern, the questions themselves are of importance.

The impact of globalisation upon security and stability can be understood as a dual process, with the Baltic states and Russia and Ukraine (in parts) benefiting from 'thick globalisation' and its attendant sources of stability. They are integrating into the 'functioning core' of the globalised world – a core that embodies rule sets, norms and ties that bind it in mutually assured dependence. Such 'thick globalisation' is characterised by network connectivity, financial transactions, liberal media flows. In this secure environment collective security systems underpin stable governments and populations enjoying rising living standards. 'Thin globalisation' occurs in the non-integrating gap that constitutes a strategic threat environment for the functioning core. It is a source of insecurity as it allows for politically repressive regimes to consolidate, regimes which can be characterised in extreme cases by the prevalence of widespread poverty, disease and mass murder. The Central Asian republics lie between the non-integrating gap and the functioning core, whilst the states of the South Caucasus, Moldova, and Belarus are as dependent on Russia as they are on the West to marry them to the stabilising benefits of 'thick globalisation'.

The security dynamics which shape international relations and the levels and quality of stability within the former Soviet bloc are complex, inter-related and very difficult to isolate. Moreover, their causal factors and consequences are hard to discern. This book has attempted – however imperfectly – to at least identify some of the key debates and outline the evolving context within which the foreign and security policies of the former Soviet states are elaborated. Perhaps ultimately, the degree to which the former Soviet republics can be integrated into the global political economy will be critical to stability in this region.

Bibliography

ABALKIN, Leonid I (1994) 'Ekonomicheskaya bezopasnost Rossii: ugrozy i ikh otrazhenie', *Voprosy ekonomiky*, no. 12: 4–13.

ALEXANDROVA, Olga, Götz, Roland, and Halbach, Uwe (2003) *Rußland und der postsowjetische Raum*, Rußland und der postsowjetische Raum Baden-Baden: NOMOS Verlagsanstalt.

ALLISON, Roy (2000) 'Subregional Cooperation and Security in the CIS', in Dwan and Pavliuk 2000: 149–76.

—— and Johnson, Lena (eds) (2001) *Central Asian Security: The New International Context*, London and Washington: Royal Institute of International Affairs and Brookings Institution Press.

ALSAUSKAS, Juozas (2000) 'The Baltic Naval Squadron – BALTRON', *Baltic Defence Review*, vol. 2000, no. 3: 33–7.

ARBATOV, Alexei G (1994) 'Russian National Interests', in Blackwill and Karaganov 1994: 55–76.

ARCHER, Clive (1999) 'Nordic Involvement in the Baltic States' Security: Need, Motives, and Success', Copenhagen Peace Research Institute (COPRI); http://www.ciaonet.org/wps/sites/copri.html.

—— (2000) *EU and the Common Strategy to Russia: A Bridge Too Far?*, Camberley: Conflict Studies Research Centre (CSRC), February 2000, F69/3.

—— and Jones, Christopher (1999) 'The Security Policies and Concepts of the Baltic States – Learning from their Nordic Neighbours?', in Knudsen 1999: 167–82.

ARNSWALD, Sven and Jopp, Mathias (2001) *The Implications of Baltic States' EU Membership*, Helsinki: The Finnish Institute of International Affairs; Berlin: Institut für europäische Politik.

ARON, Leon R (1998) 'The Foreign Policy Doctrine of Post-Communist Russia and Its Domestic Context', in Mandelbaum 1998: 23–63.

—— (2001) *Yeltsin: A Revolutionary Life*, New York: St. Martin's Press.

ARTÉUS, Gunnar and Lejins, Atis (eds) (1997) *Baltic security. Looking towards the 21st century*, Riga: Latvian Institute of International Affairs; Stockholm: Försvarshögskolan.

ASMUS, Ronald (1996) 'NATO Enlargement and Baltic Security', presentation at 'The Baltic Sea Region and the New European Security Structure' conference, Stockholm, 19 November 1996; www.usis.usemb.se/BalticSec/ASMUS.htm

AUSTIN, Daniel F C (1999) *NATO Expansion and the Baltic States*, Camberley: Conflict Studies Research Centre (CSRC), February 1999, G70.

AVERY, Graham and Cameron, Fraser (1998) *The Enlargement of the European Union,* Sheffield: Sheffield Academic Press.

AYOOB, M (1995) *The Third World Security Predicament: State Making, Regional Conflict, and the International System,* London: Lynne Rienner.

BABILUNGA, N V and Bomeshko, B G (1993) *Bendery rasstrelyanye nepokorennye,* Tiraspol: T G Shevchenko Transnistrian State-Corporate University.

BAKER, James C (1997) 'Non-Proliferation Incentives for Russia and Ukraine', *Adelphi Papers,* 309: 55–79.

BALEANU, V G (2000) *In the Shadow of Russia: Romania's Relations with Moldova and Ukraine,* Camberley: Conflict Studies Research Centre (CSRC), November 2000, G85.

BARAJŪNAS, Eitvydas (2000) 'Baltic Security Co-operation: a Way Ahead', *Baltic Defence Review,* vol. 1999, no. 3: 43–62.

BARANOVSKY, Vladimir (ed.) (1997) *Russia and Europe: The Emerging Security Agenda,* Oxford: Oxford University Press and SIPRI.

BARSKY, Jennifer (1999) 'Drawing the Line in the Snow: Finnish Frontier Guards Internationalize Activities',*The Washington Times International Supplements,* 23 April 1999.

BASHKIROVA, Elena (1998) 'Democracy, Foreign Policy and the Media in the Russian Federation', Individual Fellowship Paper http://www.nato.int/acad/fellow/96-98/f96-98.htm.

BEISSINGER, Mark R (1997) 'State Building in the Shadow of an Empire State', in Dawisha 1997: 157–85.

BELAPAN (2001) 'The Viewer', 8–14 August 2001.

BLACK, J L (1986) *Origins, Evolution and Nature of the Cold War: an Annotated Bibliographical Guide,* Oxford: Oxford University Press.

BLACK SEA ECONOMIC CO-OPERATION (BSEC) (1997) Report of the Ninth Meeting of the Ministers of Foreign Affairs, Istanbul, 30 April 1997.

BLACKWILL, Robert D and Karaganov, Sergei A (eds) (1994) *Damage Limitation or Crisis?: Russia and the Outside World,* Washington: Brassey's.

BLANK, Stephen J (1998a) *NATO Enlargement and the Baltic States: What Can Great Powers Do?,* Carlisle: U.S. Army War College Strategic Studies Institute.

—— (1998b) 'Rhetoric and Reality in NATO Enlargement,' in Blank 1998a: 5–48.

—— (1998c) 'Russia and the Baltics in the Age of NATO Enlargement', *Parameters,* vol. 28, no. 3, Autumn 1998: 50–68. .

—— (2000) *Rethinking the Nordic–Baltic Security Agenda: A Proposal,* Camberley: Conflict Studies Research Centre (CSRC), November 2000, G88.

BLEIERE, Daina (1998), 'Latvia and the Future of European Security', in Blank 1997: 119–146.

BOGOMOLOV, Oleg (1996) 'National Interests in Russian Foreign Policy', *International Affairs* (Moscow), vol. 42, no. 2: 1–24.

BONVICINI, G, Greco, E, Von Plate, B and Rummel, R (eds) (1998) *Preventing Violent Conflict: Issues from the Baltic and Caucasus,* Baden-Baden: Nomos Verlagsgesellschaft.

BOWERS, Stephen (1993) 'The Partition of Moldova', *Jane's Intelligence Review,* October 1993: 435–7.

BRADLEY, Bryan (2002) 'Baltics Increasingly Confident as EU and NATO Enlargement Nears', Agence France Presse, 27 Jan 2002.

BROK, Yvonne (2001) 'Schengen: Nothing New for Finland',*Euro Views International Magazine*, 27 April 2002.
—— and Kuprijanko, Alexander (2001) 'Patrolling the Border', *Euro Views International Magazine*, 27 April 2002.
BROWNING, Christopher S (2001) 'A Multi-Dimensional Approach to Regional Cooperation: The United States and the Northern European Initiative', Copenhagen Peace Research Institute (COPRI); www.copri.dk/ publications/ WP/ WP%202001/15–2001.doc
BRUBAKER, Rogers (1994) 'Nationhood and the National Question in the Soviet Union and Post-Soviet Eurasia: An Institutionalist Account', *Theory and Society*, no. 23: 47–78.
BRZEZINSKI, Zbigniew (1989) *The Grand Failure: the Birth and Death of Communism in the Twentieth Century*, London: Macdonald.
—— (1997) 'A Geostrategy for Eurasia', *Foreign Affairs*, September/October 1997, vol. 74 (1): 26–42.
—— (1998) 'A Plan for Europe', *Foreign Affairs*, vol. 76, no. 5, 1998: 50–64.
BUKVOLL, Tor (2001) 'Off the Cuff Politics – Explaining Russia's Lack of a Ukraine Strategy', *Europe–Asia Studies*, vol. 53, no. 8, December 2001: 1151–8.
BURNS, Richard Dean (1986) 'Foreword', in Black 1986a.
BUZAN, Barry, Waever, Ole and De Vilde, Jaap (1998) *Security: A New Framework for Analyses*, London: Lynne Rienner.
BYMAN, Daniel and Van Evera, Stephen (1998) 'Why They Fight Hypotheses on the Causes of Contemporary Deadly Conflict', *Security Studies*, vol. 7, no. 3: 1–50.
CARR, E H (1966)*The Bolshevik Revolution 1917–1923*, vol. 3, London: Macmillan.
CARYL, Christian (1998) 'Who Makes Russia's Foreign Policy Anyway?', *US News and World Report*, 16 February.
CASTLE, Stephen (2001a) 'Poland: New Guard of Fortress Europe', *Independent on Sunday*, 8 April 2001.
—— (2001b) 'Back to the Wall...', *Financial Times*, 2 August 2001: 20.
CENTRE FOR EUROPEAN INTEGRATION STUDIES (2001) 'EU and Georgia – New Perspective', Tbilisi, vol. 2, no. 9.
CERNEY, Phillip G (2000) 'The New Security Dilemma: divisibility, defection and disorder in the global era', *Review of International Studies*, vol. 26: 623–46.
CHAMPION, Marc (2002) 'Europeans Fear Bush's Signaling of Unilateralist Foreign Policy', *Wall Street Journal*, 4 February 2002.
CHANG, Steve (1995) 'Regime Transition in the Asia/Pacific Region: Democratisation as a Double-Edged Sword', *The Journal of Strategic Studies*, vol. 18, no. 3, September 1995: 52–67
CHUBARIAN, A O (1997) 'Novaia istoriia "Kholodnoi Voiny"', *Novaia i noveishaia istoriia,* no. 6, 1997: 8–9.
CLEMENS, Walter J (2001) *The Baltic Transformed: Complexity Theory and European Security,* Lanham: Rowman and Littlefield.
CLEMMESEN, Michael H (1999) 'NATO Interoperability and the Baltic Defence College', *Baltic Defence Review*, vol. 1999, no. 1: 116–27.
—— (2001) 'The Colonel's Course – A Shortcut to Defence Development', *Baltic Defence Review*, vol. 2001, no. 5: 7–11.
COHEN, Ariel (2001) 'The Reason for Concern: Latest Tendencies of the Russian Policy in the South Caucasus',*Central Asia and the Caucasus*, vol. 14, no. 2: 7–12.

COHEN, Richard (2001) 'Cooperative Security: From Individual Security to International Stability', in Cohen and Mihalka 2001: 1–27.

—— and Mihalka, Michael (2001) Garmisch-Partenkirchen: The Marshall Center Papers, no. 3.

COLTON, Timothy and Legvold, Robert (eds) (1992) *After the Soviet Union: From Empire to Nations*, New York: W. W. Norton.

COUNCIL ON FOREIGN AND DEFENCE POLICY (CFDP) (1997) 'Will the Union be Reborn? The Future of the Post-Soviet Region', Cambridge: J. F. Kennedy School of Governance, Harvard University, Strengthening Democratic Institutions Project, June 1997.

DAHRENDORF, Ralf (1990) ' Transitions: Politics, Economics and Liberty', *The Washington Quarterly*, vol. 13, no. 3, Summer 1990: 133–42

DALBIÙŠ, Juris (1996) 'Baltic Cooperation – the Key to Wider Security', *NATO Review*, vol. 44, no. 1, January 1996: 7–10.

DANILOV, Dmitrii (2001) 'The EU's Rapid Reaction Capabilities: A Russian Perspective', Seminar on ESDP, 10 September 2001, Brussels: Centre for European Security Studies; www.eusec.org

DANOPOULOS, Constantine P and Zirker, Daniel G (eds) (1996) *Civil–Military Relations in the Soviet and Yugoslav Successor States*, Boulder: Westview Press.

DARCHIASHVILI, David (2000) *Politicians, Soldiers, Citizens [Politikosebi, Jariskatsebi, Mokalakeni]*, Tbilisi University (in Georgian).

DAWISHA, A I and Dawisha, Karen (eds) (1995) *The Making of Foreign Policy in Russia and the New States of Eurasia*, Armonk: M E Sharpe.

DAWISHA, Karen (1997) *The International Dimension of Post-Communist Transitions in Russia and the New States of Eurasia*, Armonk: M E Sharpe.

—— and Parrott, Bruce (1997) *The End of Empire? The Transformation of the USSR in Comparative Perspective*, Armonk: M E Sharpe.

—— (1997) *Democratic Changes and Authoritarian Reactions in Russia, Ukraine, Belarus and Moldova*, Cambridge University Press.

DE NEVERS, Renée (1993) 'Democratisation and Ethnic Conflict', *Survival*, vol. 35, no. 2: 31–48.

—— (1994) 'Russia's Strategic Renovation', *Adelphi Papers*, no. 289, July 1994.

—— (1998) 'Conflict Prevention in Multi-Ethnic Societies: The Impact of Democracy Building', in Bonvicini *et al.* 1998: 99–129.

DE SPIEGELEIRE, Stephan (2002) *Recoupling Russia: Staying the Course, Europe's Security Relationship with Russia*, IISS/CEPS European Security Forum Paper, 14 January 2002.

DEMPSEY, Judy (2001) 'World News–Europe: Poles Juggle the Hard and Soft Approach to Border Patrol...', *Financial Times*, 16 April 2001.

—— (2002) 'NATO Plans to Admit Five States As Members', *Financial Times* (online edition), 27 Jan 2002.

DEMURIN, Mikhail (2001) 'The Prospects of Russian–Latvian Relations', *International Affairs*, vol. 47, no. 1: 72–9.

DEPARTMENT FOR INFORMATION AND PUBLICATION (2001) 'Region – Problems and Prospects', Yerevan: Government of Armenia.

DEUTSCHE PRESSE-AGENTUR (DPA) (2000) 'Poland "Open" to Europatrols on Eastern Border After EU Entry', 14 November 2000.

DIEHL, Jackson (2002) 'Our Cold War Hangover', *Washington Post*, 18 March 2002.

DI PALMA, Giuseppe (1990) *To Craft Democracies*, Oxford: University of California Press.

DOYLE, Michael (1986) 'Liberalism and World Politics', *American Political Science Review*, vol. 80, no. 4, December 1986: 1151–69.

DUKES, Paul (2000) *The Superpowers: A Short History*, London: Routledge.

DWAN, Renata and Pavliuk, Oleksandr (eds) (2000) *Building Security in the New States of Eurasia. Subregional Cooperation in the Former Soviet Space*, Armonk: M E Sharpe.

ECONOMIST (2000) 'Poverty in Eastern Europe: The Land that Time Forgot', 23 September 2000.

—— (2001) 'A New Misery Curtain', 2 June 2001.

EELRAND, Helen (2001) 'Ühisõppusseadis Baltimaad NATO-valmis', *Eesti Päevaleht*, 7 September 2001.

EESTI STATISTIKAAMET (2001) '2000. aastal väliskaubanduse käive suurenes', 9 March 2001.

EIDINTAS, Alfonsas, Zalys, Vytautas and Senn, Alfred Erich (1998) *Lithuania in European Politics: The Years of the First Republic, 1918–1940*, New York: St Martin's Press.

ELAGIN, V (2001) 'A Difficult Road from Tallinn to Moscow', *International Affairs*, vol. 47, no. 3: 152–60.

ENTERLINE, Andrew J (1996) 'Driving While Democratising', *International Security*, vol. 20, no. 4: 183–96.

FAIRBANKS, Charles (1995) 'The Postcommunist Wars', *Journal of Democracy*, vol. 6, no. 4: 18–34

FAMINSKI, I (1994) 'Otkritaya ekonomika i vneshneekonomicheskaya bezopasnost', *Voprosy ekonomiki*, no. 12: 65–78.

FEDERAL BROADCAST INFORMATION SERVICE (FBIS) (1995a) 'Kozyrev Remarks on Helping Compatriots Viewed', FBIS-SOV-95-096-S, 18 May 1995.

—— (1995b) 'Collective Security Documents from CIS 10 Feb Summit', FBIS-SOV-95-097-S, 19 May 19, 1995.

—— (1995c) 'Yeltsin Endorses Strategic Policy Toward CIS States', FBIS-SOV-95-180, 16 September, 1995.

—— (1995d) 'Strategic Policy Toward CIS Published', FBIS-SOV-95-019, 28 September, 1995.

—— (1996a) 'Defense Minister Gives Reasons for not Signing CIS NATO Documents', FBIS-SOV-96-160, 20 August 1996.

—— (1996b) 'Ukraine Still Lukewarm on CIS', FBIS-SOV-96-204, 21 October 1996.

—— (1996c) 'Tuleyev Interviewed on Cooperation with CIS', FBIS-SOV-96-218, 6 November 1996.

—— (1996d) 'Foreign Ministry Confirms No Territorial Claims on Ukraine', FBIS-SOV-96-222, 14 November, 1996.

–– (1996e) 'Russian Defence Minister Opposes Sharing Sevastopol', FBIS-SOV-96-231, 27 November 1996.

—— (1996f) 'Kuchma Addresses OSCE Summit in Lisbon', FBIS-SOV-96-241, 16 December 1996.

—— (1997a) 'Horbulin: Integration into Europe in National Interest', FBIS-SOV-97-008, 12 January 1997.

—— (1997b) 'Ukrainian Security Council Secretary Stresses Integration Into Europe', FBIS-SOV-97-008, 14 January 1997.

FEDOROV, Yuri (1998) 'Interest Groups and Russia's Foreign Policy', *International Affairs* (Moscow), vol. 44, n. 6:173–183.

—— (2000) 'Baltic Security in the Regional and the Wider European Context', in Grier *et al.* 2000: 29–44.

FELDMAN, Merje (2000) *Does the EU Offer Security?: European Integration in the Estonian Identity Discourse*, Copenhagen Peace Research Institute (COPRI); www.copri.dk/publications/WP/WP%202000/34–2000.doc

FIERKE, Karin and Wiener, Antje (1999) 'Constructing Institutional Interests: EU and NATO Enlargement', *Journal of European Public Policy*, vol. 6, no 3: 721–42.

FILIP, M (1998) 'Przed kim zamykamy granice', *Rzeczpospolita*, 29 January 1998.

FLETCHER, Martin (2002) 'New Curtain rises in Eastern Europe', *The Times*, 28 February 2002.

FORDHAM, Benjamin O (1998) 'Economic Interests, Party, and Ideology in Early Cold War Era US Foreign Policy', *International Organization*, vol. 52, no. 2, Spring 1998: 359–96.

FRIEDMAN, Julian R (1970) 'Alliance in International Politics', in Friedman *et al.* 1970: 3–32.

—— , Bladen, Christopher and Rosen, Steven (eds) (1970), *Alliance in International Politic*, Boston: Allyn and Bacon.

FUKUYAMA, Francis (1989) 'The End of History', *The National Interest*, vol. 16: 3–16.

—— (1992) *The End of History and the Last Man*, Harmondsworth: Penguin.

FURMAN, D (ed.) (1998) *Belorussiya i Rossiya: obshchestva i gosudarstva*, Moscow: Prava Cheloveka.

GADDIS, John Lewis (1997) *We Now Know: Rethinking Cold War History*, Oxford: Clarendon Press.

GARTEN, Jeffrey E (1997) 'Business and Foreign Policy', *Foreign Affairs*, vol. 76, no. 3: 67–79.

GILPIN, Robert (1975) *U.S Power and the Multinational Corporation*, London and Basingstoke: Macmillan.

—— (1987) *The Political Economy of International Relations*, Princeton: Princeton University Press.

GLEDITSCH, Nils Petter (1992) 'Democracy and Peace', *Journal of Peace Research*, vol. 29, no. 4: 369–77.

GOBLE, Paul A (1994) 'Russia as a Eurasian Power: Moscow and the Post-Soviet Successor States', in Sestanovich 1994: 42–51.

GOLDGEIER, James and McFaul, Michael (1992) 'Core and Periphery in the Post-Cold War Era', *International Organization*, no. 46: 466–91.

GOROBETS, A (2001) 'Ukraine Imposes Visa Regime For Several CIS Countries', *Pravda*, 19 December 2001.

GÖTZ, Roland (2002) *Russlands Erdgas und die Energiesicherheit der EU*, SWP-Studie, Berlin: Stiftung Wissenschaft und Politik.

GOWA, Joanne (1994) *Power, Trade and War*, Princeton: Princeton University Press.

GRABBE, Heather and Hughes, Kirsty (1998) *Enlarging the EU Eastwards*, London: The Royal Institute of International Affairs.

GRACHEVA, Vera (2000) 'Significance of the Hague, Oslo, and Lund Recommendations Regarding the Rights of National Minorities in the CBSS Region', presentation at the CBSS Working Group on Assistance to Democratic Institutions, Moscow, 30–31 March 2000.

GRIBINCEA, Mihai (1998) *Trupele Ruse ën Republica Moldova: Factor Stabilizator Sau Sursă De Pericol*, Chişinău: Civitas.

GRIER, Samuel, Almeida, Manuel and Forander, Nils (eds) (2000) *Security in the Northern European Region: 1999 PfP International Research Seminar*, Rome: NATO Defence College.

GUROFF, Gregory and Guroff, Alexandr (1995) 'The Paradox of Russian National Identity', in Szporluk 1995: 78–100.

GURR, Ted Robert (ed.) (1993) *Minorities at Risk: A Global View of Ethnopolitical Conflict*, Washington: United States Institute of Peace Press.

HALL, Alan (2000) 'EC Mulls Border Patrol Corps', *The Scotsman*, 12 October 2000: 11.

HANNE, Gottfried (1998) 'Der Transnistrien-Konflikt: Ursachen, Entwicklungsbedingungen und Perspektiven einer Regulierung', *BIOst*, no. 42.

HANSSON, Ardo (1997) 'The Baltic States: Performance Much Improved', *The Stockholm Report on East European Economics*, Stockholm: School of Economics.

HARTELIUS, Dag (1998) *Sub-Regional Security Cooperation in the Baltic Sea Space: Time to Move Ahead*, East–West Institute Policy, Brief No. 1.

HEIMSOETH, Hans Jürgen (2000) 'The Role of the Council of Baltic Sea States in Promoting Regional Cooperation', presentation at 'The 5th Anniversary Stockholm Conference on Baltic Sea Region Security and Cooperation' conference, Stockholm, 19 October 2000; www.usemb.se/bsconf/2000/heimsoeth.html

HERD, Graeme P (ed) (2000) *EU Enlargement in the North: Security Dynamics in Nordic–Baltic–EU–Russian Relations in the New Century*, Camberley: Conflict Studies Research Centre (CSRC), February 2000, F69.

—— (2002) 'Lithuania Continues Pursuing NATO', in Nelson and Markus 2002: 207–21.

—— and Huang, Mel (2001) *Baltic Security in 2000*, Camberley: Conflict Studies Research Centre (CSRC), May 2001, G95.

—— (2002) 'Latvia's Year in Defence: 2000', in Nelson and Markus 2002: 191–206.

—— and Weber, Martin (2001) 'Forging World Order Paradigms: "Good Civilization" versus "Global Terror"', *Security Dialogue*, vol. 32, no. 4, December 2001: 504–6.

HEYWOOD, Andrew (1997) *Politics*, Basingstoke: Macmillan.

HILL, Fiona (2001) 'A Not-So-Grand Strategy: United States Policy in the Caucasus and Central Asia since 1991', Brookings Institution, February 2001.

HOFF, Ove H G (2001) 'NATO and the Baltic Preparations After Invitation to Join the Alliance', *Baltic Defence Review*, vol. 2001, no. 6, 21–9

HOLMES, Leslie (1997) *Post-communism: An Introduction*, Cambridge, Polity Press.

HOLOBOFF, Elaine (1995) 'National Security in the Baltic States: Rolling Back the Bridgehead' in Parrott 1995: 111–33.

HOLTOM, Paul (2002) 'A Litmust Test for Europe?: Constructing Kaliningrad's Identity in Moscow, Brussels and Kaliningrad', unpublished PhD Thesis, University of Birmingham: 158–92.

HOSKING, Geoffrey (1999) 'The Russian People and the Soviet Union', in Hosking and Service 1999: 214–23.

—— and Service, Robert (1999) *Reinterpreting Russia*, London: Arnold.

HUANG, Mel (2002) 'Estonia Reassesses Russia's Threat', in Nelson and Markus 2002: 173–89.

HUBEL, Helmut (1999) 'The European Union, the Baltic States and Post-Soviet Russia: Theoretical Problems and Possibilities for Developing Partnership Relations in the North-eastern Baltic Sea Region', in Knudsen 1999: 241–56.

—— (ed.) (2002) *EU Enlargement and Beyond: The Baltic States and Russia,* Nordeuropäische Studien, No. 18, Berlin.

HULDT, Bo (1996) 'Summation', presentation at 'The Baltic Sea Region and the New European Security Structure' conference, Stockholm, 19 November 1996; www.usis.usemb.se/BalticSec/HULDT2.htm

HUNTINGTON, Samuel P (1991) *The Third Wave: Democratisation in the Late Twentieth Century,* London: University of Oklahoma Press.

—— (1993) 'The Clash of Civilisations', *Foreign Affairs,* vol. 72, no. 3: 22–49.

—— (1996a) *The Clash of Civilisations and the Remaking of the World Order,* New York: Simon and Schuster.

—— (1996b) 'Democracy for the Long Haul', *Journal of Democracy,* vol. 7, no. 2, April 1996: 3–13.

ILVES, Toomas Hendrik (1999) 'Estonia as a Nordic Country', speech delivered at the Swedish Institute for International Affairs, Stockholm, 14 December 1999.

INBAR, E and Sheffer, G (eds) (1997) *The National Security of Small States in a Changing World,* London: Frank Cass.

INSTITUT MIROVOI EKONOMIKI I MEZHDUNARODNYKH OTNOSHENII (RAN) (1994) *Aktualnie problemy vneshneekonomicheskoi bezopaznosti Rossii,* Moscow: RAN.

INTERFAX NEWS SERVICE (1996) 'Military Experts Warn of NATO Infiltration of Black Sea', 18 December 1996.

—— (1997a) 'More to Lose than Gain from Treaty with Ukraine', 28 May 1997.

—— (1997b) 'Russia to Compensate for Withdrawn Nuclear Weapons', 28 May 1997.

—— (1997c) 'Russia to Pay Ukraine $100,000,000 Year for Navy Base', 29 May 1997.

INTERNATIONAL AFFAIRS (1996), 'National Interests in Russian Foreign Policy', Moscow, no. 2: 1–24.

INTERNATIONAL MONETARY FUND (IMF) (1994) World Economic Outlook, October 1994.

—— (2001) *Direction of Trade Statistics Yearbook.*

ISAKOVA, Irina (1998) *The CIS and Europe: Evolving Security Relationship,* Centre for Defence Studies, No. 45, London: Brassey.

ITAR-TASS NEWS AGENCY (2001) 'Russia–Finland Border Rarely Quiet – Putin', 3 September 2001.

IVZHENKO, Tatyana (1996) 'Kuchma and Yeltsin are Trying to Lead the Russian–Ukrainian Out of Deadlock', *Nezavisimaya Gazeta,* 23 October 1996.

JACK, Andrew and Norman, Peter (2001) 'World News–Europe: EU Expansion Drives Debate on Kaliningrad's Fate', *Financial Times,* 18 January 2001: 2.

JOENNIEMI, Pertti and Prawitz, Jan (eds) (1998)*Kaliningrad: The European Amber Region,* Hampshire: Ashgate.

JONES, Stephen F (1996) 'Adventurers or Commanders? Civil–Military Relations in Georgia Since Independence', in Danopoulos and Zirker 1996: 31–52.

JONSON, Lena, (1997) 'Russian Policy in Northern Europe', in Baranovsky 1997: 305–24.

KANGAS, Roger (1996) 'CIS Integration: A Gradual Approach', *OMRI Analytical Brief*, vol. 1, no. 50, 29 March 1996.

KARAGANOV, Sergei A (1994) 'Russia's Elites', in Blackwill and Karaganov 1994: 41–53.

KARBALEVICH, Valery (1999) 'Natsionalno-gosudarstvennye Interesy Respubliki Belarus', in Zaiko 1999: 55–88.

KARP, Aaron (2001), *Is America a Baltic Power?*, University College, Sweden.

KASSIANOVA, Alla (2001) 'Russia: Still Open to the West? The Evolution of the State Identity in the Foreign Policy and Security Discourse', *Europe–Asia Studies*, vol. 53, no. 6, September 2001: 821–40.

KAUFMAN, Stuart J (2001) *NATO, Russia, and the Baltic States*, Program on New Approaches to Russian Security, PONARS Policy Memo, no. 216.

KAUPPILA, Laura (1999) *The Baltic Puzzle: Russia's Policy Towards Estonia and Latvia 1992–1997*, unpublished dissertation, University of Helsinki; ethesis.helsinki.fi/julkaisut/val/yhtei/pg/kauppila/index.html

KAZOCINS, Janis (1999) 'The Baltic Battalion Five Years On: Cornerstone of Baltic Military Co-operation or Expensive White Elephant?', *Baltic Defence Review*, vol. 1999, no. 2: 47–54.

KHIRIPUNOV, Igor and Matthews, Mary M (1996) 'Russia's Oil and Gas Interest Group and its Foreign Policy Agenda', *Problems of Post Communism*, May/June 1996: 38–47.

KHRUSHCHEV, Nikita (1959) 'On Peaceful Co-existence', *Foreign Affairs*, vol. 38, no. 1: 1–18.

KING, Charles (2000) *The Moldovans: Romania, Russia and the Politics of Culture*, Stanford: Hoover Institution Press.

KIPP, Jacob W (1998) ' "From Prague"...After Paris and Madrid' in Blank 1998a: 49–70.

KIRICHENKO, S (1994) 'Evolutsiya i perspektivy ekonomicheskikh otnoshenii Rossii so stranami SNG', *Svobodnaya mysl*, no. 9: 3–14.

KNUDSEN, Olav F (ed.) (1999) *Stability and Security in the Baltic Sea Region*, London: Frank Cass.

—— (2000) 'From National, Via Regional, to European Security: Actors, Challenges, and Recommendations', in Grier *et al.* 2000: 17–28.

KOCHER, Scott A (1997) 'The Baltic States in the European Security Framework', *Atlantic Council of the United States*, vol. 8, no. 6, 27 June 1997.

KOHUT, Zenon E (1994) 'History as a Battleground. Russian–Ukrainian Relations and Historical Consciousness in Contemporary Ukraine', in Starr 1994: 123–45.

KOLCHIN, Sergei V (1995) 'Rossiya–blizhe zarubezhe: vzaimootnosheniya, interessy, tseli politiki', *Mirovaya ekonomika i mezhdunarodnie otnosheniya*, no. 4: 47–56.

KOMISINA, Irina (2001) 'Prospects for Integration of the South Caucasus States into the European Union',*Central Asia and the Caucasus*, vol. 13, no. 1: 105–13.

KOMMERSANT DAILY (1997) 'Yeltsin, Kuchma Seal Agreement with Blood – Hunting with Yeltsin made Kuchma More Compliant', 18 November 1997.

KONDRAKOV, S (1996) 'National Interests in Russian Foreign Policy', *International Affairs* (Moscow), vol. 42, no. 2: 1–24.

KÖRBER FOUNDATION (2002) *The Baltic Sea. A Region of Prosperity and Stability?* The 121st Bergedorf Round Table, Hamburg.

KORTUNOV, Sergei V (1998), *Russia's National Identity in a New Era*, Cambridge, Mass.: J. F. Kennedy School of Governance, Harvard University, Strengthening Democratic Institutions Project, September 1998.

KOZARYN, Linda D (2002) 'US Considers "Train and Equip" Program for Georgia', American Forces Press Service, 27 February 2002.

KOZHOKIN, Evgueny (2000) 'A Russian View', in Grier *et al.* 2000: 173–80.

KOZYREV, Andrei (1995) *Preobrazhenie*, Moscow: Mezhdunarodnye Otnosheniia.

KRAMER, J M (1993) ' "Energy Shock" from Russia Jolts Baltic States', *RFE/RL Research Report*, no. 17, 23 April 1993: 41–9.

KRAMER, Mark (1997) *Kaliningrad Oblast, Russia, and Baltic Security*, Program on New Approaches to Russian Security, PONARS Policy Memo, no. 10.

KRIVAS, Andrius (1999) 'Towards Interoperability: Actions at Home', *Baltic Defence Review*, vol. 1999, no. 1: 103–14.

KRUPNICK, Charles (ed.) (2002)*Almost NATO: Partners and Players in Central and Eastern European Security*, Rowman and Littlefield, forthcoming.

KRUPP, Elena (2002) 'Kasyanov Promises to Run the Blockade', *Izvestia*, 7 March 2002.

KUZIO, Taras (2000) 'Geopolitical Pluralism in the CIS: The Emergence of GUUAM', *European Security*, vol. 9, no. 2 (Summer 2000): 81–114.

—— (2001) 'Russia Continues to hold up Border Demarcation', Endnote, RFE/RL Newsline, 30 October 2001, *European Security*, (July 2001), vol. 10, no. 2: 111–26.

—— (2002) 'Russia Gives Ukraine a Helping Hand in its Elections', Endnote, RFE/RL Newsline, 22 January 2002.

—— , Kravchuk, Robert and D'Anieri, Paul (1999) *Politics and Society in Ukraine*, Boulder: Westview Press.

—— and Moroney, Jennifer D P (2001) 'Ukraine and the West: Moving from Stability to Strategic Engagement', *European Security,* July 2001.

LAANEMÄE, Mart (1998) 'Post-Madrid Estonian Security Policy', in Blank 1998a: 147–56.

LAPIDUS, Gail W (ed.) (1995) *The New Russia: Troubled Transformation*, Oxford: Westview Press.

—— , Zaslavsky, Victor and Goldman, Philip (eds) (1992) *From Union to Commonwealth: Nationalism and Separatism in the Soviet Republics*, Cambridge: Cambridge University Press.

LAPTYONOK, Oleg (1999) 'Plurality of Foreign Policy Vectors of Belarus in New International Setting', *Belarus in the World*, vol. 4, no. 4: 42–5.

LAPYCHAK, Christina (1995) 'Crackdown on Crimean Separatism', *Transition*, vol. 1, no. 8, 26 May 1995: 2–5.

LARRABEE, F Stephen (1999) *NATO Enlargement After the First Round*, Santa Monica: RAND, RP-786.

—— (2001) 'NATO Enlargement: Prague and Beyond', presentation at the IISS/CEPS European Security Forum, Brussels, 9 July 2001; www.eusec.org/larrabee.htm

LAURISTIN, Marju and Vihalemm, Peeter (eds) (1996) *Return to the Western World: Cultural and Political Perspectives on the Estonian Post-Communist Transition*, Tartu University Press.

LEJINS, Atis and Ozolina, Zaneta (eds) (1997) *Small States in a Turbulent Environment: The Baltic Perspective*, Riga: Latvian Institute of International Affairs.

LENIN, Vladimir I (1993) *Imperialism, The Highest Stage Of Capitalism: A Popular Outline,*London: Lawrence.

LEONARD, Dick (2001/2) 'EU Enlargement – Dangers from Schengen', *Europe*, December 2001/January 2002: 3–4.

LEPIK, Lauri (2002) 'The Accession of the Baltic States to the European Union', at the 'First Baltic–German Dialogue' conference, Berlin, 2–4 November 2001; Berlin: Stiftung Wissenschaft und Politik: 20–23.

LIEN, Richard (2002) 'Russian Forces to Tackle Kaliningrad', Agence France Presse, 7 March 2002.

LIEVEN, Dominic (1999) 'Russia as Empire: a Comparative Perspective', in Hosking and Service 1999: 9–20.

—— (2000) *Empire: The Russian Empire and its Rivals*, New Haven: Yale University Press.

LIGHT, Margot (1996) 'Foreign Policy Thinking', in Malcolm *et al.* 1996: 33–101.

LIKLIKADZE, Koba (2000) Bulletin: *The Army and Society in Georgia*, CIPDD, March 2000.

LINKEVIČIUS, Linas (1999) 'Participation of Lithuanian Troops in International Peace Support Operations', *Baltic Defence Review*, vol. 1, no. 1: 86–91.

LOEB, Vernon (2002) 'Footprints in the steppes of Central Asia: New bases indicate US presence will be felt after Afghan War', *Washington Post*, 9 February 2002.

LOSHCHININ, V (interview with) (1996) 'The Baltic States: The Situation is Often Discouraging', *International Affairs*, vol. 42, no. 1: 48–54.

LUKANOV, Yuri (1996) *Tretyi Prezydent: Politychnyi Portret Leonida Kuchmy*, Kyiv: Taki Spravy.

LUKASHENKA, Alyaksandr (1998) *Belarus and the CIS: A Path Towards a Common Vision*, Geneva: East European Development Association.

LUKIN, Vladimir P (1994) 'Russia and its Interests', in Sestanovich 1994: 106–15.

LYKSHIN, S and Svinarenko, A (1994) 'Razvitie ekonomiki Rossii i ee restruktur-izatsiya kak garantiya ekonomicheskoi bezopasnosti', *Voprosy ekonomiki*, no. 12: 115–25.

LYNCH, Allen C (2001) 'The Realism of Russia's Foreign Policy', *Europe–Asia Studies*, vol. 53, no. 1, January 2001: 7–33.

MACMILLAN, John (1996) 'Democracies Don't Fight: A Case of the Wrong Research Agenda', *Review of International Studies*, vol. 22: 275–99.

MAIN, Steven (1998) *Instability in the Baltic Region*, Camberley: Conflict Studies Research Centre (CSRC), June 1998, S37.

MALCOLM, Neil (1996) 'Foreign Policy Making', in Malcolm *et al.* 1996: 101–67.

—— *et al.* (eds) (1996) *Internal Factors in Russian Foreign Policy*, Oxford: Oxford University Press.

MALISHEVA, Dina (2001) 'Security Problems in the Caucasus', *Central Asia and Caucasus*, vol. 13, no. 1: 41–56.

MANDELBAUM, Michael (1998) *The New Russian Foreign Policy*, New York: Council on Foreign Relations.

MANSFIELD, Edward D and Snyder, Jack (1996) 'The Effects of Democratisation on War', *International Security*, vol. 20, no. 4: 196–207.

MARGERUM HARLEN, Christine (1999) 'A Reappraisal of Classical Economic Nationalism and Economic Liberalism', *International Studies Quarterly*, vol. 43: 733–44.

MARKUS, Ustina (1995) 'Black Sea Fleet Dispute Apparently Over', *Transition*, vol. 1, no. 13, 28 July 1995: 30–5.

MCFAUL, Michael (1995) 'Revolutionary Ideas, State Interests and Russian Foreign Policy', in Tismaneanu 1995: 27–54.

—— (2001) *Russia's Unfinished Revolution: Political Change from Gorbachev to Putin*, Ithaca: Cornell University Press.

MCGWIRE, Michael (1997) 'Russia and Security in Europe', in Dawisha 1997: 68–100.

MEDVEDEV, V (1997) 'Problemy ekonomicheskoi bezopasnosti', *Voprosy ekonomiki*, no. 3: 11–127.

MICHALOPOULOS, Costantine and Tarr, David G (1994) *Trade in the New Independent States*, Washington: The World Bank.

MIHALKA, Michael (2001) 'Cooperative Security: From Theory to Practice', in Cohen and Mihalka 2001: 28–67.

MIHKELSON, Marko (1996) 'Eesti on Venemaa tõsiseim oponent: Avaliku arvamuse kÜsitlus toetab Kremli agressiivsust Balti riikide suhtes', *Postimees*, 17 May 1996.

MIKENBERG, Eero (2000) 'Pskov, Leningrad Regions and Estonia: Trans-border Cooperation or Competition?', in Herd 2000, ch. 4: 20–9.

MILBANK, Dana (2002) 'Uzbekistan Thanked for Role in War: US, Tashkent Signs Cooperation Pact', *Washington Post*, 15 March 2002.

MILL, John Stuart (1951) *Utilitarianism, Liberty and Representative Government*, New York: Dutton.

MITCHELL, R Judson (1978) 'A New Brezhnev Doctrine: The Restructuring of International Relations', *World Politics*, vol. 30, no. 3 (April 1978): 366–90.

MOISEEV, Eugenie (1997) *International Legal Framework of CIS Cooperation [Mezhdunarodno-pravovie Osnovi Sotrudnichestva Stran SNG]*, Moscow: Yurist (in Russian).

MØLLER, T D (2000) 'BALTBAT – Lessons learned and the Way Ahead', *Baltic Defence Review*, vol. 2000, no. 3: 38–42.

MORAN, Theodore H (1996) 'Grand Strategy: The Pursuit of Power and the Pursuit of Plenty', *International Organization*, vol. 50, no. 1: 175–205.

MORIKAWA, Jun (1997) *Japan and Africa: Big Business and Diplomacy,* London: Hurst and Company.

MORONEY, Jennifer D P (2001) 'Frontier Dynamics and Ukraine's Ties to the West', *Problems of Post-Communism*, March–April 2001, vol. 48, no. 2: 15–24.

—— (2002) 'Defining and Sustaining Ukraine's Strategic Partnerships', *Journal of Ukrainian Studies,* May 2002.

—— and Closson, Stacy (2002) 'NATO's Strategic Engagement with Ukraine in Europe's Security Buffer Zone', in Krupnick 2002: 199–230.

—— and Konoplyov, Sergei (2001) 'Western Support for GUUAM in Europe's Security Gray Zone', *National Security and Defense*, no. 7, 2001: 68–71.

—— , Kuzio, Taras and Molchanov, Mikhail (2002) *Ukrainian Foreign and Security Policy: Comparative and Theoretical Perspectives*, Westport: Greenwood/Praeger.

MORRISON, James W (1994) 'Vladimir Zhirinovskiy. An assessment of a Russian Ultra-Nationalist', McNair paper 30, Washington: National Defense University.

MOSHES, Arkady (2002) 'Russia, EU Enlargement, and the Baltic States', in Hubel 2002: 309–20.

MOTYL, Alexander (ed.) (1992) *The Post Soviet Nations: Perspectives on the Demise of the USSR*, New York: Columbia University Press.

MURADIAN, Igor (2001) *Contradictions of the Policy of Atlanticism and the Problems of Regional Safety [Protivorechia Politiki Atlantizma i Problemi Regionalnoi Bezopasnosti]*, Yerevan: Antares (in Russian).

NAROCHNITSKAYA, Natalya (1992) 'Russia's National Interests', *International Affairs* (Moscow), vol. 38, no. 8: 134–43.

NEDELCIUC, Vasile (1992) *Respublika Moldova*, Chişinău: Universitas.

NEIL, Malcolm and Pravda, Alex (1996) 'Democratisation and Russian Foreign Policy', *International Affairs*, vol. 72, no. 3: 537–52.

NELSON, Dan and Markus, Ustina (eds) (2002) Brassey's Central and East European Security Yearbook 2002, Washington: Brassey's.

NEW YORK TIMES (2001) 'Europe Ponders Uniform Security for Its Borders', 7 October 2001.

NOREN, James H and Watson, Robin A (1992) 'Interrepublican Economic Relations After the Disintegration of the USSR', *Soviet Economy*, vol. 8, no. 2: 89–129.

NORKUS, Renatas (1998a) 'Preventing Conflict in the Baltic States: A Success Story That Will Hold?', in Bonvicini *et al.* 1998: 135–67.

—— (1998b) 'Testing Regional Cooperation and Security in the Baltic Sea Rim', in Bonvicini *et al.* 1998: 264–90.

NOUGAYREDE, Natalie (2002) 'As EU Expands, Moscow Worries About Its Baltic Enclave', *Manchester Guardian Weekly*, 20 March 2002.

NUYAKSHEV, V (2002) 'Baltic Fleet Commander Worried Over NATO War Games', ITAR-TASS News Agency, 10 March 2002.

ODOM, William (1998) *The Collapse of the Soviet Military*, New Haven: Yale University Press.

OLCOTT, Martha Brill, Åslund, Anders and Garnett, Sherman W (1999) *Getting it Wrong: Regional Cooperation and the Commonwealth of Independent States*, Washington DC: Carnegie Endowment for International Peace.

OLDBERG, Ingmar (1997) 'No love is lost – Russia's relations with the Baltic states', in Artéus and Lejins 1997: 152–85.

—— (1998) 'The problems and prospects of the Kaliningrad region', in Joenniemi and Prawitz 1998: 1–31.

—— (ed.) (1999a) *At A Loss – Russian Foreign Policy in the 1990s*, FOA-R–99–01091–180-SE, Stockholm: Swedish Defence Research Establishment.

—— (1999b) 'Russia and Its Western Neighbours in the Context of NATO Enlargement', in Oldberg (1999a): 33–62.

—— (2001) *Kaliningrad: Russian exclave, European enclave*, FOI-R-0134–SE, Stockholm: Swedish Defence Research Institute.

ONEAL, John R and Russett, Bruce (1997) 'The Classical Liberals Were Right: Democracy, Interdependence, and Conflict, 1950–1985', *International Studies Quarterly*, vol. 41: 267–94.

OOLO, Antti (1999) 'Kaitsekolledzh tõstab ohvitseride taset', *Eesti Päevaleht*, 20 February 1999.

—— (2001) 'Tallinna lahes 35 miini vähem', *Eesti Päevaleht*, 15 November 2001.

ÕUN, Mati (2001) *Eesti Vabariigi kindralid ja admiralid*, Tallinn: Tammiskilp.

OZOLINA, Zaneta (1999) 'The Impact of the European Union on Baltic Cooperation', Copenhagen Peace Research Institute (COPRI); www.copri.dk/publications/WP/WP%201999/3–1999.doc

PAPPE, Yakov (1997) 'Neftyanaya i gazovaya diplomatiya Rossii', *Pro et Contra*, vol. 2, Summer 1997: 55–71.

PARISH, Steve (1996) 'Chaos in Foreign Policy Decision-Making', *Transitions*, 17 May 1996: 30–3.

PARROTT, Bruce (1995) *State Building and Military Power in Russia and the New States of Eurasia*, Armonk: M E Sharpe.

—— (1997) 'Perspectives on Post-Communist Democratisation', in Dawisha and Parrott 1997: 1–39.

PAVLIUK, Oleksandr (1997) 'Ukraine and Regional Cooperation in Central and Eastern Europe', *Security Dialogue*, vol. 28, no. 3, September 1997: 347–61.

—— (2000) 'GUUAM. The Maturing of a Political Grouping into Economic Cooperation', in Dwan and Pavliuk 2000: 33–56.

PBS 'NEWS HOURS WITH MARGARET WARNER' (2002) 'New Allies', 12 March 2002.

PERLEZ, Jane (1996) 'Ukraine Caught in a Tug-of-War Between East and West', *New York Times*, 24 October 1996.

POLAND BUSINESS REVIEW (2002) 'Polish–Kaliningrad Flight Connection deal and New Highway...', 12 March 2002.

POLUKHOV, Elkhan (1997) 'Contract of the Century', *Caucasian Regional Studies*, UNDP Georgia, issue 1: 9–32.

POPESCU, Nicu (2001) 'Scenarios of NATO Enlargement and MAP States', *Integrare Europeana*, 10 October 2001.

POULSEN-HANSEN, Per (1996) 'NATO, EU, and the Baltic Sea Region', presentation at 'The Baltic Sea Region and the New European Security Structure' conference, Stockholm, 19 November 1996; www.usis.usemb.se/BalticSec/POULSEN.htm

POZDOROUKIN, Vladimir (2000) 'Problems of Supply and Development of the Kaliningrad Oblast in the Context of EU Expansion Eastwards', *Lithuanian Foreign Policy Review*, vol. 6, no. 2.

PRIZEL, Ilya (1997) *National Identity and Foreign Policy: Nationalism and Leadership in Poland, Russia and Ukraine*, Cambridge: Cambridge University Press.

—— (1998), *National Identity and Foreign Policy: Nationalism and Leadership in Poland, Russia and Ukraine*, Cambridge: Cambridge University Press.

PUHELOINEN, Ari (1999) *Russia's Geopolitical Interests in the Baltic Sea*, Helsinki: Finnish Defence Studies No. 12.

PUSHKOV, Aleksei K (1996) 'National Interests in Russian Foreign Policy', *International Affairs* (Moscow), vol. 42, no. 2: 1–24.

RASIZADE, Alek (2001) 'Oil from Azerbaijan – Trap for the West?', *Central Asia and the Caucasus*, vol. 13, no.1: 178–93.

REBAS, Hain (1999) 'Can the Baltic States be Defended? An Essay on Macrohistory and Semantics', *Baltic Defence Review*, vol. 1999, no. 1: 24–35.

REISS, Mitchell (1995) *Bridled Ambition: Why Countries Constrain their Nuclear Capabilities*, Baltimore: Johns Hopkins University Press.

REITER, Dan and Stam, Allan C (III) (1998) 'Democracy, War Initiation, and Victory', *American Political Science Review*, vol. 92, no. 2, June 1998: 377–89.

RIA-NOVOSTI NEWS SERVICE (1997) 'Presidents of Russia and Ukraine Sign Joint Declaration', 1 June 1997.

ROBINSON, Neil (2002) *Russia: A State of Uncertainty*, London: Routledge.

RONIS, Aivis (1996) 'Is There Any Alternative to NATO Enlargement – the Latvian View', presentation at 'The Baltic Sea Region and the New European Security Structure' conference, Stockholm, 19 November 1996; www.usis.usemb.se/BalticSec/RONIS.htm

ROSE, Richard, Mishler, William and Haerpher, Christian (1998) *Democracy and Its Alternatives*, Cambridge: Polity Press.

ROZANOV, Anatoly (1998) 'Vneshnyaya politika Belorussii: predstavleniya i Realnosty', *Pro et Contra*, vol. 3, no. 2, Spring 1998: 68–80.

RUMER, Eugene (1994) *The Building Blocks of Russia's Future Military Doctrine*, Santa Monica: RAND Corporation.

RUSSETT, Bruce *et al.* (1993)*Grasping the Democratic Peace: Principles for a Post-Cold War World*. Princeton: Princeton University Press.

RUSTOW, Dankwart (1970) 'Transitions to Democracy: Toward a Dynamic Model', *Comparative Politics*, vol. 2, no. 3: 337–63.

SAKWA, Richard and Webber, Mark (1999) 'The Commonwealth of Independent States, 1991–1998: Stagnation and Survival', *Europe–Asia Studies*, vol. 51, no. 3: 379–415.

SALMON, Trevor C (2000) 'Issues in European Union Enlargement', in Herd 2000: 6–10.

SAMSONOV, K (1994) 'Elementy kontsepsii ekonomicheskoi bezopasnosti', *Voprosy Ekonomiki*, no. 12: 14–24.

SANDS, David (2001) 'Latvian Urges Limit on Ties to NATO', *Washington Times*, 12 December 2001.

SAPRONAS, Robertas (1999) 'BALTBAT and Development of Baltic Defence Forces', *Baltic Defence Review*, vol. 1999, no. 2: 55–70.

—— (2000), *The Costs of NATO Enlargement to the Baltic States*, Individual EAPC Fellowship Paper; www.nato.int/acad/fellow/98–00/sapronas.pdf

SAVIN, V (1995) 'Torgovlya otnosheniya i vneshekonomicheskaya politika', *Vneshnyaya torgovlya*, no. 5: 13–15.

SCHIMMELFENNIG, Frank (1999) *The Double Puzzle of EU Enlargement: Liberal Norms, Rhetorical Action, and the Decision to Expand to the East*, ARENA Working Paper 99/15.

SCHWELLER, R L (1992) 'Domestic Structure and Preventive War. Are Democracies More Pacific?', *World Politics*, vol. 44, no. 2, January 1992: 235–69.

SEMJONOV, Aleksei (1996) 'Estonia: Nation Building and Integration – Political and Legal Aspects', Copenhagen Peace Research Institute (COPRI) http://www.copri.dk/publications/WP/WP%202000/8-2000.doc.

SERGOUNIN, Alexander (1999) *Regional Cooperation as a Security Factor in Northeastern Europe: A Russian Perspective,* Nizhny Novgorod: Nizhny Novgorod Linguistic University.

—— (2000) *Russia and the European Union: The Northern Dimension*, Program on New Approaches to Russian Security, PONARS Policy Memo, no. 138.

—— (2002), *The United States' Northern Dimension? Prospects for a U.S.–Russian Cooperative Agenda in Northern Europe*, Program on New Approaches to Russian Security, PONARS Policy Memo, no.232.

SESTANOVICH, Stephen R (ed.) (1994) *Rethinking Russia's National Interests*, Washington: Centre for Strategic and International Studies.

SHARAPO, A V (2000) 'Rossiisko–Belorusskaya Integratsiya i Obshchestvennoye Mneniye', *Belorussky Zhurnal Mezhdunarodnogo Prava i Mezhdunarodnykh Otnoshenii*, no. 1: 63–7.

SHEVTSOVA, Lilia (1995) 'Russia's Post-Communist Politics: Revolution or Continuity?' in Lapidus 1995: 5–36.

SHUTOV, A (ed.) (1998) *Soyuz Belarusi i Rossii: vybor sdelan*, Minsk: Polymya.

SILVESTROV, Sergei N and Filatov, Vladimir I (1994) 'Vneshneekonomicheskaya politica i sistemny vzgliad', *Rossiiski ekonomicheski zhurnal*, no. 10: 46–58.

SIMON, Jeffrey (2001) *Roadmap to NATO Accession: Preparing for Membership*, Washington: Institute of National Security Studies.

SIROTSKY, Anatoly (2000) 'Tamozhenny Soyuz: Plany i Realii', *Belorussky Zhurnal Mezhdunarodnogo Prava i Mezhdunarodnykh Otnoshenii*, no. 1: 68–71.

SLEVIN, Peter (2002) 'Some War Allies Show Poor Human Rights Records', *Washington Post*, 5 March 2002.

SMITH, Alan (1993) *Russia and the World Economy: Problems of Integration*, London: Routledge.

SMITH, Benjamin (2001) 'U.S., Russia Allegiance In War on Terror May Stall Baltic States' Entry Into NATO', *Wall Street Journal*, 5 October 2001.

SMITH, Graham *et al.* (1998) *Nation Building in the Post-Soviet Borderlands: The Politics of National Identities*, Cambridge: Cambridge University Press.

SMITH, Mark A (1994) *Russian Hegemony in the Near Abroad*, Camberley: Conflict Studies Research Centre (CSRC), July 1994, F40.

SMITH, Robert F (1960) *The United States and Cuba: Business and Diplomacy, 1917–1960*, New Haven: New College and University Press.

SMOLANSKY, Oles M (1995) 'Ukraine's Quest for Independence: the Fuel Factor', *Europe–Asia Studies*, vol. 47, no. 1: 49–58.

SMORODINSKAYA, Natalia (2001) *Kaliningrad Exclave: Prospects for Transformation into a Pilot Region*, Moscow: Institute of Economics, Russian Academy of Sciences.

SNYDER, Jack (2000) *From Voting to Violence: Democratisation and Nationalist Conflict*, New York: W W Norton.

SOCOR, Vladimir (1992a) 'Creeping Putsch in Eastern Moldova', *RFE/RL Research Report*, 17 January 1992: 8–13.

—— (1992b) 'Russia's Fourteenth Army and the Insurgency in Eastern Moldova', *RFE/RL Research Report*, 11 September 1992: 41–8.

—— (1993a) 'Dniester Involvement in the Moscow Rebellion', *RFE/RL Research Report*, 19 November 1993: 25–32.

—— (1993b) 'Moldova: Another Major Setback for Pro-Romanian Forces', *RFE/RL Research Report*, 26 February 1993: 15–21.

—— (1993c) 'Russia's Army in Moldova: There to Stay?', *RFE/RL Research Report*, 18 June 1993: 42–9.

SPECTER, Michael (1997) 'Setting Past Aside, Russia and Ukraine Sign Friendship Treaty', *New York Times*, 1 June 1997.

SPRUDS, Andris (2002) 'Perceptions and Interests in Russian–Baltic Relations', in Hubel 2002: 345–70.

STANKEVICH, Sergei B (1994) 'Towards a New "National Idea"', in Sestanovich 1994: 24–32.

STARR, S Frederick (ed.) (1994) *The Legacy of History in Russia and the New States of Eurasia*, Armonk: M E Sharpe.

STENLUND, Peter and Nissinen, Marja (1999) *A Northern Dimension for the Policies of the European Union*, Virtual Finland, Ministry of Foreign Affairs.

STENT, Angela (2002) *American Views on Russian Security Policy and EU–Russian Relations*, Paper prepared for the 'Russia's Security Policy and EU–Russia Relations' IISS/CEPS European Security Forum, Brussels, 14 January 2002.

STOCKHOLM INSTITUTE OF TRANSITION ECONOMICS (SITE) (2002) *Baltic Economic Trends*, vol. 1.

STOCKHOLM INTERNATIONAL PEACE RESEARCH INSTITUTE (SIPRI) (1997) *SIPRI Yearbook, 1997*, Oxford University Press.

—— (1998) *SIPRI Yearbook, 1998*, Oxford University Press.

—— (2001) *SIPRI Yearbook, 2001*, Oxford University Press.

STRANGA, Aivars (1997) 'Baltic–Russian Relations: 1995–Beginning of 1997', in Lejins and Ozolina 1997: 184–237.

STRANGE, Susan (1992), 'States, Firms and Diplomacy', *International Affairs*, vol. 68, no. 1: 1–15.

SUTELA, Pekka (2002) 'The Linen Divorce, The Baltic Countries outside the Post-Soviet Space', in Alexandrova *et al.* 2002.

SYSOEV, G and Shumilin, A (1997) 'Ministerstvo Strannikh Del', *Kommersant*, no. 44 (250), 2 December 1997: 39–40.

SZAYNA, Thomas S (2001) *NATO Enlargement 2000–2015: Determinants and Implications for Defense Planning and Shaping*, Santa Monica: RAND Project Air Force.

SZPORLUK, Roman (ed.) (1995) *National Identity and Ethnicity in Russia and the New States of Eurasia*, Armonk, M E Sharpe.

TAKHNENKO Galina (1992) 'Anatomy of a Political Decision: Notes on the Marshall Plan', *International Affairs* (Moscow), July 1992: 111–27.

TALI, Peeter (1999) 'Balti riigid suurendevad Baltbati tulejõudu', *Eesti Päevaleht*, 5 April 1999.

TAMMERK, Tarmu (2002) 'Estonian Government Sworn Into Office', Agence France Press, 28 January 2002.

TARULIS, Albert (1959) *Soviet Policy towards the Baltic States: 1918–1940*, University of Notre Dame Press.

TARZI, Shah M (1991) 'Multinational Corporations and American Foreign Policy: Radical, Sovereignty-at-Bay, and State-Centric Approaches', *International Studies*, vol. 28, no. 4: 359–71.

TIMMERMANN, Heinz (2000) 'Rußlands Politik gegenüber der EU (I) Eine schwierige Partnerschaft im Zeichen des patriotischen Konsenses Osteurops', *Osteuropa*, vol. 50, no. 7/8: 750–7.

—— (2001)*Kaliningrad: Eine Pilotregion für die Gestaltung der Partnerschaft EU–Russland?* SWP-Studie, Berlin: Stiftung Wissenschaft und Politik.

TISMANEANU, Vladimir (ed.) (1995) *Political Culture and Civil Society in Russia and the New States of Eurasia*, Armonk: M E Sharpe.

TOLZ, Vera and Teague, Elizabeth (1992) 'Russian Intellectuals Adjust to Loss of Empire', *RFE/RL Research Report*, vol. 1, no. 8, 21 February 1992: 4–8.

TORBAKOV, Igor (2002) *Eurasia Insight*, 12 November 2001.

TRACEVSKIS, Rokas M (2002) 'Kaliningrad Visa Issue Aired', *The Baltic Times*, 14 March 2002.

TRAVKIN, Nikolai (1994) 'Russia, Ukraine and Eastern Europe', in Sestanovich 1994: 33–41.

TRAYNOR, Ian (2001) 'Putin's Trojan Horse Alarms Fortress EU', *The Guardian*, 15 February 2001.

TRENIN, Dmitri (1998) 'Military Tools and CSBMs in Conflict Prevention in the Post-Soviet Area,' in Bonvicini *et al.* 1998: 223–43.

—— (ed.) (2000) *Russia and Basic European Security Institutions: at the Threshold of the XXI Century [Rossia i Osnovnie Instituti Bezopasnosti v Evrope: Vstupaia v XXI Vek]*, Moscow: S&P (in Russian).

TYLER, Patrick (2002) 'In Caucasus Gorge, A Haven for Muslim Militants', *New York Times*, 28 February 2002.

UKRAINIAN WEEKLY (1996a) 'Moscow Meetings Make Progress on Russian–Ukrainian Friendship Treaty', 6 October 1996.

—— (1996b) 'Kuchma and Yeltsin Hold Working Meeting', 27 October 1996.

UNITED NATIONS DEVELOPMENT PROGRAMME (UNDP) (2001) *Human Development Report*.

UNITED STATES DEPARTMENT OF STATE (DOS) OFFICE OF RESEARCH (2000a) *Opinion Analysis*, M-162–00, 13 September 2000.

—— (2000b) *Opinion Analysis*, M-162–00, 20 September 2000.

UPRESA NEWS (1995) 'Ukrainian, Russian Defense Ministers Exceed Expectations', 24 November 1995.

—— (1996) 'Agreement Between the Russian Federation and Ukraine on the Black Sea Fleet', 14 June 1996.

UŠACKAS, Vygaudas (1996) 'NATO's Role in Baltic Security: A Lithuanian View', presentation at 'The Baltic Sea Region and the New European Security Structure' conference, Stockholm, 19 November 1996; www.usis.usemb.se/BalticSec/USACKAS.htm

VAHL, Marius (2001) *Just Good Friends? The EU–Russian Strategic Partnership and the Northern Dimension*, CEPS Working Documents, no. 166, Brussels: Centre for European Policy Studies.

VALDEZ, Jonathan (1995) 'The Near Abroad, the West, and National Identity in Russian Foreign Policy', in Dawisha and Dawisha 1995: 84–109.

VAN HAM, Peter (1994) *Ukraine, Russia and European Security: Implications for Western Policy*, Paris: Institute for Security Studies of the Western European Union.

—— (ed.) (1995) *The Baltic States: Security and Defence After Independence,* Paris: The Institute for Security Studies of Western European Union, Chaillot Paper 19.

VAREIKIS, Egidijus and Žygelyte·, Jūrate (1998) 'The Eastern Baltic Subregion: Conflict and Cooperation',*Lithuanian Foreign Policy Review*, no. 2, http://www.lfpr.lt/982/6.doc.

VÄYRYNEN, Raimo (1999) 'The Security of the Baltic Countries: Cooperation and Defection', in Knudsen 1999: 204–22.

VIHALEMM, Peeter (1996) 'Changing National Spaces in the Baltic Area', in Lauristin and Vihalemm 1996: 129–62.

VON SYDOW, Björn (1999) 'The Baltic Defence College: Strengthening Baltic Defence Structures through Education', *Baltic Defence Review*, vol. 1999, no. 1: 9–13.

WALT, Stephen M (1987) *The Origins of Alliances*, Ithaca: Cornell University Press.

WATERS, Trevor (1996) 'Moldova: Continuing Recipe for Instability', *Jane's Intelligence Review*, September 1996: 398–401.

—— (1998) 'The Republic of Moldova: Armed Forces and Military Doctrine', *The Journal of Slavic Military Studies*, vol. 2, no. 2, June 1998: 80–97.

WOLF, Reinhard (1996) 'Correspondence', *International Security*, vol. 20, no. 4: 176–83.

XINHUA NEWS AGENCY (2001) 'Russia to Reduce Border Troops, Toughen Control of Chechnya', 5 February 2001.

—— (2002) 'EU Willing to Reach Deal With Russia on Kaliningrad', 6 March 2002.

YABLOKOV, Alexey V (2000) 'Environmental Security: Problems for the Russian Northwest', in Grier *et al.* 2000: 121–40.

YELTSIN, Boris (1997) 'Kontseptsiya Federatsii Natsionalnoy Bezopasnosti Rossiyskoi', *Rossiiskaya Gazeta*, 26 December 1997.

YEREMENKO, Alla (1998) 'Presidenty i argumenty', *Zerkalo Nedeli*, no. 5 (174), 31 January 1998: 1–2.

ZAIKO, Leonid (ed.) (1999) *Natsionalno-gosudarstvennye Interesy Respubliki Belarus*, Minsk: Analytichesky Tsentr 'Strategiya'.

ZAKARIA, Fareed (1997) 'The Rise of Illiberal Democracy', *Foreign Affairs*, vol. 76, no. 6: 22–43.

ZALYS, Vytautas (1998) 'The Return of Lithuania to the International Stage', in Eidintas *et al.* 1998: 59–110.

ZLOTNIKOV, L and Shlyndikov, V (eds) (1999) *Ekonomicheskaya politika: analiz i alternativa*, Minsk: Bestprint.

ZURAWSKI VEL GRAJEWSKI, Przemyslaw (2000) 'Polish–Ukrainian Co-operation in the Context of the Future Membership of Poland in the European Union', CPCFPU Occasional Paper 45/2000, December 2000.

Newspapers, television and miscellaneous media

AP FLUX (Moldova)

Army and Society in Georgia (Caucasus Institute for Peace, Democracy, and Development – CIPDD)

Baltic Independent (BI) (Estonia)

Baltic Observer (BO) (Latvia)

Baltic Times (BT) (Latvia)

Basapress (Moldova)

BBC Monitoring (BBC) (UK)

Byulleten Belarus Segodnya (Belarus)

Byulleten Mezhdunarodnykh Dogovorov (BMD) (Russia)

Dagens Nyheter (DN) (Sweden)

Dilis Gazeti (Georgia)

Diplomatichesky Vestnik (Russia)

Droni (Georgia)

Eesti Päevaleht (EPL) (Estonia)

Financial Times (FT) (UK)

Finansovye Izvestiya (FI) (Russia)

Handelsblatt (Germany)

Independent (UK)

Interfax (Russia)

ITAR-TASS (Russia)

ITAR-TASS World Service (Russia)

Izvestiya (Russia)
Jamestown Monitor (USA)
Jane's Foreign Report (UK)
Kommersant (Russia)
Kommersant-Vlast (Russia)
Krasnaya Zvezda (KZ) (Russia)
LETA (Latvia)
Mayak Radio (Russia)
Moldovan Radio
Moscow News (MN) (Russia)
Moskovskiye Novosti (Russia)
Neue Zürcher Zeitung (NZZ) (Switzerland)
New York Times (USA)
Nezavisimaya Gazeta (NG) (Russia)
Nezavisimoe Voennoe Oboozrenie (Russia)
NG-Dipkurier (Russia)
NG-Stsenarii (Russia)
Novoye Vremya (NV) (Moldova)
Official Journal of the European Communities (OJEC) (EU)
OMRI Daily Digest (Czech Republic)
Postimees (Estonia)
Pravda (USSR, Russia)
Resonanci (Georgia)
RFE/RL Balkan Report (Czech Republic/USA)
RFE/RL Caucasus Report (Czech Republic/USA)
RFE/RL Newsline (Czech Republic/USA)
RFE/RL Security Watch (Czech Republic/USA)
Rossiiskaya Federatsiya (Russia)
Rossiiskaya Gazeta (RG) (Russia)
Rossiiskiye Vesti (RV) (Russia)
Rossiya (Russia)
Russian TV
Rzeczpospolita
Sakartvelos Respublika (Georgia)
Segodnya (Russia)
Sovetskaya Belorussia (Belarus)
Sovetskaya Rossiya (SR) (Russia)
Soyuz Belarus-Rossiya (Russia)
SPB Vedomosti (Russia)
Tagesspiegel (Germany)
Voprosy Ekonomiki (Russia)
Vremya Novostei (VN) (Russia)
Wall Street Journal (WSJ) (USA)
Washington Post (USA)
Yeni Yuzil (Georgia)

Index